to Francine,
who saw me through it.

TEIKYO WESTMAR UNIV. LIBRARY

ANXIETY
AND MUSICAL
PERFORMANCE

Da Capo Press Music Series

ANXIETY AND MUSICAL PERFORMANCE

On Playing the Piano from Memory

by DALE REUBART

91-1963

DA CAPO PRESS • NEW YORK • 1985

Library of Congress Cataloging in Publication Data

Reubart, Dale.
  Anxiety and musical performance.

  (Da Capo Press Music series)
  Bibliography: p.
  Includes index.
  1. Music — Memorizing. 2. Piano — Instruction and
study. I. Title.
  MT82.R5   1985   781.6′3   84-21422
  ISBN 0-306-76253-6

Copyright © 1985 by Dale Reubart

Published by Da Capo Press, Inc.
A Subsidiary of Plenum Publishing Corporation
233 Spring Street, New York, N.Y. 10013

All Rights Reserved

Manufactured in the United States of America

PREFACE

Several years ago, while strolling on one of Vancouver's many beaches, I came upon a contest somewhat extravagantly billed as *The World Frisbee Championship*. One of the featured tests was the "Accuracy Event," in which participants were given five chances to throw the plastic disk through a large tire. As it happens, my aim is fairly decent, and the tire didn't seem to be situated too far from where I would have to stand, so after sizing up the first few entrants (who performed miserably), I decided to compete. At the outset, I was "on," and my first and second shots went cleanly through the tire. However, when the announcer saw that he finally had a contestant who was not a total klutz, he began drumming up an audience, a crowd began to form, and almost immediately, I choked up. I literally could feel my coordination draining from my body; my arms, my feet refused to move as they should, and the results were predictable. The third shot was wide, the fourth was worse, the fifth hit the announcer on the head, the crowd dispersed, and I slunk back into my well-deserved "frisbee-an" anonymity, never to re-emerge.

I spent a lot of time during the next few days trying to analyze why, after two accurate throws, I had failed so ignominiously in the next three. Actually, the answer is quite simple. I had originally entered as a lark, but when I realized that I actually had a chance to win, the stakes became much higher. Throwing a frisbee had always been a totally unconscious act on my part; my feet, arms and torso moved with an inner timing of their own that on occasion allowed me to get the thing more or less where I had aimed it. But now, with the ante raised, there was nothing unconscious about the situation; on the contrary, I could not have been more self-conscious, and that state of mind had somehow rendered useless all my unconscious knowledge of how to throw a frisbee. If I had been a little more aware earlier of what I actually do while engaged in that activity, I may have fared considerably better in the competition, since even under pressure, I

vii

probably would not have forgotten which foot to move first, when to release the frisbee, how to coordinate my arm motion with that of my feet, and so on.

It was also around that time that I regularly became extremely nervous prior to a concert. I am not blessed with a natural piano technique, and no matter how long or hard I practiced, I could never attain the secure feeling that my fingers would work well (or even passably) at any given performancce. Almost invariably, my initial "warming-up" period during a concert was sheer torture; particularly during concerto appearances, I often felt a total disconnection between my hands and mind. While pondering the frisbee experience, I was suddenly struck by the thought that perhaps some of the inner tensions that had disabled my natural coordination in the contest were also largely responsible for my stage fright (or, as it is now called, performance anxiety). It was then only a short step to the conclusion that if I could re-orient my practicing toward the goal of bringing as much as possible of my knowledge of piano playing (and music making in general) into a state of consciousness, the stage fright might be alleviated somewhat since, for all my nervousness, I did, after all, know how to play the piano.

Over the next couple of years, I focused my attention on developing practice techniques designed to achieve that end, and experienced far greater success than I possibly could have anticipated. For a short while, my playing sounded a little over-controlled, but I soon felt free to "let myself go" again, and found that the spontaneity, inspiration, or whatever you may wish to call it, had returned, revitalized and richer than it ever had been. Since then, for the last several seasons, I have certainly felt apprehensions prior to a performance, but debilitating stage fright is a thing of the past.

Of course, the fact that this method worked for me does not guarantee that anyone else who practices exactly as I do will have even the slightest degree of success in reducing his level of performance anxiety; I suspect that every pianist's stage fright is as unique as his fingerprints. Still, a book such as this one, which discusses the many components of performance anxiety and describes the amazing array of remedies currently available to counter that syndrome, will obviously be of tremendous assistance to those interested in (and afflicted by) the phenomenon of stage fright. Pianists now have available a single source book — long overdue — which will direct them to virtually all the significant research, current and previous, on the subject, including, of course, that of its author. Furthermore, there is such a catholicity of ideas presented here that any reader is bound to be intrigued and influenced by at least some of them. The resulting voyage of self-discovery will surely lead to a greater understanding of one's own pianistic problems, and ultimately, to their solution.

Robert Silverman
Professor of Piano,
The University of British Columbia

FOREWORD

All the world's a stage,
And all the men and women merely players:
They have their exits and their entrances;
And one man in his time plays many parts. . . .

Shakespeare, *As You Like It*

As usual, Shakespeare is right, and one could say that Dale Reubart has written a book for all the players: he has written for each of us. What he has to say — and says so well — helps make all of our performances much more enjoyable than they would otherwise be.

Though Professor Reubart directly addresses the pianist beset by anxiety in the face of performing from memory, it is easy to read between the lines to see that the anxiety the pianist feels is his variation on a theme common to us all.

Who does not vividly recall the mixed feelings — mostly of terror — associated with first piano recitals, débuts in school plays, participations in debates, and making a graduation speech? My sweaty palms and dry mouth then were nothing compared to my first graduate school presentation, my first paper at a conference, or my first lecture before 400 students. The first poetry readings I gave seemed as if they would never end. And my first date . . . and when I said, "I do . . . ." All these experiences and many others we all share were performances in which we wore many masks to disguise or hide from our anxieties.

Today, thanks in part to Dale Reubart's work, we can better understand and respond to anxieties that threaten our performances — no matter what role we play.

Frederick Candelaria
Professor of English
Simon Fraser University

TABLE OF CONTENTS

Introduction

When I first thought of writing this book in 1979, my way seemed clear. Although I saw a number of ramifications which the subject implied, and suspected that there would probably be others which I was not able to foresee, I did not even fathom what byways I would explore before I could feel even remotely ready to write. Such surprises seem inevitable whenever serious inquiries are entertained, no matter what the field. I had experienced them often enough when engaging musical topics. It was only reasonable, therefore, that I would experience even greater surprises when I became involved with adjunctive disciplines as well. That is certainly true; the way led me into deep and intriguing waters.

My original intention was to write one-half a book, leaving the other half to be written by a friend who, as a clinical psychologist, had had experience in treating performance-anxious pianists. In my half of the book I was to discuss simply and succinctly the thought processes which appeared most desirable for the pianist to experience while performing from memory. From my own introspection, based upon nearly fifty years of performing and forty years of teaching, that seemed straightforward enough. However, it occurred to me that my own thought processes, derived from introspection, might not reflect the norm. (I fully recognized that, as my career as a performer had not always been without its problems, my thought processes alone might not represent the best of all models.)

The second problem which I encountered almost immediately was that, although I had long recognized both conscious and out-of-awareness functions during performance, no one agreed as to what consciousness was or, in many cases, whether the mind is involved at all in anything outside of conscious awareness.

I undertook the second of these questions first: What are the limits of consciousness? Clearly there may never be agreement on this issue. To some writers, existence is *predominantly* non-aware; to others, consciousness is of cosmic proportions. Countless others see the lower limits of awareness somewhere between these two extremes. For my purposes, I was in need of a description which was sufficiently easy to comprehend without being simplistic, and clear enough in its delimitations that it could be discerned apart from the world of non-awareness which most people recognize. While those who embrace other points of view may not agree with the construct that I settled upon, it was expedient that I make a choice. The clarity with which I could discuss equally complex issues was at stake. Even this first hurdle was anything but easy, as the reader might guess.

A solution to the first of my two initial problems needed not only a great deal of introspection but, as well, questions (both oral and written) put to quite a number of successful North American colleagues. The questionnaires were especially revealing. After reading Maslow, and becoming convinced of the wisdom of polling the "Olympic gold medal winners," I found confirmation for most of my suppositions in the diverse responses to my queries by pianists who enjoy reputations for reliability as well as excellence in performance. What are the pianist's thought processes during performance when he is at his best? If common denominators could be discovered, would it not be wise to model after such thought processes wherever possible? Would not those whose "crooked" thinking stands in the way of their potential achievement come closer to its realization with such knowledge? Perhaps, but even then the problem of staying on the right track, apparently, can remain. That knowledge may not be enough.

Why does one become mentally "derailed" when the perceived threats of performance are encountered — even when he knows upon what his thoughts should dwell? Ah, that's another question — a question which begged answers not only from my own experience as a performer and teacher but, as well, from as yet unperformed empirical studies: studies which subsequently followed with the intent of providing some elucidation, if not incontrovertible evidence. It also begged answers from the immense field of psychological theory, as I found out.

Studying the psychological literature I soon found that there were undoubtedly many therapies that would be appropriate to the control of stage fright — many effective approaches to the alleviation of performance anxiety which would depend upon individual circumstances. I therefore decided that the book should include a survey of as many of these therapeutic approaches as possible, and that it might best be written by me alone. That is not to say that I sought understanding only from books. I asked for and received much invaluable insight and advice from professionals in psychology, audiology and the speech sciences, medicine, physiology, physiotherapy, anatomy, the neural sciences, and even in such apparently remote fields as nuclear physics.

Although I first considered conscious and out-of-awareness functions in playing the piano from memory (Chapters Three and Four), I realized that, first, I must discuss the experience of anxiety itself so that the performer with stage fright might better understand what it is that is causing his misery (Chapter One). I then turned my attention to causation; the origins of the anxious response (Chapter Two). This was followed by a discussion of many other factors, both hereditary and environmental (musical and otherwise), which either cause/encourage or preclude/mitigate performance anxiety (Chapters Five and Six). These chapters are intended for the teacher and parent who might thus become aware of what he can and cannot contribute to the problem of performance anxiety, its possible control, or its minimization. Chapters One through Six were then followed by four others which, except for Chapters Seven and Eight, I had not initially intended to write: chapters which outline ways that may be found helpful in putting an end to debilitation by stage fright. These last chapters naturally consider readjustments in the pianist's musical and technical style as well as self-help somato-psychic/ psychophysical strategies and psychological interventions, on the premise that, unless all is well with one's musical and technical approaches to piano playing, nothing else can be more than a band-aid on the problem.

The book is frankly addressed to the piano teacher and to the performing pianist who know the meaning of performance anxiety — who have observed a form of human misery that all too often thwarts the noble effort to communicate through the art of music. While the pianist, performing from memory, plays the central role, the reader may find that the relevance of the material contained herein is not limited to the pianist, or even the musician.

I owe more of a debt to more people than I had anticipated. That should have come as no surprise but it did. I had imagined myself as a "lone eagle soaring in a boundless sky," in need of nothing more than my own wings. I was wrong. It did not take long for me to discover that I needed help and support of various kinds in this, my "maiden flight"; I received it in abundance. Would that I could speak my eternal thanks adequately. My dear wife, Francine, must be first on my list: the person without whom my zeal may have faltered. Her love, calm support and unflagging interest in the project kept me going. Our many hours of discussion kept the spark ever alive. Next, comes Frederick Candelaria, "Renaissance man" extraordinaire, who read each chapter of the book several times, at various stages of development, offering invaluable criticism, advice and encouragement. Others, to whom I owe a great debt are Betty Highley Reubart, Gregory Butler, J. Evan Kreider, and John H. V. G. Gilbert, who read the manuscript and commented constructively; and Margaret Kendrick, with whom I conferred at length on questions of a professional nature. There were many others, also, who contributed much through their personal contact and stimulating ideas. It is truly as Yerkes has said: "One chimpanzee is no chimpanzee."

Chapter 1

THE ANATOMY
OF STAGEFRIGHT

Whoever is educated by anxiety is educated by possibility,
and only he who is educated by possibility is educated according
to his infinitude. Søren Kierkegaard, *The Concept of Anxiety*.[1]

Performance and Anxiety.

One of the most exhilarating experiences I know of is performing
in public, especially when there is a magnificent piano under my
fingers, great music in my head, and the feeling that there are no
technical obstacles. Although there may well be other factors involved, I like to think that it is the pure joy of sharing the rewards of
an aesthetic experience that makes the undertaking so gratifying.
That has always been my view, at least — a view shared by many
pianists.

There is a factor which can and does make public performing
less pleasurable, nevertheless, and on the worst occasions turns it into
an excruciating nightmare: "stage fright." I have known very few
performers who have escaped it entirely: some who have learned to
deal with it successfully through therapy of one kind or another, quite
a number who have merely accepted it as a way of life, and others
who have experienced debilitating agony from it to the extent that
stage fright has ended their careers. In many cases the only reason
there could possibly be for continuing to perform is for the occasional
experience of supreme joy suggested above. Certainly a lifetime of
dedication to the art would be pointless if stage fright were the only
return on the investment.

1

Stage fright. Psychologists more appropriately call it "performance anxiety," since it is not necessary to be on stage to experience it. Regardless of what one calls it, it is questionable whether anxiety associated with musical performance is unique. It may be that its neurotic form is different from other types of anxiety only in terms of the threats which motivate it. Although many psychologists recognize hundreds of distinct varieties of anxiety, I have not been convinced that their symptoms differ other than in degree of reaction. Many of the more severe forms of anxiety seem to share common roots, whether or not the anxiety is manifest in performance.And the sources of therapeutic relief from performance anxiety may not differ significantly, except in subject matter and mode of presentation, from those that are effective for other forms of anxiety.

Psychological Persuasions.

Not the least of the problems facing the uninitiated researcher in the present field is that of evaluating the numerous and disparate points of view that are represented by the various psychological persuasions. Fundamentally, these persuasions may be reduced to two generic branches with opposite viewpoints: those in which anxiety and other emotional disturbances are seen as intrapsychic affairs requiring analysis as to origins, nature, and dynamics of the particular symptoms; and those which are concerned solely with the observable, measurable symptoms of anxiety, irrespective of their possible origins. Subsumed under the first category are the psychoanalysts (psychiatrists and dynamic psychologists), and under the second the behavioral psychologists (including the cognitive-behaviorists). Under each of these generic headings is a larger number of major and lesser psychological disciplines which point to an even greater number of therapeutic approaches.[2] For present purposes I have limited myself to the major points of view: psychoanalytic, behavioral/ cognitive-behavioral, and existential-humanistic.

While it is difficult enough for a layman to cover a large segment of this vast literature with comprehension, it is even more difficult to avoid developing some biases. When I have taken a biased stance, at times, it is because a particular point of view seemed more pertinent to the conditions of musical performance, more meaningful to the musical mind in matters which seem to relate specifically to it. Hopefully, that is where my prejudices have ended. It will become apparent soon enough, however, that I have not been able to accept an explanation of performance anxiety or methods for its control which ignore the role of mind — of mental processes — of conscious versus subconscious mentation. It will also become apparent that I am in sympathy with a more humanistic point of view — a point of view which is well demonstrated by Gordon W. Allport, who writes:

> Emulation of an older science never creates a newer science. It is only unquenchable curiosity about some persistent phenomenon of nature that does so. Individuality, I argue, is a legitimate object of curiosity, especially at the human level, for it is here that we are overwhelmed by this particular natural phenomenon. I venture the opinion that all of the animals in the world are psychologically less distinct from one another than one man is from other men. There are, of course, many areas of psychology where individuality is of no concern. What is wanted is knowledge about averages, about the generalized human mind, or about types of people. But when we are interested in guiding, or predicting John's behavior, or in understanding the Johnian quality of John, we need to transcend the limitations of a psychology of species, and develop a more adequate psychology of personal growth.[3]

What is Anxiety?

Perhaps the most widely-held view of anxiety is that it is "diffuse apprehension."[4] According to Rollo May:

> Anxiety is the apprehension cued off by a threat to some value that the individual holds essential to his existence as a personality. . . . Its special characteristics . . . are the feelings of *uncertainty* and *helplessness* in the face of the danger. The nature of anxiety can be understood when we ask *what* is threatened in the experience which produces anxiety.[5]

This, of course, is a distinctively psychoanalytic point of view.

By comparison with the conceptualizations represented by May, the behaviorists seem coolly detached and "classicistic." They eschew all reference to psychoanalysis and, although the individual's past history and genetic constitution are taken into account as response modifiers, they ignore anxietal origins prior to the paired stimuli (unconditioned and conditioned) which occasioned them. When anxiety is manifest, they take note of its physiological, cognitive, and overt behavioral components which are measured and assessed. The assessment is then used to define the quality and quantity of the particular anxiety manifestation. It is apparent that, while the behavioristic and psychoanalytic camps may share a common concern for observable and measurable symptoms, they share little else. B. F. Skinner expresses the behaviorist's point of view of anxiety as follows:

> Anxiety, as a special case of emotion, should be interpreted with the usual caution. When we speak of the *effects of anxiety*, we imply that *the state itself is a cause* [italics mine], but so far as we are concerned here, the term merely classifies behavior. It indicates a set of emotional predispositions attributed to a special kind of circumstance.[6]

Definitions. Profusion/Confusion.

There are many words commonly used interchangeably with "anxiety" — words used to mean the same thing but which are not always synonymous. Before proceeding it would be well to clarify some of these and place them in their proper contexts.

As already indicated, the term "stage fright" is anxiety placed in a particular setting. "Apprehension" is a word that psychologists often use synonymously with anxiety, although, at times, one has the feeling that there should be an anticipatory connotation to it. It is used often enough as a substitute, however, that it may well appear here with the same meaning.

"Threat" is one of the causes of anxiety, as is "stress," according to professional usage, although the latter is sometimes confused with anxiety even among scholars and scientists.[7] But, as Rollo May points out, "Anxiety is how the individual relates to stress, accepts it, interprets it. Stress is a halfway station on the way to anxiety. Anxiety is how we handle stress."[8] Intimately bound up with anxiety is how one *interprets* both threat and stress.

"Worry" is another common expression: "I'm worried about my

performance tonight," or, "That passage worries me." Worry is the way anxiety is expressed cognitively; it accompanies anxiety as negative thought (generally quite confused, taking the form of negative self-talk and catastrophizing). There would be no worry without anxiety.

The words "panic" and "terror" are both used to indicate extremes of anxiety — feelings which almost every reader has probably experienced at one time or another, whether or not as performing pianists.

Anxiety versus Fear.

There is much difference of opinion concerning the words "anxiety" and "fear." Are they the same or do they imply different emotional responses? Many psychologists, like Borkovec, make no distinction:

> While various investigators have attempted to distinguish between fear and anxiety at both the theoretical and empirical level, we are in agreement with Spielberger [1972] that the distinction is meaningless unless the response patterns of the two emotions differ and that little attention has yet been devoted to the identification of those differential patterns.[9]

May thinks otherwise, making the following comparison between fear and anxiety:

> However uncomfortable a fear may be, it is experienced as a threat which can be located spatially and to which an adjustment can, at least in theory, be made. The relation of the organism to a given object is what is important, and if that object can be removed, either by reassurance or appropriate flight, the apprehension disappears. But since anxiety attacks the foundation (core, essence) of the personality, the individual cannot "stand outside" the threat, cannot objectify it. Thereby, one is powerless to take steps to confront it. One cannot fight what one does not know. In common parlance, one feels caught, or if the anxiety is severe, overwhelmed; one is afraid but uncertain of what one is afraid.[10]

In short, "One *has* a fear" of something but "One *is* anxious."[11] And as Karen Horney points out:

> Fear and anxiety are both proportionate reactions to danger, but in the case of fear the danger is a transparent, objective one and in the case of anxiety it is hidden and subjective. That is, the intensity of the anxiety is proportionate to the meaning the situation has for the person concerned, and the reasons why he is thus anxious are essentially unknown to him.[12]

Freud's formulations are similar:

> I shall avoid going more closely into the question of whether our linguistic usage means the same thing or something clearly different by *"Angst* anxiety", *"Furcht* fear" and *"Schreck* fright"*. I will only say that I think *"Angst"* relates to the state and disregards the object, while *"Furcht"* draws attention precisely to the object. It seems that *"Schreck"*, on the other hand, does have a special sense; it lays emphasis, that is, on the effect produced by a danger which is not met by any preparedness for anxiety. We might say, therefore, that a person protects himself from fright by anxiety.[13]

Existential[14] versus Neurotic Anxiety.

Most psychotherapists distinguish two kinds of anxiety, existential ("natural" or "normal") and neurotic. Existential anxiety is shared by everyone and is manifest in terms of wariness toward the natural dangers which confront all human beings: sickness and disease, natural disasters, death. It has its roots in the instinct of self-preservation. Freud notes, "On what occasions anxiety is felt — that is to say in the face of what objects and in what situations — will of course depend to a large extent on the state of a person's knowledge and his sense of power *vis-à-vis* the external world."[15] Usually, the response to normal anxiety is relatively weak.

Neurotic anxiety, on the other hand, is apprehension that is disproportionate to the objective threat. That is, it is anxiety where specific threats are either ambiguous or unknown, and the responses out of proportion to the danger recognized by society — in which the responses are generated by the individual's *interpretation* rather than by the actual threat they impose. As May puts it:

> It is, of course, this development of anxiety in amounts out of proportion to the actual danger, or even in situations where no ostensible external danger exists, which constitutes the problem of neurotic anxiety.[16]

Stage fright is normally such an anxiety.

Manifestations of Anxiety in Musical Performance.

Those who have experienced performance anxiety need not be reminded. But, for the sake of completeness I here outline a few impressions that are commonly expressed by those who do experience it. Most of these manifestations are common to all forms of anxiety, although a few are particularly recognizable to the musician playing from memory.

The pattern and symptoms of performance anxiety are familiar: apprehension sometimes days before the performance, often increasing as the day nears, with a crescendo in the last hours before the concert is to begin. It is called "catastrophizing," that is, irrational worry which crowds out constructive thought. In some individuals anxiety manifests itself in loss of appetite, inability to sleep, and, in very extreme cases, upset stomach and vomiting. The greatest worry is usually about forgetting the music, losing one's place, the mind "going blank," a state of mental confusion and disorientation, the head "swimming," the total inability to focus attention. Equivalent manifestations are reported by athletes, public speakers, parachute jumpers, and students anticipating an important examination. When such an exaggerated state is carried into the concert the worst often does happen. If "forgetting" and loss of control occur, they are accompanied by a feeling of desperation and panic, the painful feeling of embarrassment, of being totally alone and forsaken in the misery of the moment, of being paralyzed, helpless and powerless. This feeling is often accompanied, in turn, by an impulse to "bail out," of wanting to run away, to be almost anywhere other than where one is at that moment. The seconds seem like minutes and the minutes like hours.

The muscles become rigid and all technical flexibility is lost. There is no joy in the music, only despair. And add to this the concomitant feelings of social inadequacy, alienation, and competitive failure, and one does not wonder why the effort so often ends in disillusionment. The feelings are all too familiar to those who have suffered uncontrolled anxiety.

Physiological Arousal and Phylogenetic Roots.

Our bodies are programmed to respond automatically to danger in ways which will permit us to fight or flee a threat most advantageously. When a danger is encountered all the organs of the body are put on the alert by the autonomic nervous system, each contributing its part to the preparations for "battle or retreat." The same is true whether they are fear or anxiety reactions. The resultant physiological responses are the most frequently measured, since they are manifest in ways that are easiest to monitor, some efficaciously during musical performance.

That our neurophysiological reactions are geared more to dangers encountered in the primeval forest than to the threats encountered on the concert platform, is one of the phylogenetic miscalculations of nature. Sometimes autonomic responses seem to the pianist's advantage, but more often than not they are strangely incongruous and frequently counterproductive. An increase in heart rate is due to the increase in blood that is being pumped to the skeletal muscles. A rise in blood pressure results from peripheral vasoconstriction (to minimize bleeding if the organism is wounded in battle) which, in turn, causes cold hands, fingers and feet.

Cold sweat precedes the warm sweat of actual muscular activity. Sweating in the palms of the hands and in the soles of the feet, where one does not normally perspire, is to better equip us for a speedy departure from the threatful scene. An increase in sweat gland activity brings about lower galvanic skin resistance, resulting in increased electrical activity in the skin (a useful source of information for measuring anxiety levels).

The purpose of deep and rapid breathing, which usually accompanies anxiety, is to provide more oxygen for the muscles and cardiovascular system in general. Loss of appetite and, occasionally, vomiting are part of the operation to inhibit digestive functions so that more blood will be available for the skeletal muscles. Dryness in the mouth is a sympathetic response to the suspension of gastric juice flow. There is a rise in the amount of sugar supply for energy, and an increase in adrenal activity (both needed for an effective "fight or flight").

The increased contraction of all the large skeletal muscles, while an advantage to strength in an ensuing battle, can be disastrous for piano playing. Even muscles excessively contracted in support of posture can take their toll in fatigue. Hypertension, the bane of the pianist's technical existence, is particularly a problem during periods of high anxiety. We will see later that reducing muscular tension is an important step in the effective relief of anxiety; that, very often, by releasing excessive muscular contraction, the feedback loop between mind and body can be interrupted with a corresponding release from anxiety.

Overt Behavioral Responses.

Counted among overt behavioral responses to anxiety are, naturally, the number and extent of the mistakes that occur in a performance. Pianists like to forget these, of course. But they are often taken into account in assessing the behavioral component of performance anxiety although they are rather awkward to evaluate;[17] certainly their measurements are very inexact.

The same can be said for other behavioral manifestations which may occur before and during a performance. Those that might be visually or audibly perceived are backstage pacing, fidgeting, an awkward, unnatural walk to the piano, stiff and uncharacteristic posture at the instrument, fiddling with hands and the piano bench, wiping the hands, hands shaking, a deadpan expression combined with paleness, shrugging the shoulders, quick, restless movements of the arms and hands to and from the keyboard, knees shaking and feet trembling on the pedals; moistening lips, subvocalizing.These, and other manifestations, are seldom ignored by psychologists. But, while they are indicative of anxiety, they are unwieldy and imprecise from both the standpoint of statistics and meaningful evaluation.

Psychosomatic Manifestations of Chronic Anxiety and Tension.
Roberto Assagioli writes:

> Music[al performance] can, and often does, have injurious effects on the performers themselves, who are subjected to a combination of harmful elements: muscular and nervous fatigue as a consequence of intense technical study and the excessive quantity of music, both heard and performed; the anxiety caused by public performances; the particular contrast of psychological attitudes required by the performance itself, which demands on the one hand perfection of technique, concentrated attention, and self-control; and on the other an emotional identification with the mood expressed by the music, needed to produce that warmth of expression, that powerful suggestion which fascinates the audience. For these reasons performing musicians need, more than anybody else, to train their will, to control their emotions and to help themselves, or be helped, by a judicious use of relaxation and of all available means of psychotherapy.[18]

While Assagioli's statement now seems a bit naive and exaggerated, it is true that the long-range deficit to psychological and physical health can be great if chronic anxiety and tension are allowed to persist unchecked over a protracted period.

Although numerous psychosomatic problems are reported as consequences of prolonged and severe anxiety,[19] I have seen no data which link serious physical maladies *solely* to musical performance anxiety. Instances of severe heart condition are well known among performers (including a few instances of fatal attacks during performance), but, so far as I have been able to ascertain, the causes have not been traced specifically to anxiety that is performance-rooted to the exclusion of apprehension simultaneously stemming from other sources. Peptic ulcers and other gastrointestinal disorders are reported, as are rare cases of diabetes mellitus brought about by chronic anxiety and the overproduction of sugar in the system. High blood pressure, one of the numerous manifestations of hypertension, is another deficit that is often associated with a pattern of excessive anxiety. However, in all such cases reported among musicians, investigation would no doubt reveal that a high level of neurosis already pervades the life of the individual, and that performance merely adds to it. While there is no question that the level of anxiety commonly sustained by performers is extremely high, if it is heaped upon an already anxious life, a variety of serious illnesses can be expected. No performer can hope for much relief from anxiety until he brings his whole life under control.

Aside from the occasional somatic response that may occur during periods of high anxiety (noted above), the earliest manifestations of chronic performance anxiety would seem to be psychological. Most conspicuous is the tendency to inhibition; and if inhibition is allowed to persist and compound, along with corollary intrapsychic disturbances, serious psychological and physiological consequences can result. After all, inhibition is a form of escape — a means of avoiding the dreaded anxiety. As Karen Horney puts it, "An inhibition consists in an inability to do, feel or think certain things, and its function is to avoid the anxiety which would arise if the person attempted to do, feel or think those things."[20] Whether the impulse to escape is conscious or subconsious makes no difference; the easiest way to avoid the anguish of severe anxiety, for very many people, is to avoid the stimuli which occasion it. Carried to sufficient lengths, and if exposure to the perceived threats is unavoidable (as with many professional musicians), severe emotional disturbances are very possible consequences, along with such false escape mechanisms as drug abuse and alcoholism. Inhibition is merely a manifestation of one's inability to cope with anxiety — a consequence of ineffectual efforts to override the feelings of helplessness in a confrontation with perceived threats. Although my present concern is with the solo pianist, the problems of anxiety and inhibition are clearly matters of concern for all professional musicians, as evidenced by the recent study done with the Vienna Symphony Orchestra.[21] In that study, the stress factors encountered by orchestral musicians under varying conditions were noted and measured, indicating the range of anxiety that can occur in that profession. Since there is no room for inhibition under conditions of professional orchestral employment, daily confrontation with extreme performance anxiety can place an unendurable strain on mind and body.[22]

Living with Anxiety; an Existentialist Viewpoint.

What should one do about anxiety in performance? Take steps to get rid of it? At times, at least, that would seem to be the answer. How wonderful it would be to walk on stage, sit down at the piano, and have done with that pounding heart, sweaty palms, and the rest. Or would it? The question is, would it be wise to rid oneself of it altogether? The answer is clearly No, as most performers would agree. Without some anxiety, "getting up" for a concert becomes impossible, for the music is robbed of all its excitement and intensity, both for the performer and for the audience: the performance is flaccid, lethargic, and devoid of the spirit that is essential for communication.

At one point or another anxiety seems to identify with enthusiasm — with excitement. Just where one stops and the other begins is difficult to say. One would certainly not want to get rid of anxiety at the expense of excitement. That would be pointless. Such a thing could happen, one must assume, since the feeling of high excitement is easy to confuse with the feeling associated with a healthy level of anxiety. Conceivably, their roots are the same, even though the psychoanalysts might find a distinction somewhere in the psyche. But perhaps, after all, the distinction is only in the way one responds to a stressful situation — how one interprets it. It is quite possible that any given set of stimuli could be stressful on one occasion and inspiring on another. The audience, the milieu, the music are all challenges which could be variously interpreted depending upon the performer's attitudes — his self-regard. Conceivably, one person might see a challenge as an inspiration, while another responds to the same challenge as a threat. Even if anxiety and excitement should prove to be two discrete manifestations, however, there could not be more than a small step separating them.[23] The factors which could cause the differences in interpretation are discussed below.

If one should assume that excitement is merely a form of anxiety that is expressed positively, then anxiety, under certain conditions, can be regarded as a salutary component of living. It goes without saying that life, like music, would be intolerably dull without some "dissonance" — and are not the dynamics of dissonance and anxiety virtually the same?[24]

Something similar to the foregoing is implied by the existentialists. Rollo May, for instance, expresses the optimistic belief (after Kierkegaard) that anxiety is an essential part of life, impossible to eliminate because of our nature as human beings — even if we wanted to. He proposes that anxiety supplies essential creative energy derived from precisely the "dissonance" that I have mentioned, and that, instead of running away from anxiety, it is wisest to "move through it," achieving a measure of self-realization in the process.[25] Interestingly enough, it is exactly this mood of resigned acceptance which stands behind almost all therapeutic approaches. Few therapies, if any, are designed to remove anxiety entirely. Their object in general is to modify it and to keep it contained within manageable limits.

Anxiety or Vigilance

When all is said and done, nothing would be gained and a great deal lost if all traces of performance anxiety were to be eliminated. It is obvious, at least to the experienced performer, that a degree of anxiety (or excitement, certainly) must be present if there is to be enough intensity to convey the musical idea persuasively. Two questions remain, however: "How much is enough?" and "How little is too little?" "How much is too much?" is a question easily answered by anyone who has been debilitated by performance anxiety.

The conclusion reached many years ago by R. M. Yerkes and J. D. Dodson was that, up to a point, the effective realization of a task increases as the level of anxiety (arousal) increases; however, when it increases beyond a certain point, efficiency decreases.[26] This is known as the Yerkes-Dodson Law and has been tested many times since 1908 by Broadhurst (1957), Easterbrook (1959) and others. Broadhurst determined that the law held true only for more difficult tasks.[27]

According to Solso, "Arousal tends to keep active our capacity to perceive sensory events"[28]; and this increasing awareness of "relevant cues" to the progressive exclusion of others that are irrelevant probably accounts for the increasing effectiveness. Easterbrook postulates that, when anxiety increases beyond a maximum level of tolerance, selectivity in the processing of stimuli becomes so narrow that even essential cues are overlooked.[29] The inverted U is often used to illustrate the law:

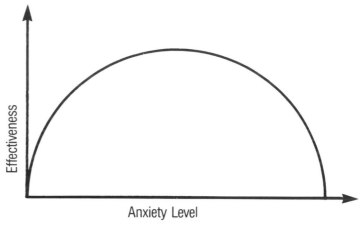

Anxiety Level

Figure 1.1

Anxiety which is too low for effective realization of the task (lethargic) is illustrated by the low end of the curve at the left. As arousal increases efficiency improves until the peak at the center, after which, as it continues to mount, effectiveness decreases until the point beyond which performance gets out of hand. Graphically speaking, the desirable place to be is at or near the center, although anywhere between the inner extremes of low and high arousal would allow one to function without impairing the result. Obviously, it would be best to avoid the extremes of anxiety that would jeopardize effectiveness; but, on the other hand, calmness to the point of lethargy would also be undesirable, at least from the musical point of view.

It seems to me that the word "vigilance" is one which best

identifies the level of anxiety that is ideal for performance. Although the word has been used primarily to characterize the wary attitude of lower animals toward their environment, it also suffices well to suggest a desirable level of anxiety in human beings. To be vigilant is to be maximally alert without the attendant neurotic symptoms (at least that seems to be the implication), a level of apprehension which prepares the individual to adapt quickly without excessive "worry" — a position on the inverted U which is comfortably situated in the central portion of the curve. Howard Liddell has observed that vigilance supplies the energy for conditioned reflexes.[30] It is precisely this state of alert readiness that is highly desirable for the performing pianist. Anxiety below the level of vigilance results in lethargy — above it, panic.

Anxiety and Courage.

Finally, every pianist must recognize the essential need for "courage" in his encounters with performance-related anxiety. It is a need he shares with all creative and re-creative people. The painter, the author, the actor, the physicist, and everyone else who is involved with the creative process knows that it takes courage to make that first line on a clean, white canvas, to type that first line on a sheet of blank paper, to respond on cue with the first words of a role, or to submit a new formula to its first test. That was perhaps the most eloquent message to come out of *The First International Conference for the Study of Tension in Performance* in September of 1981 — a point made dramatically clear by the veteran British actor, Sebastian Shaw.[31] Most experienced pianists realize that performing takes courage; they expect it and accept it as an *essential* part of their artistic existence — an existence which draws persuasive power from the interface between the creative impulse and its realization. It is not simply the courage to face extra-musical threats — "task-irrelevant ideation"; it is the courage to face the vast unknown which is implicit in the work of art — in the creative act. The experienced artist is inspired by it; it is his "joy."[32] The novice can easily be overawed by it and succumb to the anxiety that lurks potentially in such a confrontation. The reward for taking the risk, nevertheless, is the possible "peak experience"[33] – "ecstacy."[34] Under optimum circumstances the experience can be one of joy and excitement, rather than of anxiety. Such experiences are within the reach of many, if not all, pianists.

NOTES AND REFERENCES

1. Søren Kierkegaard, *The Concept of Anxiety*, trans. Reidar Thomte (Princeton, N. J.: Princeton University Press, 1980), p. 156.
2. Over 250, according to Richie Herink (ed.), *The Psychotherapy Handbook* (N. Y.: New American Library, 1980).
3. Gordon W. Allport, *Becoming: Basic Considerations for a Psychology of Personality* (New Haven and London: Yale University Press, 1955).
4. Sigmund Freud, Kurt Golstein, Karen Horney, and Rollo May, among others.
5. Rollo May, *The Meaning of Anxiety*, revised edition (N. Y.: Washington Square Press, 1977), p. 180.
6. B. F. Skinner, *Science and Human Behavior* (N. Y.: Macmillan, 1953), p. 180f.
7. For example, Maximilian Piperek (ed.), *Stress and Music* (Vienna: Wilhelm Braumueller, 1981).
8. May, *op. cit.*, p. 98.
9. Thomas D. Borkovec, "Physiological and Cognitive Processes in the Regulation of Anxiety," in Gary E. Schwartz and David Shapiro (eds.), *Consciousness and Self-Regulation*, vol. 1 (N. Y.: Plenum Press, 1976), pp. 266f.
10. May, *op. cit.*, p. 181.
11. *Ibid.*, p. 182.
12. Karen Horney, *The Neurotic Personality of Our Time* (N. Y.: W. W. Norton and Co., 1937), p. 38.
13. Freud, Sigmund, *Introductory Lectures on Psychoanalysis* (Middlesex, England: Penguin Books, 1973), p. 443.
14. J. F. T. Bugental, *The Search for Authenticity*. Enlarged Edition (N. Y.: Irvington Publishers, Inc., 1981), pp. 22ff; pp. 94ff.
15. Freud, *op. cit.*, pp. 441f; see also Bugental, *op. cit.*, pp. 22ff.
16. May, *op. cit.*, p. 117.
17. Sylvia S. Appel, "Modifying Solo Performance Anxiety in Adult Pianist" (*Journal of Music Therapy*, Vol. XIII, No. 1, Spring, 1976, 2-16); Margaret J. Kendrick, et al, "Cognitive and Behavioral Therapy for

Musical Performance Anxiety" (*Journal of Consulting and Clinical Psychology*, Vol. 50, No. 3, 1982), 353-362.

18. Roberto Assagioli, *Psychosynthesis* (N. Y.: Penguin Books, 1976, first published in 1965), p. 245.
19. May, *op. cit.*
20. Horney, *op. cit.*, p. 46.
21. Piperek, *op. cit.*
22. For a fuller discussion of the psychosomatic ramifications of chronic anxiety see: Kenneth R. Pelletier, *Mind as Healer, Mind as Slayer* (N. Y.: Delta Books, 1977); Hans Selye, *The Stress of Life*. Revised edition (N. Y.: McGraw-Hill, 1976).
23. For an interesting comparison of excitement and anxiety see Pelletier, *op. cit.*, p. 206.
24. In fact, could it be possible that the amount of anxiety experienced by the musician is somehow related to the amount of dissonance in the music he plays? An interesting thought which tempts speculation. See Piperek, *op. cit.*, p. 16.
25. May, *op. cit.*
26. R. M. Yerkes and J. D. Dodson, "The Relation of Strengths of Stimulus to Rapidity of Habitformation" (*Journal of Comparative Neurological Psychology*, 1908, 18) 459-482.
27. P. L. Broadhurst, "Emotionality and the Yerkes-Dodson Law" (*Journal of Experimental Psychology*, 1957, 54) 345-352.
28. Robert L. Solso, *Cognitive Psychology* (N. Y.: Harcourt Brace Jovanovich, Inc., 1979), p. 137.
29. J. A. Easterbrook, "The Effect of Emotion on Cue Utilization and the Organization of Behavior" (*Psychological Review*, 1959, 66) 183-201.
30. Howard Liddell, *The Role of Vigilance in the Development of Animal Neurosis*. In Paul Hoch and Joseph Zubin (eds.), *Anxiety* (N. Y.: Grune and Stratton, 1949), pp. 183.197.
31. *The First International Conference on Tension in Performance*, Kingston upon Thames, England, September, 1981.
32. Rollo May, *The Courage to Create* (N. Y.: Bantam Books, 1976), pp. 44f.
33. A. H. Maslow, *Motivation and Personality*, second edition (N. Y.: Harper and Row, 1970).
34. Carl R. Rogers, *On Becoming a Person* (Boston: Houghton Mifflin Co., 1961).

Chapter 2

WHY SHOULD I BE
SO NERVOUS?

It is certainly not unusual for a pianist to have worked long and hard, studied thoroughly, and practiced ever so diligently, only to have the performance jeopardized by extreme nervousness (as anxiety is often called). How often he has hoped against hope that he would not be visited by that demon who leaves him feeling helpless. How often he has resorted to rituals of all sorts, including many naive home remedies, because someone has assured him that they would help him to control stage fright. One time apprehension remains harmlessly in the background, contributing just the right amount of "edge" to the performance. The next time, with no less care taken in preparation, anxiety envelopes him like a shroud, draining away every ounce of confidence. What is it that causes this unexpected state of vulnerability? Whence comes this anxiety, these unpredictable and irrepressible attacks of nervousness? The specific sources would be too numerous to mention, and even if it were possible, an atomistic analysis and list of origins would accomplish little. I have preferred, instead, to focus upon three general sources of anxiety — sources from which most if not all apprehensions seem to emanate, whether or not they involve musical performance: the survival instinct, the social-cultural matrix, and, for the performer specifically, one's education and training in music together with the experience of performing itself.

Origins of Neurotic Anxiety.

All anxiety is rooted, ultimately, in the survival instinct. It is implicit in the organism's capacity to react to threat, regardless of the threat's origin. This capacity is expressed instinctively in terms of *Normal anxiety* (see above, Chapter One). As May notes, "The only assumption necessary is that the human organism has the capacity to react to threats, a capacity which its ancestors possessed likewise."[1] *Neurotic anxiety*, nevertheless, is learned. According to May, "The capacity for anxiety is not learned, but the quantities and forms of anxiety in a given individual are learned."[2]. A myriad of stimuli impinge upon the human organism throughout life starting, it appears, *during the prenatal period*.[3] Whether or not these stimuli are interpreted as threats depends upon the interaction of the individual's innate capacity to respond with the personality and character traits he has acquired or is in the process of acquiring. Recent research suggests that the personality traits themselves may indeed be initiated during the prenatal period.[4]

The starting point of neurotic anxiety notwithstanding, the origins undoubtedly arise from a social matrix, the first being the interpersonal relationship of mother and child, a social matrix which eventually expands to include the entire immediate family.[5] It is within that microcosm that the earliest patterns of anxiety are nurtured. It is there, depending upon such pre-existent variables as shyness, sensitivity, feelings of insecurity and dependence, that the first potentially threatful stimuli are observed and evaluated for noxiousness. And it is quite conceivable that the interpretations which result may eventuate in patterns of neurotic anxiety that are ultimately associated with musical performance.[6] The influence of family socio-dynamics, from the prenatal period through infancy and early childhood, cannot be underestimated as a determinant of performance anxiety in later years. If anxiety is essentially a reaction to a threat to values, as May observes, "The essential values are originally the security patterns existing between the infant and these significant persons."[7] Undoubtedly, the die is cast even before the first piano lesson is taken.

Individual Differences and Anxiety Susceptibility.

It is abundantly clear that, at this juncture, no one really knows for certain which personality traits are inherited and which are acquired. To the behaviorists, naturally, personality traits are manifest as behaviors which result from the environment. On the other hand, psychologists of Albert Ellis's persuasion have made a strong appeal for the recognition of personality traits as innate endowments.[8] Observing the on-going polemics is rather like watching an amusing (and vexing) game whose object is to throw pet theories through a hoop. I can see the possible importance of the "game" for some scientists in terms of future hypotheses but, in my restricted view of the play, it makes little difference who is the winner. When the dust settles I think we will find, simply, that every human organism is filled with inherited potentials — with genetically-determined predispositions which, depending upon the environment, will produce one personality trait or another if and when compatible stimuli are encountered. That is to say, every person is born with capacities which may or may not be responsive to the stimuli which he encounters in the environment; that such determinants operate at the personality level as surely as they do in the domain of musical "talent." This point of view will be met throughout this book. It is explored much more fully in Chapter Six.

There is no doubt that the heredity/environment issue has been further muddied by Thomas Verny's book in that it places the origins of personality and character in the period between conception and birth rather than before conception or after birth.[9] For the field of psychology that is tantamount to a paradigm shift. If true (which Verny's evidence would seem to indicate), then environment is the determining factor even when the organism is being acted upon by stimuli while still in the womb. Inherited characteristics, logically, would then be only those that are present at conception. Based upon this assumption, I believe a good case remains for the assertion that the *predispositions* to traits of personality, character, etc., are inherent in the individual even though the traits themselves are not.

Studies that have been done with identical twins have not settled the controversy of heredity versus environment, either. Even where such twins have been raised in totally disparate environments after birth, they did share the same environment for the previous nine months.[10] And while physiological and neurological duplications may be expected and rationalized in terms of DNA encoding, such shared traits as attitudes, values, and tastes, might be partially explained by the social environment which they shared during the prenatal period. Whether such traits as shyness, sensitivity, emotionality, and receptivity are inherited or acquired *in utero*, on the other hand, is a question which has not yet been answered. Possibly it does not matter at this point, although it is obvious that such factors as these are critical determinants of susceptibility to anxiety. They are organismic variables, and whatever may be their source, such individual differences account ultimately for the wide range in human responses to "danger."

Anxiety as a Learned State.

While the human organism is born with the *capacity* to react to threat, the reactions themselves are learned. Probably soon after conception this capacity is tested for the first time by at least one stimulus capable of eliciting some kind of response, whether it be oxygen deprivation caused by maternal cigarette smoking, or by maternally-produced catecholamines passed on to the unborn child via the bloodstream.[11]

Freud saw the birth trauma and the separation from the mother as the first stimulus to anxiety. Although it now seems that it may not be the first, certain psychoanalysts (particularly the neo-Freudians) see it as the most crucial one, inasmuch as the separation from the mother represents the first disturbed interpersonal relationship — a disturbance which typifies those that will be encountered throughout life. Most psychologists of this persuasion see this type of disturbance as the basis of all anxiety.[12]

After this initial separation the child continues to be exposed to a barrage of potentially-threatening stimuli, all capable of producing anxiety, all originating one way or another in the cultural matrix. For several years the family continues to be his only world. Nonetheless, it is reasonable to assume that, even before the larger cultural milieu is encountered directly, he will have anxiety-producing experiences passed on to him from the outside world by parents and other elders of the family. In other words, it is very likely he will be affected by macrocosmic stimuli even before he engages the macrocosm firsthand.

Although the inherent capacity to respond to noxious stimuli might be exercised at any time from conception onward, the nature of a response as well as the stimulus which induced it are determined by maturation.[13] The following points of maturation (after birth) have been recognized in numerous studies:

> *Five to twelve months*: emerging objectivation of the environment when specific stimuli elicit corresponding fears (e.g., the sudden appearance of an unfamiliar face) where formerly the responses had been diffuse and undiffentiated reactions to sudden, intense, and unusual stimuli for which the infant had no coping mechanisms (e.g., a loud noise, or the feeling of being dropped).
>
> At this juncture the first attempts at avoidance behavior are manifest (e.g., turning the head to avoid seeing the source of its fear). These escape-avoidance maneuvers can ultimately lead to inhibitions — behavioral manifestations which may contribute to shyness.
>
> *Post-infant period*: Gradual emergence of self-awareness and the corresponding awakening of the imagination. Imaginary dangers, the awareness of self in relation to others, the concepts of competition, status, prestige, ridicule, success and failure become factors whose dynamics elicit threat stimuli. Henceforth, no threat sources are closed to him.[14]

Culture and Pervasive Anxiety.

I have often used a bit of imagery with students for the purpose of analyzing a technical problem, and have found recently that comparable imagery might be used in an analysis of performance anxiety.

Hypothetically, if a technical maneuver requires contraction of a muscle to an intensity of fifteen in order for a playing unit to move in a given direction with a force of fifteen, and that muscle has the capacity of thirty, then there is no problem with fatigue or coordination so long as all the muscles involved are starting at or near zero. However, if the opposing set of antagonistic muscles that are involved in the action are already contracted to a degree of fifteen when *at rest*, then the motivating muscle must contract to a degree of thirty to bring about a force effect of fifteen. That is obviously not the most efficient way to execute the movement. Analagously, if a player hopes to keep his anxiety level within the desirable boundaries represented by the Yerkes-Dodson curve (above), but goes into the performance with a "pervasive anxiety"[15] level that is already within that range, any additional anxiety motivated by the level of threat of the performance could push him over into the region of panic.

Unfortunately, strong reactive anxieties like those associated with performance, taking important examinations, or being interviewed for a new job, rarely start from zero. Most are heaped upon some level or other of pervasive anxiety (or "free-floating" anxiety) acquired simply by living in the cultural milieu. This has always been so, and, as many contemporary psychologists have noted, never before have the levels of threat and stress sustained by man been greater than in that absorbed by twentieth-century society. Excessive pervasive anxiety is now the major threat to mental and physical health in the Western world.[16]

It was obviously this alarming state of affairs which prompted Auden to write *The Age of Anxiety* in 1948, perhaps the most eloquent social comment to emerge from the chaotic cultural conditions of the post-World War II era.[17] But the psychology of modern Western society did not begin with the Second World War, however much the stress-filled conditions with which we now live may have been exacerbated by that cataclysm. May (building upon the writings of Hallowell, Gardner Murphy, Karl Mannheim, and others) traces the origins of our modern dilemma to the Renaissance whence originated our current system of values that emphasizes competitiveness, individualism, and the need to triumph (at the expense of others, if necessary).[18] Most of us, as a result, struggle with fear of failure in the face of competition, emotional isolation in a culture where the appearance of strength is a virtue, and, often, distrust of those who represent the competition. Upon this base are built manifold other sources of stresses and threats (e.g., greed, disproportionate ambition, etc). If one adds to these "potential threats to survival" the accelerating pace of life, the rapidly deteriorating environment, the constant threat of war and nuclear holocaust, the rising noise level, and a multitude of other factors which are added to the cultural pressures, it is no wonder that the musician finds himself confronted with degrees of anxiety which are already just within the desirable limit before he engages the anxieties that are peculiar to the performance. The shared insanity with which we are burdened is what Fromm calls the "socially-patterned defect."[19] So long as we all share it we are all normal; failure to cope with it implies mental illness. To alleviate or evade these threats and stresses — ah, that's the point!

Never have efforts to control stress been more widespread than today. Self-help books fill shelves of countless bookstores, brilliant minds have turned their attention to the problems of consciousness and new modes of learning [20], and millions of people are actively engaged in routines of benefit to stress alleviation: exercise, dietary vigilance, meditation, and many of the therapy-oriented regimens that are discussed in Chapter Nine.

"Organismic" Values; "Introjected" Values; Quality.

A vast source of potential anxiety lurks in the space between the identification of values and their achievement. I wish to emphasize again, however, that it is not anxiety to be avoided, lest one wish to eliminate a great deal from life that makes it worth living. It is anxiety which can end in joy if the values being pursued are a reflection of one's own human-ness uninhibited by simultaneous efforts to grasp values that are contradistinctive.

Any discussion of values is, itself, fraught with danger (and potential anxiety, incidentally). Like so many other words dealt with in this book, the one now being considered has many definitions. My own formulations agree with those of Carl Rogers[21] and Abraham Maslow,[22] to whom I owe an obvious debt. The consideration of values is central to both their points of view (views which they share, in many respects). It will become increasingly self-evident that I find their theories particularly effective in my analysis of anxiety and the maintenance of psychological equilibrium in musical performance.

By the time a child encounters the culture at large he has already assembled a fairly significant assortment of values, some of which he brought with him into the world, and a great number which he acquired from his cultural microcosm. The ones he brought with him are "organismic," while the ones he acquired environmentally are "introjected."[23] The former are values associated with his functioning as a human being — with his "basic needs,"[24] while the latter are those which he has adopted from the cultural milieu because their adoption by him promised approval by the society which had embraced them. They are culturally-conceived values which "may be widely discrepant from what he is experiencing."[25]

Organismic values tend to vary according to the basic needs for which one is seeking gratification. When one set of basic needs has been gratified (physiological, safety, love, or esteem needs) values shift; i.e., what was of value in the attainment of gratification for one set of needs is superceded by values associated with higher-level needs. Self-actualization, which is sought after all other needs have been gratified, is the highest of these basic needs. For the self-actualizing person, everyone and everything is considered from the point of view of intrinsic value, rather than from a point of view that is formulated from sources outside oneself.

Introjected values are those that are taken over from the cultural milieu; they are the cause of some of the human being's greatest problems. To Rogers, the pursuit of introjected values is the major deterrent to self-fulfillment. And certainly, from the point of view of "noxious stimuli," if these values become prime motivators, they can represent perhaps the greatest single cause of neurotic anxiety. "Because these concepts are not based on his own valuing, they tend to be fixed and rigid, rather than fluid and changing."[26] Neurotic anxiety arises when these conceived values interfere with fulfillment of those that are organismic.

It is often tempting to associate organismic with human values and introjected with materialistic values but this is misleading and simplistic. After all there is nothing wrong with modern (material) technology so long as its value is conceived as a service to the pursuit of organismic values. The problem with modern society is that it tends to direct attention to the technology as an object desirable for itself alone. That tendency, if it continues, will probably destroy society as we know it. But I find the word processor (computer) I am writing upon at the moment the greatest boon to creative writing that I have ever encountered. As such, it can only enhance life for me and, hopefully, for some others. I can see how many people "get hooked" on the object as an intrinsic value, nevertheless — something to be desired for itself. The automobile is another well-known object of misplaced values. So is money but, in Western society at least, even the dedicated artist must have money to buy food to survive to create.

In this society, of course, if a person's organismic values happen to produce rich materialistic rewards, he is quite fortunate. After all, one can envy the successful financier whose inner needs are gratified by the challenges of high finance. If his highest needs are aesthetic, however, and he would rather pursue artistic values above all else, his life and work could be pretty untenable. The same can be said for those students of piano who study and practice (sometimes quite industriously) because they have accepted the value-judgments of their parents — values which often run counter to organismic values that might be better served in the financial world, on the athletic field, in a machine shop, or in a dental laboratory.

It is not difficult to adopt introjected values over organismic values; almost everyone has, to one extent or another. The pressure to adopt conceived values is sometimes very subtle — very beguiling (as in some forms of advertising). On the other hand, it can also be coercive. Acceptance by peers and by society is often contingent upon the adoption of values they have fashioned (moral and social values, for example), and a great deal of courage is necessary to resist.

The reader perhaps wonders why I have spent so much time on the subject of values. The relationship of a pianist's system of values to anxiety should be clear; however, the quest of values and, in particular, the struggle inherent in the dichotomy between organismic and introjected values is fraught with the dissonance that is the source of anxiety in performance.

Values are inseparably blended with quality. The quality inherent in any value can only be experienced, never fully described, even though R. M. Pirsig[27] has come as close to defining it as anyone I have read in recent years. The quest of quality is, after all, the goal of the artist. But tension again lurks in the space between the conception of quality and its realization – tension which, for the pianist, is fuel for anxiety. It is obviously an aspect of anxiety with which one must learn to live and cope. The pianist is in trouble who believes that only perfection can represent quality.

Origins of Anxiety in Unrealistic Challenges.

When I was a boy, I wanted to be a major league baseball player; and that was my father's hope, too, until I was in my early teens. For some reason which I could not understand at the time, he suddenly stopped pushing me in that direction and joined my mother, whose wish had always been that I would be a pianist like her. I never quite understood my father's change of heart until, at age eighteen, I still weighed only 130 pounds, not really enough for my six-foot frame or for any professional baseball pretensions I still might have had. He was right. A career in baseball would have been unthinkable considering my stature alone, to say nothing of my lack of natural ability. I have wondered ever since what the course of my life might have been had I persisted in my ambitions. Undoubtedly it would have been extremely disappointing. I was perhaps fortunate that my zeal was less than fanatical. The challenges were unrealistic; and even before I quit playing daily under my father's watchful eye, I was having trouble with "stage fright" whenever I walked to the plate for my turn at bat. I realize in retrospect that I would not have been good enough to play on the high school team, let alone professional sports. Had I been a little bit better, I might have had enjoyment in play commensurate to the amount of time it took for practice; but under the circumstances, my time was much better spent at the piano, where I learned my real interests lay.

Homespun autobiographies like this one could be endlessly duplicated, I am sure, all with similar moralistic consequences. Some, no doubt, may not have turned out so well. I am sure the reader knows of many such instances — instances where unrealistic challenges were pursued with disappointing, even tragic results. There are many cases of it in music, but such instances are certainly not limited to musical endeavors.

Obviously, one must have realistic challenges in order to achieve higher goals. In pianistic studies, I have always advocated (for myself and students) that there should be some piece in the practice repertoire at all times which is *just beyond* one's capabilities at that moment, technically, emotionally, musically, and perhaps even intellectually. If the challenge is too great, of course, discouragement and anxiety can result; just enough, and there can be new and rapid growth. The same is true of all endeavors, I am sure, although it probably would not be wise to attempt the leap across a deep chasm that is ten feet across when one's previous record was nine feet.

Pursuing unrealistic challenges often results in high anxiety and frustration. Even small challenges can sometimes create a proportionate amount of apprehension, but, if the desire is strong, and the challenges are realistic, the outcome is generally salutary.

Musical Origins of Performance Anxiety.

Although much of the anxiety one experiences in performance may have extra-musical origins, there is no question that a great deal also stems from experiences related to music itself. Musical insecurity which occasions performance anxiety can usually be traced to two sources: inadequate levels of musical awareness, and physical/technical deficiencies. Each of these categories is subdivisible into inherent and acquired problems. Musical difficulties which may have inherited roots are: 1) low auditory awareness, 2) low capacity for musical imagery, 3) low rhythmic awareness, and 4) low intellectual capacity. Inherent physical/technical problems originate in coordinative weakness and in incompatible physical structures.

As stated below (Chapter Six), it is probable that a *predisposition* to auditory stimuli is inherited whereas pitch acuity is acquired; that is, acute pitch discrimination seems to result from exposure to a stimulating and enriched sonorous environment by the child (perhaps before and after birth) whose aural faculties are predisposed to sound over other sensory signals. The acuity seems to develop during the period from infancy to about eight years of age. I postulate throughout these pages that, of all musical faculties, auditory sensitivity is probably the most important to the pianist. Certainly, lack of confidence in tonal memory is one of the root causes of anxiety in performing from memory.

Related to tonal memory and pitch acuity is the ability to internalize musical images. Most people can remember a tune and, even when there is little capacity to reproduce it, they will recognize it when they hear it. However, the performing pianist must be able to image the total musical texture with which he is involved. This ability probably is acquired, although pitch acuity and a good melodic memory must be assumed. Inability to perceive more than a melodic line would be sufficient cause for alarm for any pianist playing from memory.

Although I could very well be wrong, I believe that rhythmic awareness may not be inherited either. Rather, like pitch acuity, an inclination toward rhythmic stimuli may be inherited, with its manifestation in terms of bodily response acquired. To date I know of no evidence to support or refute such a hypothesis.

A fine teacher I know once asked, "Why is it that I can teach a person to play in time, but I cannot teach him to play rhythmically?" The answer is clear. Rhythm is a holistic concept — a feeling in the body; playing in time is an intellectual process which presupposes a linear mode of thought. A pianist who has not established rhythm as a bodily response might learn to play in time, but he will never play with convincing rhythm. This incapacity can be another major cause of performance anxiety, taking all the ramifications of rhythm into account.

The reader will note that, although I have placed other values above intellectual functions for the performing pianist, I have not implied disuse or distrust or denigration of the intellect. I have merely placed other values above it *at the moment of performance*. A great deal more will be encountered in Chapters Five and Six regarding intellectual involvement in musical study and practice. It is obviously an essential function in all judgments related to musical conception and execution — judgments which, for the most part, must predate the performance. In addition, of course, there are intangible contributions made by the inquiring intellect to all facets of taste and discernment. It is important to note in the final analysis that pianists with high intellectual capacity and broad interests have usually been among those best able to cope with anxiety in performance.

It seems certain that good coordination is inherited. Otto Ortmann has observed, "I am inclined to believe that the readiness with which relaxation sets in between movements, be they movements of fingers, hand, or arm [i.e., coordination], is a fair index of kinesthetic talent as applied to the piano."[28] The same may be said about kinesthetic talent as it relates to any activity in which the human being is physically engaged (including playing baseball). There can be no question that many people are born with fine coordination for piano playing just as there are many whose coordination ill-suits them for playing the instrument.[29] That unsuitability is frequently the cause of considerable performance anxiety, especially when technical challenges have not been carefully weighed against coordinative potential.

Finally, one must consider the possibility of structural incompatibility, body to instrument, as a cause of performance anxiety. More often than young pianists would like to know, their body structures stand in the way of complete fulfillment as pianists because they are not "made right" for the instrument. Christoph Wagner, of the *Hochschule für Musik* in Hannover has spent a number of years developing ways of measuring the size and range of movement of fingers, hands, and arms, relating these measurements to the physiognomy and technical exigencies of various musical instruments (including the piano).[30] He has invented and constructed an array of sophisticated instruments for accurately measuring supination and pronation of the forearm, abduction and adduction of fingers, wrist, and other pertinent skeletal articulations, the lengths of fingers, phalanges, the distances between fingers at full abduction of the hand knuckles, etc. His investigations have led him to methods by which to diagnose or predict problems of unusual muscular tension inherent in the association of an individual with specific musical instruments. He has been equally successful in his efforts to determine whether or not a particular instrument is right for the person wishing to study it, and in identifying the tension-based disabilities of experienced musicians. He is convinced, as am I, that such incompatibility might occasion performance anxiety, since muscular tension can be the cause as well as a result of anxiety. Obviously, so long as a pianist stays within the technical boundaries dictated by the structure of his playing apparatus, there is no particular problem; but, as with the limits imposed by coordination, if challenges are accepted which cause those boundaries to be exceeded, frustration and anxiety are likely to ensue. This subject, as well, is further discussed in Chapter Six.

Sources of Anxiety in the Educational Experience.

Although most anxiety is learned by experiential encounters with threat and stress, much is acquired by learning from the cultural milieu. Behavioral psychology recognizes three sources of fear (anxiety) response of which two involve learning from other human beings: by means of "modeling," and through instruction and information.[31] Demonstrations of performance anxiety (modeling) by other people, particularly members of the peer group, can often condition the young pianist to *expect* to be anxious in performance. If the young pianist observes anxious behavior as a prevalent response to the conditions of performance, he will indeed learn to be anxious when these conditions are encountered. If he has not known before what makes these conditions threatening, he will learn. And do not think that the impressionable young student will not pick up the fear of threat that is conveyed in the demeanor of parents and teacher.

Information gleaned from conversation and personal revelations, according to some psychologists, is the largest source of anxious behavior. Possibly if a youngster never hears about performance anxiety, he may never know what it is. At least that is the belief held by behavioral psychologists. Nevertheless, I am not entirely convinced that it is a *major* source of performance anxiety. In my experience as a teacher of performing pianists, shielding the student from the idea of performance anxiety has never prevented it from occurring when other anxiety-inducing factors were present already (e.g., self-doubt, technical insecurity, unrealistic challenges, etc.). Of course it is possible that knowledge about performance anxiety had been acquired long before I interceded. It is amazing how such information does get around.

Somato-psychic Origins of Performance Anxiety.

As suggested above, a major source of anxiety is the muscular tension which exists in the body before a threat is encountered.

Hypertension of the skeletal muscles is a chronic ailment of modern man and, whether it is the cause or result of pervasive anxiety, it is frequently responsible for increased susceptibility to threat. If muscles are tensed inordinately, the brain may be sent danger signals which alert the autonomic nervous system to a possible threat, which sends defensive signals back to the skeletal muscles for further contraction, etc. The resultant feedback loop thus both initiates anxiety and feeds it until the loop is interrupted. And, since relaxed muscles are simply those that are not contracted, the first step toward escaping or alleviating the anxiety is obviously to relax. Clearly, relaxing muscles before a real threat is perceived would be the logical way of avoiding neurotic anxiety in the first place.It is for that reason that nearly all therapies start with relaxation techniques — relaxation techniques either to interrupt the feedback loop that sustains a neurotic anxiety, or to reduce the chances of its formation before a potential threat has been encountered.

Piano Technique as a Source of Anxiety.

The indomitable Carola Grindea is convinced that excessive tension in piano technique is the foremost cause of performance anxiety.[32] I certainly agree that it makes a large contribution to it, whether or not it is the major one. A large number of internationally renowned pianists play with what might be regarded as an inordinate amount of muscular tension without its noticeably detracting from their artistic achievements.Who is to say if their accomplishments would be greater or less without the attendant physical tension? When such a high level of tension is sustained by most such artists it is generally offset by other factors which seem to neutralize the tension as a source of anxiety. Obviously, such a state of affairs should not be advocated; to do so with a student even of considerable talent would be presumptuous and irresponsible. Grindea is obviously correct in her judgment that immense effort is wasted and enormous amounts of anxiety are induced because of piano techniques that ignore the role of relaxation and "balance" in playing. For most of "us mortals," the best advice is always to seek the lowest level of tension that is possible short of jeopardy to the musical outcome. A great deal more is said on this subject in Chapter Eight. For now it is sufficient to recognize tension in piano technique itself as a significant source of anxiety.

Origins of Performance Anxiety in Low Self-Esteem.

There are two states of mind which will start performance anxiety faster than any others. One is, "I'm a rotten pianist"; and the other is, "I'm a rotten person." No other convictions will bring on stage fright more quickly. Such cognitive self-statements are at the heart of nearly all failures in performance, no matter what the fundamental origins of anxiety. Probably the biggest problem a teacher has to face with a student is that of low self-esteem — the student's feeling that he is not good enough. Often it originates in the musical experience itself, but occasionally it is rooted much more deeply in feelings of personal unworthiness. Both feelings are difficult to assess and often may be beyond the capacities of even the most sincere and most empathetic teacher to deal with.

Whatever the original source, low self-esteem as a pianist is ultimately the outgrowth of a bad experience in performance. One learns performance anxiety from the performance. To the individual who feels "safe" and secure in life, the first bad performance may not appear as a catastrophe. Self-respect most likely will be uninjured and the next performance viewed with optimism. But if the person's basic need for security is not thoroughly satisfied, a minor mishap may set the tone for excessive anxiety each time the threats of performance are encountered.[33] Because personal esteem is shaky in the first place, he will be convinced of his inadequacy and will be totally subjugated by his own negative self-statements.

That original bad experience in performance might be earned or unearned. In spite of every precaution, no matter how well prepared, a bad experience can befall the young pianist early in his career. We all know that. Nevertheless, the odds against it are greatly increased if preparation has been thorough. A mishap may occur but it is less likely. All things being equal, the performance will be successful and the future promising with respect to other performances. However, as is too often the case, early performances in the career of a student are not thoroughly prepared, with too many musical and technical problems left unresolved, so that loss of control is practically inevitable. One can say, in this case, that the bad experience which set off the anxiety syndrome was earned, perhaps more by the teacher than by the student. In any case the victim is the student who is very likely to be the pianist typified at the outset of this chapter — a pianist who cannot assume that the next performance will go well because of a pattern that started early in his career. Whereas there are effective measures for alleviating the condition, obviously it would have been preferable to avoid the pattern in the first place. Taking steps to avoid it should be a goal of every teacher and parent. One of the aims of this book is to indicate ways in which that might be accomplished.

NOTES AND REFERENCES

1. Rollo May, *The Meaning of Anxiety* (N.Y.: Washington Square Press, 1977), p. 191.
2. *Ibid.*, p. 192.
3. Thomas Verny, *The Secret Life of the Unborn Child* (Toronto: Collins, 1981).
4. *Ibid.* In the Freudian view, neurotic anxiety has its foundation, at least symbolically, in the birth trauma and in the fear of castration. The complex rationales for this point of view need not concern us here. Such formulations may now be in need of revision, anyway, in light of the evidence given by Verny — evidence which implies that, while the birth trauma must be taken into account, incipient neurotic anxiety can and does begin earlier.
5. Particularly significant is the role of the father who becomes known through the sound of his voice. *Ibid.*, p. 31.
6. Among other things, the adverse effect upon the unborn child of maternal smoking and drinking has been noted. *Ibid.*, pp. 20f, p.71. Music heard *in utero* can evidently have either a salutary or adverse effect, as well. *Ibid.*, pp 21f.
7. May, *op. cit.*, p. 193.

8. Albert Ellis and John M. Whiteley (eds.), *Theoretical and Empirical Foundations of Rational-Emotive Therapy* (Monterey, California: Brooks/Cole Publishing Company, 1979), pp. 17ff.

9. Verny, *op. cit.*

10. In one well-publicized case, male twins in their forties displayed similar tastes and attitudes, as well as similar appearances, behavior and speech mannerisms, even though they had been separated at birth and had had no further contact whatsoever until middle age.

11. Verny, *op. cit.*, pp. 43f.

12. Erich Fromm, *The Sane Society* (N. Y.: Fawcett Premier, 1955); Karen Horney, *The Neurotic Personality of Our Time*, (N. Y.: W. W. Norton and Co., 1937); Harry Stack Sullivan, *Conceptions of Modern Psychiatry* (Washington, D. C.: William A. White Psychiatric Foundation, 1947).

13. A summary analysis of children's fears and anxieties is given in May, *op. cit.*, pp. 88ff.

14. See: A. L. Gesell, *The Individual in Infancy*, in Carl Murchison (ed.), *The Foundations of Experimental Psychology* (Worcester, Mass.: Clark University Press, 1929); A. T. Jersild, *Child Psychology*, Rev. ed. (N. Y.: Prentice-Hall, 1940); and Jerome Kagan, Richard Kearsley, and Philip Zelazo, *Infancy: Its Place in Human Development* (Cambridge, Mass.: Harvard University Press, 1978).

15. Joseph Wolpe, *Psychotherapy by Reciprocal Inhibition* (Stanford: Stanford University Press, 1958).

16. See: Fromm, *op. cit*; Horney, *op. cit.*; May, *op. cit.*, Chapter Six; Kenneth Pelletier, *Mind as Healer, Mind as Slayer* (N. Y.: Delta Books, 1977); Hans Selye, *The Stress of Life*. Revised edition (N. Y.: McGraw-Hill, 1976).

17. W. H. Auden, *The Age of Anxiety: A Baroque Eclogue* (London: Faber and Faber Limited, 1948).

18. May, *op. cit.*

19. Fromm, *op. cit.*

20. For example: Martha Davis, Elizabeth R. Eshelman, and Matthew McKay, *The Relaxation and Stress Reduction Workbook* (Richmond, Calif.: New Harbinger Publishers, 1980); Gay Hendricks and James Fadiman (eds.), *Transpersonal Education* (Englewood Cliffs, N. J.: Prentice-Hall, 1976); Sheila Ostrander and Lynn Schroeder, *Super Learning* (N. Y.: Delta, 1979).
21. Carl R. Rogers, *Freedom to Learn* (Columbus, Ohio: Charles E. Merrill, 1969).
22. A. H. Maslow, *Motivation and Personality*. Second edition (N. Y.: Harper and Row, 1970).
23. Rogers, *op. cit.*, pp. 242ff.
24. See Maslow's discussion of basic needs, *op. cit.*, pp. 35-47.
25. Rogers, *op. cit.*, p. 245.
26. *Loc. cit.*
27. Robert M. Pirsig, *Zen and the Art of Motorcycle Maintenance* (N. Y.: Bantam Books, 1979; originally published in 1974).
28. Otto Ortmann, *The Physiological Mechanics of Piano Technique* (N. Y.: E. P. Dutton, 1962; originally published in 1929), p. 120.
29. Is it possible that the preconditions for rhythmic excellence and fine coordination are allied in the same DNA molecule? I don't know that this question has been answered. Since good coordination is largely a matter of timing, such an alliance is certainly implied.
30. Ch. Wagner, "Die Messung rheologischer Grössen an Gelenken der menschlichen Hand in vivo." In F. Hartmann, *Biopolymere und Biomechanik von Bindegewebssystemen* (Berlin/New York: Springer, 1974).
31. G. Terence Wilson and K. Daniel O'Leary, *Principles of Behavior Therapy* (Englewood Cliffs, N. J.: Prentice-Hall, 1980), pp. 150ff.
32. Carola Grindea (ed.), *Tensions in the Performance of Music*. Second edition (London: Kahn and Averill, 1982).
33. In the analysis of Maslow the need for self-esteem cannot be fulfilled if safety needs are not sufficiently satisfied. *Op. cit.*, pp. 39-46.

Chapter 3

CONSCIOUSNESS, PERCEPTION AND ATTENTION

Ask any experienced pianist (baseball pitcher, high jumper, or reader of poetry, for that matter) what condition is essential to the success of his performance and he will usually say it is the ability to concentrate. Ask him precisely what he wants to concentrate upon, however, and most frequently he has difficulty defining it. He will mention things like "the music," "the sound," "communication with the audience," or other abstract concepts which, while fraught with meaning for him, are nevertheless vague generalities that are hardly informative for the person who has never experienced musical performance at its best, if he has experienced it at all.

Concentration and attention, for most people, usually imply some kind of conscious effort — conscious in the sense of noticing something and, if what is noticed is of sufficient moment, remembering all or part of it for at least a short period of time. That is, what is noticed might be recalled upon reflection.[1] I "notice" the melodic line at this point, the tension in the harmonies here, the technical strategy which has proven successful in this passage or that. I remember how well such and such a passage sounded at my last concert or I recall the incessant coughing of the lady sitting on the front row. Such acts of mind, in my view, involve consciousness. Anything that cannot be recalled at all may never have been conscious in the first place and, so far as I am concerned here, has functioned outside of conscious awareness; i.e., it was unconscious, subconscious, a function of "bodily awareness"[2] or of "reactivity."[3]

That which is to be concentrated upon, then, is that which should be noticed. And, in many cases, that which is noticed may be recalled upon reflection at a future time, *depending upon the degree of affective response involved in the "noticing."* "Noticings" without emotive connotations often tend to elude retrieval and perhaps, in time, are lost to conscious recall altogether.[4] Whatever should be its fate with regard to long-term memory, nevertheless, that which is noticed, at the moment of noticing, must be regarded as an act of conscious awareness. This, at least, is the tack I have taken in this book. Although for some it may seem simplistic, this paradigm is useful in the ensuing discussion.[5]

Performing from Memory: Conscious or Subconscious?

Some years ago Lilias MacKinnon wrote: "Consciousness [is] the centre of practice; subconsciousness the centre of performance."[6] This assertion, echoed by a number of pedagogues and technical theorists over the years, is well taken and, to a degree, accords with the realities of performance. Even cursory consideration of the act of piano playing reveals that only a fraction of what is done during performance can be brought under conscious surveillance. A myriad of decisions and physical adjustments must be made during every moment of the performance which are beyond the capacity of any conscious mind to mediate — to notice. It is true that each of these decisions and adjustments must be considered in practice, (more or less, depending upon one's level of experience) but most must have been "worked in" by performance time.

MacKinnon did *not* say that one must practice with consciousness and perform without it. Obviously, the performance must have a "mind" behind it, regardless of the automaticity which ultimately governs the course of much of the executionary functions. No intelligent and experienced performer wishes to place his performance on "automatic pilot" with no conscious guidance whatsoever (although there are numerous occurrences of it every day). The hazards which this practice invites are well known.[7]

But the question remains, What should I be noticing during a performance if I am to be at my best? If consciousness must play its part, what should be its role?

Performing from memory is not unlike driving an automobile in heavy traffic. By the time the exigencies of complex traffic patterns are encountered all of the automatic processes that are essential to the effective handling of the vehicle must be well established, albeit adaptable to the changes that occur in that environment. Obviously, consciousness must be present. Notice must be taken of all unexpected environmental changes — to the shifting conditions of the environment which are beyond those dictated by the routine of unobstructed driving. It is the conscious mind which notes these fluctuating conditions, signalling its commands to the automatic processes which, one trusts, stand in alert and malleable readiness to meet the ever-changing needs of an environment in flux. The level of vigilance is almost always proportionate to the complexity of traffic. Think for a moment what might happen should a person drive in heavy traffic without noticing the changing conditions of that traffic. Think also of what can occur if the techniques of steering, braking, and shifting gears have not been sufficiently prepared. There can be commensurate ramifications if a musical performance proceeds without conscious awareness or without adequate preparation of those processes which must function out of awareness.

Conscious of What?

I once sat as outside examiner for a Ph. D. candidate in psychology who had prepared an excellent dissertation on the control of performance anxiety in music. One of the questions I felt her dissertation did not answer, however, concerned thought processes that might be advantageous for the pianist playing from memory; i.e., thought processes not involved with the self. (I did not realize at the time that, in the milieu of academic psychology, such questions could be inappropriate.) Specifically my question was, "What aspects of my performance should I be thinking about while I am playing?" It was an honest query begging for an answer — a question which had been hounding me, both as a teacher and as a performer, for a long time. In that particular milieu the response dealt only with "task-relevant ideation" as opposed to "task-irrelevant ideation," jargon which, at the time, meant little to me. I was genuinely interested, nevertheless, in what she would consider "task relevant" (other than that involving interrelationship of the self and its environment). The question has continued to pique my curiosity, eliciting much introspection as well as numerous queries to other experienced pianists. My question, to myself and to my performing colleagues, has been: When you have been performing at your best, what, specifically, have you found yourself concentrating upon? In other words, what foci of attention have you found to be most desirable when playing from memory? Naturally, as a performer of some experience, personal introspection has provided some viable answers, I believe. But what about other seasoned pianists, particularly the "Olympic gold medal winners" mentioned by Maslow[8] whose mentation might be unique but which may also share much in common with my own?

To satisfy my curiosity I submitted a questionnaire to a large number of accomplished pianists across North America. All were pianists acknowledged not only for their interpretations, but also for their reliability in playing from memory.

They were asked to detail their foci of attention, as accurately as possible, at those times when they felt they had been "at their best." Naturally, this is extremely difficult to pin down. I found, not surprisingly, that most of them had never thought of what they had been thinking before — it was a new experience for them. In one case, that of pianist Anton Kuerti, the question elicited such enthusiasm that he wrote an entire article on his introspection (perhaps to be published before publication of this book). I quote from the article:

> My experience has been that successful performances depend on the extent to which one can in fact transcend being overly conscious of . . . details, difficulties, special effects, etc., and reach that state in which the feelings and emotions of the music almost fully occupy one's consciousness. . . . I like to imagine the music as being alive during the performance, of displaying a will of its own, so that the precise lengths of notes, the relative dynamics and tensions and shapes are creating themselves at the instant they are heard, rather than being churned out in a preordained way. . . .
>
> Even if I often descend several levels from [such] lofty pinnacles, . . . I will try to think, during a difficult passage, not of the individual notes or motions, but of the effect I want from the entire passage; if there is a difficult leap, I think of the sound of the notes I am leaping to, not of the location or any mechanical detail; in fact I leap to the sound, not the spot, *I imagine*

> *the result, not the cause* [Italics mine]. . . .
>
> It is only the warmth of the music itself, that will thaw out cold fingers, it is only by entering wholeheartedly into the mood of the piece with the mind, that the body and the fingers can be coaxed into expressing this mood and obeying their nearly subconscious instructions without apprehension or undesired tension. Just like the proverbial centipede, we must not think of each motion of each finger consciously, or we will be paralyzed. What makes this so difficult to achieve is that the opposite applies to much of one's practice time, during which one must coldly analyze all of the mechanical details. But the ultimate success in public performance is to feel intensely that uncanny, ESP-like bond which can exist between the composer, the performer and the audience, and to learn to believe in it and immerse oneself in it with ever-growing dedication and conviction.

John Perry, the American pianist and teacher believes, "The most important thing is to concentrate with all your energy on what you are doing — listen with *all* your concentration. Then there will be no thought possible to engage in destructive worry." Rather typically, foci of his concentration were not specified in his written comments; nevertheless, in the check-list which followed he indicated that he preferred to focus upon the next phrase, tone quality and sonority, mood and projection, the character and quality of the instrument he was using, his interaction with the audience, to a certain extent the feeling in his muscles and what may be called the "flow" of the music.

While most of the responses to my questionnaire were written, a few were derived from recorded interviews. Their impromptu nature was often quite revelatory, as was the following with Canadian pianist, Robert Silverman:

> There are moments when I feel as though my playing were coming from without. I am merely the medium; the inspiration is from beyond. . . . I remember a recent all-Brahms recital, particularly Opus 118, numbers 2 and 6. At that point I was in a trance. . . . My state of concentration was so intense that I'm not even sure what I was concentrating on . . . maybe the sound; I must have been listening. I know I had some sort of inner ear to all kinds of nuances, the keyboard was just an extension of

my fingers, and I was at one with the music. . . . There was also a part of me that was a detached listener saying to himself, "This guy's pretty good. I'd like to hear him again sometime," and I must say that I heard the tape and it was damned good. But mostly, it was a moment of great humility, because I realized that, despite the fact that a tremendous amount of prior detailed preparation went into that performance, much of what I was doing then had absolutely nothing to do with those efforts. The inspiration may not have been from without, but if it was from within, I certainly did not consciously put it there. Perhaps the previous efforts were necessary in order to open the channels for that creativity to come through, but that's the most I can take credit for.

While, again, specific objects of attention were not delineated, the experience he describes is one that reappears time and again: an experience which Abraham Maslow would have called a "peak performance,"[9] and which Mihaly Csikszentmihalyi[10] would identify as a "flow experience" (discussed more fully below).

These two statements are fairly representative of the more than thirty that I received. Collectively, the responses provided me many valuable insights which, in most respects, confirmed the conclusions which I had synthesized from my own experience: that is, that the two objects of attention which, ideally, should occupy the center of attention during performance are:

1) *Musical Values.* Anything connected with the music *as an auditory experience*[11]

and

2) *Musical Gestalt.* One's "here-and-now" location within the musical structure (figure) with respect to the whole (ground).

Under the rubric "Musical Values" are included such things as sonority, mood, line and timing (to name those that appear most often), whose auditory realizations are integral to projection and communication. Matters relative to execution and technique, along with self-conscious considerations, are excluded (e.g., fingering, note identification, questions of personal acceptance, etc.). The basis for this conclusion is a synthesis of personal introspection with the expressed opinions of the "Olympic gold medalists" I have questioned. In its ideal sense it would seem to be axiomatic. Henceforth, therefore, when I speak of Musical Values, it is with such parameters in mind.

The need for conscious awareness of the musical gestalt should be obvious. The instances of a performer's *ad infinitum* repetitions of a sonata's exposition section are frequent enough to obviate further reminder. But aside from this, it would seem self-evident that structural coherence is impossible to convey unless the performer is aware of the organic interrelationships of the parts and whole as he performs. A personal experience may illustrate what I mean.

Each time I have played Liszt's B-minor Sonata I have had the feeling, as I played the two opening Gs, that I could see the entire work stretched out before me, and, perceiving the relationship of those opening notes to the *whole*, I knew exactly how those notes should be played.

Whether the musical gestalt is uppermost in the player's thinking is a question of priorities which are discussed below. It is quite possible that, for much of the time, with many pianists, musical gestalt might be found at a slightly lower level of awareness than musical values.

Concentrated Attention and the Passive Mood.

Stanislavski describes what he calls a "circle of attention" to illustrate concentrated awareness.[12] He suggests an imaginary circle of light which is surrounded by darkness. All that is within the circle may be foci of attention, he explains, with the attention restrained from straying beyond the circle's circumference. Obviously, this is a viable model not only for the actor but for any artist involved in the act of performance, especially if he is performing from memory.[13] It is something of this sort that I have implied in the foregoing: concentrated attention which is focused upon selected objects that are essential to the act of performance and communication — awareness which assumes exclusion of disruptive elements from the domain of the "circle." It is postulated here that exclusion from the "circle of attention" of these disruptive elements is a key to the maintenance of psychological equilibrium during performance, an essential step in the control of anxiety.

A child who is extremely nervous says, "I keep thinking of what chord should come next." A young woman stands back stage, extremely distraught, waiting for the buzzer that tells her to go on stage and begin the recital. She is feverishly "studying" the score, obviously trying to remember the notes of a passage that she has been turning over in her mind. A touring artist becomes totally distracted after noticing a well-known music critic sitting on the front row. Another, who has been in "top form" until intermission, finds it difficult to "put it together" afterward because he has perceived what he believes to be lack of approval in half-hearted applause. All of these are cases where irrelevant and disruptive elements have entered the "circle of attention."

But what kind of attention are we speaking of when we refer to concentration? Are we talking about wresting the musical values from the instrument, coercing and manipulating them to the demands of an indomitable will? Hardly. Almost everyone has had the experience of "trying," only to find that the goal being striven for remained frustratingly beyond reach.

As MacKinnon points out, "Conscious striving inevitably brings tension; and only when free from strain can the mechanism of memory (or recall) work unfailingly."[14] She refers to "passive attention" (a terminology used by many other writers). Gallwey speaks of "concentrating without thinking,"[15] while Arthur Koestler discusses "self-transcendent" mentation, with which he contradistinguishes "self-assertive" thought.[16] And, as Koestler observes, "Self-transcending emotions do not tend towards action [as do ones that are self-assertive], but towards quiescence."[17]

Self-transcendence cannot be achieved with self-assertive methods — with what Schultz calls "charged concepts."[18]

Passive attention and self-transcendent mentation inevitably suggest Zen[19] and Taoism: of observing, of "seeing." It is an attitude of mind where, if the will is involved at all, it is a will concerned with the result of an act rather than with the act itself.[20]

Achieving self-transcendence is the object of an artist's striving, of course, and, if concentration is best if it is upon objects that are free of self-concern, this would seem to be the logical course to follow. It is not a will-less striving, obviously, for the will is involved with the thing to be done. However, it is a willing that is passive, even when the thing willed is at the center of the "circle of attention."

I have known many young pianists who were convinced that if their wills were strong enough, and if they were thoroughly prepared, eventually they would be able to gain mastery over the act of performance through the determined exercise of their minds and muscles. How often this attitude has thwarted fulfillment of potential. Lest one conclude that passive attention with self-transcendent mentation implies mental "softness," let him be assured that achieving such an attitude in performance requires greater strength, courage and self-discipline than aggressive self-assertion. It assumes a poise that is not often achieved without long experience and, certainly, assumes consummate pianism and thorough musical preparation. In the end, the mood of passive attention is probably as important to practice as the music itself.

Multiple Cognitive Control.

It is obvious that there will always be more than one musical value in the circle of attention at any one moment, with several values demanding one's concentration at once. How is one's mind to be divided up among them, not forgetting that some small piece of conscious awareness must be reserved for the musical gestalt? Can one concentrate upon them all simultaneously? Hardly. It is unlikely that anyone can bring the *full focus* of conscious attention upon more than one thing at a time.[21] Is there some mechanism for time-allotment among them all in whatever order the exigencies of performance might dictate? How are the priorities decided? Assuming that one is successful in excluding "task-irrelevant" objects from the circle, how can he be assured that each of the remaining values receives its due?

Cognitive Psychology Looks at Attention.

Answers to some of these questions come from the field of cognitive psychology where the question of attention is the focus of much research. Chief among the issues being investigated are information-processing capacity and the question of selective attention, arousal and interest as they affect attention, control of attention, and consciousness.[22]

A number of theories have emerged to explain the apparent "bottleneck" which blocks us from attending to more than a limited amount of information at any one time. The bottleneck, attributed to neurological limitations, requires us to select from among the cues that impinge upon our sensory organs. The difficulty of attending fully to more than one voice of a fugue at one time is well known. Bringing full attention to bear upon two or more musical values simultaneously is likewise governed by limitations in this capacity (which no doubt varies among individuals).

Familiarity with the structure and meaning of the sensory input is one factor which clearly determines whether or not it will be processed, but, as observed earlier, the emotional relevance of the material (in its tendency to "arouse") is also a determinant. If a musical line is understood in terms of its structure and meaning, and if its expressive content is sufficiently appreciated, it may "grab" the attention from other musical values that are competing for attention at the same time. The brain evidently can handle a few alternatives but, if and when it is presented with too many, it makes a selection from among them based upon the criteria of meaningfulness and distinctiveness. Whereas one has some choice as to which "signal" to listen to, if there is no deliberate selectivity, the decision is made automatically by whatever mechanisms provided by nature for that purpose.[23] In other words, one can direct his attention toward one musical value or another but, should the attention not be consciously directed, the selection will be made at the subconscious level.

Cognitive psychologists give "lip-service" to consciousness but, since they seem reluctant to accept the reality of a subconscious (or unconscious), their efforts to integrate consciousness into their research on attention is limited — in fact, doomed to failure before it begins. They do dare to recognize that attention necessitates some sort of consciousness, but that is where their considerations end. While recognizing that much information from the environment is processed "automatically," they stop short of the connotation, "subconscious." Therefore, for a discussion of consciousness/subconsciousness as related to attention one must look elsewhere.

From Conscious to Subconscious and Back.

I have always been bothered by the notion of consciousness as a unified thing, with subconsciousness (unconsciousness, "reactivity," "bodily awareness," or automaticity) as the only other alternative. There have been too many instances in my own experience of "gray areas" between the conscious and subconscious: things which I must have noticed happening but which I had forgotten, and memories of incidents which, upon reflection, I could not recall noticing at the time they occurred. Such phenomena have also troubled Hilgard (among others) who observes:

> The concept of unity of the total consciousness is an attractive one, but it does not hold up under examination; there are too many shifts, as, for example, between the waking consciousness and the dream consciousness. There are also degrees of automatization achieved with practice, so that well-learned habits — such as playing a musical instrument, driving an automobile, or saying the alphabet — can go on with a minimum of conscious control once the activity is begun.[24]

Of course there are plausible explanations in terms of altered states of consciousness (discussed below), but, otherwise, one of the most convincing theories I have encountered to account for these variables is Arthur Koestler's *The Ghost in the Machine*:[25] a "scrialistic" rather than a "dualistic" (i.e., conscious/subconscious) interpretation, which sees consciousness in a gradual progression from focal consciousness to automaticity and back again. As he states it, "Consciousness is not an all-or-nothing affair but a *matter of degrees*."[26] In his view, consciousness is an emergent quality which increases or decreases by shades (as I interpret it) rather than by a step from one level of consciousness to another, or from consciousness to no consciousness. It is an elegant explanation for present purposes as it is quite easy to identify with the shades of awareness that appear in musical performance.

Koestler's hierarchic model is exemplified by the "inverted tree" which is so often used to represent other hierarchic organizations diagrammatically (government structure, military command, etc.):

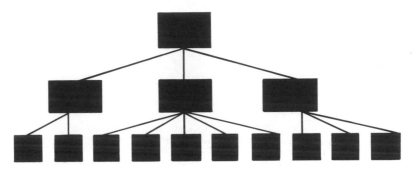

Figure 3.1

In this formulation, all thought is initiated from the top and filters down through all of the echelons to the bottom. Each node (or "holon," in Koestler's parlance), having been "triggered" by a holon in a higher echelon, functions in accordance with established "rules of the game," and triggers, in turn, the holons in a lower echelon. The "flexible strategies" issuing from the uppermost echelons contrast with the automated and specialized operations of holons in the lower echelons which, by comparison, are limited in their strategic capacities. Each holon "does its thing" (i.e., that which it has been equipped to do either by conditioning or conscious direction), "filtering" out unessential information having to do with its operation before it is fed back to the higher echelons.[27]

There is, then, a two-way flow: instructions derived from flexibly-based strategies initiated from the top (conscious decisions based, in part, upon the information received from the lowest echelons), and information about the environment, and responses to it, from below. The especially fascinating part of this conceptualization, in the end, is the opportunity it provides for an interpretation of consciousness and attention in all mentation, musical performance and otherwise.

Consciousness, as noted above, increases by degrees from the totally automatic operations at the lower echelons to what can and should be focal consciousness at the top.[28] The point that I wish to make here, however, is that it is crucial for the performer to exclude lower echelons from awareness, while bringing concentrated attention upon those at the top; that failure to do so is one of the factors involved in uncontrolled anxiety in performance. The following diagrammatic representation is freely adapted from Koestler:

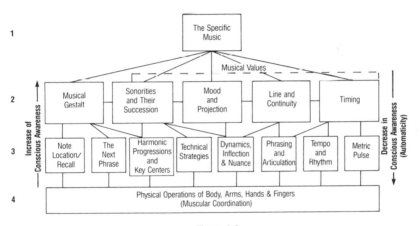

Figure 3.2

The single box (or node) at the top represents the work chosen to play. Obviously there must be a conscious decision at this level before anything else is done. The five boxes in the second level represent the foci of conscious attention discussed above.[29] Level three is the critical one. Although all such considerations (and others like them) must occupy focal attention in practice, conscious preoccupation with one or more of them in performance is hazardous (i.e., they are objects which should be excluded from the "circle of attention" during performance). Greater consideration is given in the fourth chapter to the objects making up this and level four, the latter including all of those totally automatic processes which are the products of conditioning and training (i.e., the coordinated physical operations of body, arms, hands and fingers).

While Koestler's ruminations are largely theoretical, those by another perceptive writer, David Sudnow, are views of hierarchic ordering of thought that are written from a practical vantage point. In fact, reading his two books, *The Ways of the Hand*, and *Talk's Body*, is rather like observing hierarchic mentation in action.[30] They deal ingeniously with the interrelationships of consciousness and behavior and stand in a supportive relationship to Koestler's theory. Sudnow, a professor of sociology, learned over a period of years to improvise jazz. Arranging himself strategically between two keyboards (a typewriter and a piano) he writes in depth of what his hands do in relation to his conscious thought. Often, in fact, one has the feeling that he sees his hands as enjoying an existence apart from himself; perhaps they do. That is clearly his point. His observation, "going for the sound," repeated many times as if in awe, is very close to the observation made by Anton Kuerti (above), "If there is a difficult leap, I think of the sound of the notes I am leaping to, not of the location or any mechanical detail." Obviously, what both these practicing pianists describe is the conscious observation of automatic processes (lower echelons) by focal consciousness (higher echelons). Both are standing off and watching their subconscious selves at work, a feat, by the way, which cannot be accomplished while in a "normal," everyday, routine state of consciousness.

Normal versus Altered Consciousness; The Peak Experience.

Pianist Robert Silverman suggested that he was "in a trance" on those occasions when he was truly at his best; and Anton Kuerti implied that he experienced something similar (both above). The state of "self-transcendence"[31] described by both these artists is unquestionably the same as that defined by Abraham Maslow as a "peak experience,"[32] and by Mihaly Csikszentmihalyi as a "flow experience."[33] They are states of consciousness that are recognized by most artists, mathematicians, scientists, philosophers, and many psychologists, and often discussed by them. Csikszentmihalyi observes:

There is a common experiential state which is present in various forms of play, and also under certain conditions in other activities which are not normally thought of as play. For lack of a better term, I will refer to this experience as "flow." Flow denotes the wholistic sensation present when we act with total involvement. . . . It is the state in which action follows upon action according to an internal logic which seems to need no conscious intervention on our part. We experience it as a unified flowing from one moment to the next, in which we feel in control of our actions, and in which there is little distinction between self and environment: between stimulus and response; or between past, present, and future. [34]

Maslow's views on the "peak experience" are similar: ". . . total fascination with the matter-in-hand . . . getting lost in the present . . . detachment from time and place."[35] According to him, one might expect loss of concern for the past and future, innocence, narrowing of consciousness, loss of ego, disappearance of fears, lessening of defenses and inhibition, strength and courage, acceptance (positive attitude), trust, Taoistic receptivity, aesthetic perceiving rather than abstracting, fullest spontaneity, fullest expressiveness of uniqueness, and fusion with the world.[36]

Such experiences are not necessarily limited to those in the arts and sciences. Almost everyone has entered the world of "self-transcendence" at one time or another when something totally fascinating has held him in rapt attention — when the outer world has been shut out for a period of time while full concentration was brought to bear upon whatever it was that took him "out of himself." As suggested, the reaction is not limited to the scientist, the mathematician, the artist, or the composer (although it is the Einsteins, the Oppenheimers, the Rembrandts and Beethovens who come first to mind) but, as Koestler observes, is often experienced by those of us in everyday life "when listening to Mozart, or looking at the ocean, or reading for the first time John Donne's *Holy Sonnets*."[37] It is not a world that is entered into by pre-design, nor by "self-assertive" methods, but is invariably entered as a consequence of total absorption in whatever it is that has commanded total conscious attention. It could be almost anything. For the individual with aesthetic needs, obviously, a thing of beauty is the most likely catalyst. And for the performing musician that something is the beauty of the music with which he is involved.

There is one misconception which could result from Maslow's description of the "peak experience" (above) — and this is an important point to be made. It is easily appreciated that loss of ego, fear, concern for the past and future, defenses and inhibition, etc. , can be manifestations of the "peak experience"; but it is also important to realize that that state of awareness is impossible to achieve in the first place if there is anxiety, fear, inhibition, preoccupation with self or with the past and future. These must be dismissed from consciousness *before* there is any hope that the peak experience is to be achieved. What this means for the pianist is that all technical concerns must have been eradicated; there can be no concern for the notes; and there can no longer be any doubts concerning personal worth or acceptance. The challenge for the performing artist is to eliminate all of these possible objects of concern before the concert begins.

The "flow" or "peak" experience — the moment of "self-transcendence" — clearly implies an altered state of awareness — what Charles Tart defines as a "discrete altered state of consciousness" (d-ASC). [38] Such things are not rare for any of us, of course, as we nearly all experience altered states of consciousness in one form or another nearly every day: day-dreaming, hypnagogic and hypopompic levels of awareness (i.e., the twilight between wakefulness and sleep), and other manifestations, which are not necessarily peak experiences in the Maslowian sense. Any state of awareness is altered, nonetheless, if it is a departure from the normal state in which we conduct our daily affairs, the peak experience being no exception. And far from indicating weaknesses of mind or character (as it is still so regarded by some less enlightened segments of our society), the altered state which characterizes the peak experience represents the ultimate attainment of the fully-functioning human being. It is the highest achievement of intelligence and imagination — an achievement which is fundamental to the creative act. It epitomizes that moment of self-transcendence which coincides with extraordinary insight, the "intuitive leap," "inspiration" and "ecstacy." It is quintessential to the complete aesthetic experience and must be freely entered into by the performing artist, without apprehension or inhibition, if he is to satisfy "the craving for self-transcendence"[39] that is fundamental to all artistic motivation.

Control of Attention vis-à-vis Control of Anxiety.

Control of attention and equilibrious mentation is impossible to achieve and maintain if there is anxiety. And, on the other hand, anxiety is a likely accompaniment to the musical performance if mentation is unstabilized and attention is not under control. It is rather like the proverbial "chicken and the egg." Any stimuli which are strong enough to create excessive anxiety will tend to negate efforts to concentrate attention upon musical values and the musical gestalt. And preoccupation with "task-irrelevant" details at the expense of musical considerations is a condition that is likely to culminate in an attack of anxiety.

Although the situation may seem insurmountable, it is not. Clearly, a solution to the problem can be found either by improving the quality and content of concentrated attention through education and training (musical, technical and psychological), or by taking steps to lower the level of anxiety which permeates the life-style of the individual through psychotherapy, physiotherapy, or a combination thereof. In some cases recourse to both education (or re-education) and therapy may be the most effective way to resolve the conflict. The various avenues will be explored in later chapters of the present volume (Chapters Five through Ten).

For the moment it is important to realize that anxiety and attention are interfaced; what affects one will necessarily affect the other. Excessive anxiety precludes well-focused attention; poorly-focused attention may result in uncontrolled anxiety.

Musical Fascination and Attention.

Tobias Matthay, who was also concerned about the quality of concentrated attention, made the following observation:

> True, such concentration may come almost "naturally" to
> the few possessors of that concatenation of various talents which

the public loosely gathers up into the term *genius*; and if we do possess this so-called "genius," then we may possibly succeed in giving such close attention without apparent effort, for the simple reason, that our bias towards Music is so extreme, and Music is such a keen delight to us, such a matter of life-and-death, that it is easy for us to be in this required state of keen engrossment, even, maybe, without much prompting from the teacher. But the teacher must ever be alert in such rare cases — for even a genius, we find, has frequent lapses of attention![40]

I am not convinced either that genius is a prerequisite for musical enchantment and the ability to concentrate. Musical enchantment — a sufficient enough cause for musical absorption — might be experienced by almost anybody. And certainly musical enchantment is a quality which arouses attention affectively. This, of course, brings us back to my earlier statement: that one's attention is more likely to be attracted to a stimulus that has an emotional significance. Should the beauty of a musical value be sufficiently important to the individual, concentration upon that musical value should not be a problem. If, on the other hand, the musical value is not sufficiently enchanting, perhaps other stimuli are masking it, perhaps the person is not listening to it, or perhaps he is somehow incapable of regarding it with enchantment. In any case, the musical value must eventually transcend all other values in terms of captivation before the ability to attend to it can be reasonably assured. If musical captivation evades the performer, perhaps he should ask himself why it eludes him.

Consciousness in Practice; Consciousness in Performance.

Musical values and the musical gestalt are more likely to achieve the center of attention in performance if they have been stressed in the preparation of the performance. The onus is layed upon both the teacher (who is capable of directing attention toward musical values and structure by inference and "highlighting") and the performer himself, whose attention must be self-directed toward those objects which are to be at the center of his "circle of attention." Even those aspects of the hierarchy which are in the lower echelons of mentation during performance must be brought to consciousness in practice, that is true; but their ultimate purpose, as functions in the service of higher-order mentation, must never be overlooked; e.g., fingering must serve the purposes of line, sonority, timing, as well as the needs of "note location/recall" through the haptic apparatus (see Chapter Four).

To repeat Anton Kuerti's observation (above), "Just like the proverbial centipede, we must not think of each motion of each finger consciously [during a performance] or we will be paralyzed. What makes this so difficult to achieve is that the opposite applies to much of one's practice time, during which one must coldly analyze all of the mechanical details. " Any number of pianists and pedagogues have made similar observations, from Matthay to MacKinnon, Ching and Newman, to many others. One must practice with full attention upon all the details, so that all of those processes that are to be below the level of awareness in performance will function reliably. When the performance comes, one must be able to close off the entries to the "circle of attention" with complete confidence that all of those automated functions in the lower echelons of the hierarchy will function efficaciously in response to the "flexible strategies" issuing from above. If that confidence is wanting, anxiety may not be far behind.

Listening to the Music: a Conscious Affair.

"Listening to the music" and "hearing the music" are two different things. [41] Music can be listened to only consciously, whereas music can be heard at the subconscious level. The composer, Ingolf Dahl, could not abide "canned music" as he ate in a restaurant (and many other musicians share his distaste, I am sure) since he could not just hear it — he had to listen to it; in which case the quality of the music (over which he had no control) was crucial. Most people can allow "mood music" to "wash over them" and never notice it; they only hear it, never listen to it. (It is one of the many opiates of our time.)

Unfortunately, many pianists, too, only hear the music and never listen to it. So many other facets of their performance occupy their attention that they forget how necessary it is to experience the music auditorily as they play it. Usually, they have never really listened to it in practice. And, though they have never listened to the music in practice, they still wonder why they have so much trouble focussing upon musical values in performance. Pitch acuity seems to have nothing to do with it; the person with absolute pitch is as likely not to listen as the one without it. In most cases the art of listening must be learned, it seems.

Even possession of absolute pitch is not a guaranty that all of the right things are going to be heard. Many years ago, while I was working with a student who had absolute pitch, trying to help him achieve greater and greater refinement of a particular phrase, I asked, in a moment of slight exasperation, "Don't you hear it?" His frustrated reply was, "I hear everything but the music." The significance of his answer made a profound impression upon me and I have never forgotten it.

As is reiterated in the next chapter, hearing the music can and does go on outside of conscious awareness. Listening to the music — its values and structural Gestalt — requires conscious effort: a form of attention which often must be cultivated. However, even if it is learned, should there be insufficient faith in the capacity of out-of-awareness functions to proceed unfalteringly, the ability to concentrate on the music will be hampered. One of these subconscious functions is what I call "note location/recall," a process greatly facilitated by high pitch acuity. As discussed in the next chapter, a want of faith in this function is probably the largest single deterrent to musical concentration. With high pitch acuity and faith in this process, steering the attention toward musical values is greatly facilitated. However, the necessary concentration still requires musical fascination and not a little energy.

NOTES AND REFERENCES

1. My debt to Arnold Schultz is acknowledged. His distinctions, "direct" and "indirect," or "reflective" consciousness, have been very useful here. Arnold Schultz, *A Theory of Consciousness* (N. Y.: Philosophical Library, 1973), pp. 16f.
2. *Op. cit.* , pp. 55-84.
3. Julian Jaynes, *The Origin of Consciousness in the Breakdown of the Bicameral Mind* (Boston: Houghton Mifflin Co. , 1976). Memories of events which took place outside of consciousness are often reported, recall having occurred under hypnosis or in an altered states of consciousness. Such phenomena may, exceptionally, have some relevance to musical performance but I have chosen not to muddy the waters at this point. For an explanation see: Ernest R. Hilgard, "Neodissociation Theory of Multiple Cognitive Control Systems," in Gary E. Schwartz and David Shapiro (eds.) *Consciousness and Self-Regulation*, Vol. 1 (N. Y.: Plenum Press, 1976), pp. 137-171.
4. This concept corresponds with Freud's "pleasure principle," to some degree, although it differs in that it recognizes that an adverse impression, while perhaps not always retained in long-term memory, is nevertheless an object which is likely to capture conscious attention. [See: Sigmund Freud, *Introductory Lectures on Psychoanalysis*, trans. James Strachey (N. Y.: Penguin Books, 1973; first publ. in 1963), pp. 401ff.] Schultz, *op. cit.* , accounts for this by the "charge" which accompanies either a pleasurable or displeasurable sensory encounter. Arthur Koestler, in *The Ghost in the Machine* (London: Pan Books, 1975; first pub. in 1967), p. 89, speaks of "emotional relevance. "
5. According to Eastern esoteric psychologies, consciousness has no limits. This is implied by Karl Pribram and David Bohm as well, both of whom have explained brain, mind and consciousness in terms of the hologram. See: Ken Wilber (ed.), *The Holographic Paradigm and Other Paradoxes* (Boulder and London: Shambhala, 1982). By contrast, Julian Jaynes postulates that consciousness is bound by the lexical metaphor. See: Jaynes, *op. cit.* I will have occasion to indicate below that, during periods of altered awareness, the extent of one's perception changes, so that what may have been subconscious before may become conscious.
6. Lilias MacKinnon, *Music by Heart* (London: Oxford University Press, 1926), pp. vf.

7. A pianist friend of mine tells me that once while on tour, and compelled to play a recital on a very bad piano, he mentally composed two business letters while playing his program. Although afterward he did not remember a note of what he had played, he judged that his performance must have been acceptable because he received good reviews.

8. As described in Abraham Maslow, *The Farther Reaches of Human Nature* (N. Y.: Penguin Books, 1976), p. 7.

9. Abraham Maslow, *Motivation and Personality*, 2nd edition (N. Y.: Harper and Row, 1970).

10. Mihalyi Csikszentmihalyi, "The Flow Experience," in Daniel Goleman and Richard J. Davidson (eds.), *Consciousness: Brain, States of Awareness, and Mysticism* (N. Y.: Harper and Row, 1979), p. 63.

11. It will be noted in due course that the kinesthetic experience is also an essential part of the performer's experience. However, the kinesthetic experience, under ideal conditions, should occur out of awareness, while it is through conscious awareness of the auditory experience that the performer verifies what he has done or is doing.

12. Constantin Stanislavski, *An Actor Prepares*, trans. Elizabeth Reynolds Hapgood (N. Y.: Theatre Arts Books, 1948), pp. 77ff.

13. The comparison here with the objectives of certain forms of meditation should be noted.

14. MacKinnon, *op. cit.*, p. 15.

15. W. Timothy Gallwey, *The Inner Game of Tennis* (N. Y: Bantam Books, 1974).

16. Koestler, *op. cit.*

17. *Ibid.*, p. 191.

18. Schultz, *op. cit.*

19. In particular, Eugen Herrigel, *Zen In the Art of Archery*, trans. R. F. C. Hull (N. Y.: Vintage Books, 1971; originally published in 1953).

20. A number of authors have applied Zen and Taoistic principles to activities practiced by many of us in the western world. See, especially, Gallwey, *op. cit*; and Luigi Bonpensiere, *New Pathways to Piano Technique* (N. Y.: Philosophical Library, 1952).

21. Robert L. Solso, *Cognitive Psychology* (N. Y.: Harcourt Brace Jovanovich, Inc., 1979), p. 142.

22. *Op. cit.*, p. 120.

23. Of particular interest are the researches outlined by Daniel Kahneman, *Attention and Effort* (Englewood Cliffs, N. J.: Prentice-Hall, 1973); D. A. Norman, *Memory and Attention*, 2nd edition (N. Y.: Wiley, 1976);

and Anne M. Treisman, "Selective Attention in Man" (*British Medical Bulletin*, 1964b, 20), 12-16.

24. Hilgard, *op. cit.*, p. 146.
25. Koestler, *op. cit.*
26. *Ibid.*, p. 205.
27. Koestler's discussion (*op. cit.*, pp. 3-112, particularly) is a "must read" for all thinking performers and teachers.
28. As noted above (see note 8 for example), it is quite possible to perform without any conscious attention whatsoever. In this case, the functions of even the highest echelons must have been automatized (in which case, as Koestler points out, the opportunity for flexible strategies has been relinquished).
29. Obviously a variable that is dependent upon which values the pianist considers most important.
30. David Sudnow, *Talk's Body* (N. Y.: Alfred A. Knopf, 1979), and *Ways of the Hand* (N. Y.: Bantam Books, 1979; first publ. in 1978).
31. Koestler, *op. cit.*
32. Maslow, *Motivation and Personality*, *op. cit.*
33. Csikszentmihalyi, *op. cit.*
34. *Loc. cit.*
35. Maslow, *The Farther Reaches of Human Nature*, *op. cit.*, p. 60.
36. *Ibid.*, pp. 61-68.
37. Koestler, *op. cit.*, p. 188.
38. Charles T. Tart, *States of Consciousness* (N. Y.: E. P. Dutton, 1975).
39. Koestler, *op. cit.*, pp. 195f.
40. Tobias Matthay, *Musical Interpretation* (Boston: The Boston Music Co., 1913), pp. 9f; a statement which owes much to: William James, *The Principles of Psychology* (N. Y.: Dover Publications, Inc., 1950; first published in 1890), volume 1, pp. 423f. James also observes: "Genius, in truth, means little more than the faculty of perceiving in an unhabitual way." *Ibid.*, Vol. 2, p. 110.
41. Matthay, *op. cit.*, p. 5.

Chapter 4

PERFORMANCE FUNCTIONS OUTSIDE OF CONSCIOUS AWARENESS.

Whatever is noticed in performance is conscious even when what is noticed is not retained in long-term memory. Whatever is not noticed is subconscious.[1] These are the distinctions I have chosen to use here. Whether or not one wishes to accept hierarchic order as an explanation of mentation, almost everyone recognizes that there is always some point at the lower end of consciousness where noticing seems to stop and where, if one continues downward, passing events slip more and more deeply into a state of non-awareness. Somewhere at the very top of this area of non-awareness would seem to be that stratum where experience can be monitored without being noticed (as in playing from memory, or in a variety of other types of performance). Near it is probably that stratum with which Pierre Janet was concerned: a level of cognitive functioning out of awareness which can surface in consciousness on occasion (e.g., in hypnotic experiences).[2] At the lowest extreme of non-awareness is the unconsciousness which results from a blow on the head, while somewhere between that extreme and the upper levels are those regions that are explored in dynamic psychiatry: the realms of the unconscious which reach into the darkest recesses of the human psyche, "collective" and otherwise.[3] Although these latter areas of non-awareness may well be significant at some point or other in playing from memory, I have chosen not to attempt a discussion of that relevance here. I have been concerned, instead, with the higher levels of non-awareness, which I prefer to designate "subconscious" rather than "unconscious." The distinction is henceforth indicated by the use of that word.[4] It is these "subconscious" regions, as opposed to conscious awareness, that are most important to the pianist playing from memory, at least from the standpoint of the present analysis — regions which, as Charles Tart notes, "are part of the mind, but not conscious."[5]

Who's Leading the Orchestra?

One evening in a restaurant I was listening to one of my students play dinner music. He was a fluent improviser and every night that he played he would spend several hours at a stretch chaining together snippets of one classical work after another (not just piano music), interspersed with some of the latest hit tunes. On this particular evening a small boy came to the piano to talk with him. With no interruption in the flow of the music, the two carried on a lively conversation for five minutes or more. Later I asked my student if he remembered what he had played during the time he was talking with the child. He hadn't the foggiest recollection.

Similarly, Canadian pianist Jane Coop recalls that, on a recent occasion when she was performing Beethoven's Fourth Concerto with the Toronto Symphony Orchestra, someone on the first row of the audience behind her evidently became ill. There was quite a commotion for several minutes which she could not avoid noticing. However, the music went on *without her conscious attention* all during that period. When asked how the performance went during this period she responded, "Oh, I know that it went well." When I asked, "How do you know that it did?" she responded, "I just know."

Incidents such as these are as commonplace in the field of music as they are in other walks of life — moments when well-rehearsed functions proceed at the subconscious levels of mind while conscious attention is directed toward related or even unrelated activities.[6] In the hierarchic order of mentation (referring to Figure 3.2, above) even those functions which are normally conscious (echelons 1 and 2) may operate occasionally below awareness, while conscious awareness is involved with a totally different hierarchy (e.g., the self-accompanied singer, the singing actor, or that automobile driver, again, who might also be carrying on a lively conversation with an attractive passenger as, visually, kinesthetically and perhaps auditorily, he responds to the exigencies of traffic at the subconscious level).

For the two pianists mentioned in Chapter Three, it is evident that both possessed highly developed auditory-haptic[7] coordinations (discussed below) in which they had complete faith — coordinations which could carry on the complex business of piano playing with little if any conscious participation on their part. It does seem possible that some kind of awareness can go on on the periphery even while attention is directed elsewhere (as in Jane Coop's experience) — a kind of subconscious cognition that can function while the conscious mind is otherwise occupied. The normal pattern in these circumstances, however, is for one or more of the sensory systems to monitor the environment at the subconscious level and to respond to the environment's signals according to the "rules of the game" without conscious mediation. Sometimes, as noted, the responses that continue to function out of awareness may be near enough to consciousness that, as in the case above, one "knows" that the responses have been the correct ones. However, in most cases, what has transpired at the subconscious level is beyond both cognition and memory.

Performance Functions Outside the "Circle of Attention."

There are two primary considerations in determining which functions should remain outside of awareness: what is temporally beyond the capacity of the mind to mediate, and what may be a distraction from first-priority considerations (i.e., musical values and musical gestalt). Clearly, the demands upon coordination soon reach beyond the complexity and speed possible for conscious mediation.

The same is true of what I call "note location/recall."[8] Fear of non-intervention in these processes remains one of the chief causes of performance failure. For as Julian Jaynes observes, "Consciousness is often not only unnecessary; it can be quite undesirable. [A] pianist suddenly conscious of his fingers during a furious set of arpeggios would have to stop playing."[9] As soon as he exceeds a given number of note location/recalls per second, conscious attention to the constituent parts of the action becomes impossible. Nearly all of what he does is the result of a complex coordination of auditory with haptic memory, neither of which is conscious. Remembering and locating the notes of the "furious arpeggios" implies a rate of speed which far exceeds the capacity for conscious mediation, leaving the responsibility for note location/recall entirely up to the subconscious (and automatic) side of intelligence. Anyone who is unwilling to accept this will never be able to play the piano or any musical instrument, and perhaps should question his ability to walk, or to execute any of those routine physical or behavioral maneuvers that are an integral part of everyday life. The two subconscious functions in which the pianist must acquire confidence, then, are his technique, and his auditory-haptic coordination, if the conscious mind is to be freed to consider only musical values, with some part left for the musical gestalt.

Technique.

Technique is the means by which one's musical intentions are realized. It is the bridge which connects musical ideation and fulfillment. It is, ultimately, the means by which auditory and kinesthetic perceptions are actually reconciled. Obviously, my use of this word is not limited exclusively to the implications of Czerny's "School of Velocity." Any sound that is to be controlled requires technique, whether loud or soft, fast or slow. Theoretically, any conscious attention to technique in performance subtracts from the amount of attention available for considerations of a higher priority.

It is not that temporal factors preclude concentration upon technical matters; technique often becomes the focus of attention in performance, to one degree or another, whether one likes it or not. Although some experienced pianists apparently prefer to give concentrated attention to technical strategies (judging from the poll that I took), most would rather not be so occupied. There would be unanimous agreement, I am sure, that whenever it does become necessary to concentrate upon technique in performance, it should be with the foreknowledge and confidence that all problems had been solved, and that all of the difficulties are again resolvable.It is safe to assume that rarely, and only in the ideal world, can the pianist enjoy the luxury of having technique remain entirely outside his "circle of attention." It is the ideal toward which one works; but one must be content, obviously, if it has been reduced to little more than the object of benign concern. Clearly, during the peak performance, technique recedes to the subconscious level; but, under normal conditions, one expects to have at least a corner of his conscious mind occupied with technical logistics. Further attention is given to this subject in Chapter Eight.

Note Location/Recall.

David Sudnow writes with endless fascination of his hands as they move toward "sounding places" on the keyboard without apparent conscious effort, almost, as noted in Chapter Three, as if he is observing the hands of someone else.[10] Any experienced pianist who stops to reflect on the phenomenon of his hands moving to constantly new positions on the keyboard must regard it with equal awe. The phenomenon, which we take for granted, is certainly not the product of conscious deliberation, at least beyond the most rudimentary stage of development. To play even the simplest piece demands a certain degree of automaticity in remembering and locating notes if it is to be played with any fluency or musicality whatsoever. The arms and fingers must move with ease to ever new locations on the keyboard without being guided to these locations consciously. This phenomenon, in playing from memory, is what I call "note location/recall," since remembering the notes and locating the notes on the keyboard must be an act of coordinated simultaneity. Note location/recall relies for the most part upon haptic memory, but it is normally aided by the auditory system to one degree or another even in pianists whose auditory systems are less than acute (i.e., auditory-haptic coordination).

"Chunking."

As I inferred in Chapter Three, the amount of experience a pianist has will determine which fundamentals must be consciously considered in practice and which might be taken for granted as functions of automated processes. Hypothetically, a beginner would have to give conscious consideration to the location and recall of the following notes, learning where each of the notes is found on the keyboard and, later, when playing from memory, to be aware of the melodic contour that resulted from the chaining of these notes. Each note is, for awhile, an entity, which first becomes interrelated (auditorily and haptically) with the other entities melodically:

Figure 4.1

Later the student learns that the combination of these four notes, sounded together, makes a chord. Little by little that composite structure becomes an identifiable entity in itself, the individual notes being assumed. The chord itself can then become the focus of attention with its "parts" taken for granted both at the auditory and haptic level.

Figure 4.2

The student later encounters a passage like the following:

Figure 4.3

By this time the chord can be recognized, both auditorily and haptically, as the structure underlying the series of twenty-four notes. The individual notes can sink more deeply into the subconscious (and auditory-haptic coordination), while awareness is centered upon the melodic contour and passage's chordal framework — a chord which is by now a part of the vocabulary — a structural unit in the store of long-term memories. The same can be said for the following passage further down the line of experience:

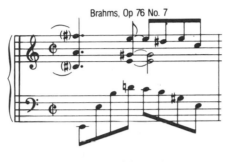

Figure 4.4

Obviously, the student who is at the level suggested by Fig. 4.1 must bring focal consciousness to bear upon locating and playing each note in practice (hopefully, interrelating them melodically), whereas by the time he reaches the level implied by Fig. 4.2 his concentrated attention can spread out, taking the individual notes as sub-structures (i.e., he now plays *the dominant-seventh chord*). By Fig. 4.3 even the chord is taken for granted as the foundation for the series of notes which, as a result, are intelligibly interrelated in the auditory and haptic systems. The same is true of Fig. 4.4 where additional structures can now be assumed. This logic, of course, can be extended to encompass the successions of chords (progressions) which are syntactically characteristic of the piano music in one style-period or another (e.g., cadence formulae), and, ultimately, can explain why pianists who have incorporated keyboard harmony and improvisation into their practice schedules are invariably amongst those whose memories are most reliable and who are among the best sight-readers.

All of the foregoing illustrates what cognitive psychologists call "chunking" as it relates to piano playing — a phenomenon which allows us to grasp increasingly larger, more complex units (chunks) as experience is acquired, by habituating greater and greater numbers of the constituent parts which make up those units.[11] The advantage to concentrated attention in piano playing is that, as smaller units combine to form chunks (e.g., as notes become chords,

and chords become passages), the rate of speed at which the new and
more complex chunks pass the "here-and-now" reduces, making them
more and more manageable as points of awareness. Where once
twenty-four separate notes (Fig. 4.3) might pass the here-and-now at
a rate of speed which made them impossible to consider individually,
now the *passage*, based upon a dominant-seventh chord and contain-
ing twenty-four constituent parts, passes the here-and-now at a rate
of speed which permits it to be consciously regarded as a compre-
hended entity. It is now a "sound:" an auditory-haptic whole,
rendered so by experience. Note location/recall takes care of the
constituent parts of the whole while conscious attention is given to the
totality. One might even say that, ultimately, as experience grows,
the process becomes "chunk location/recall" rather than note loc-
ation/recall.

Haptic vis-à-vis Auditory Acuity in Playing from Memory.

Sudnow's observations might appear, at times, to attribute the
phenomena of his hand movements solely to haptic activity. Obviously this would be a false conclusion. His repeated reference to
"going for the sound" should negate that impression. One must conclude that he assumes the participation of his auditory mechanisms in
the activity even when he seems to be solely concerned with manifestations perceived visually. Perhaps because of his high auditory
acuity, it might never occur to him that auditory perception would
not function in tandem with his haptic functions. Since he is involved
with improvisation, one can assume that his auditory and haptic
functions are already highly coordinated — coordinated, perhaps,
beyond his awareness of the fact.

Playing from memory, nonetheless, can involve a quite different
set of interrelationships between the auditory and haptic systems. It
should not, but more often, it does. Playing from memory is possible
with at least three different interrelationships:

1) Balanced, where the auditory processes stimulate com-
     plementary haptic activity (as with persons who are fluent
     in extempore playing).

2) Balanced, in which haptic memory may lead, but where

auditory memory stands in an instantaneous confirmatory and monitoring relationship to it.

3) Haptic memory which functions apart from auditory memory.

The first of these is clearly the most desirable and is common even among pianists without absolute pitch. The second is frequently encountered among pianists with good ears who have not developed the practice of extemporization. The third is probably the most widespread and is particularly prevalent among pianists who distrust their auditory senses.

Two experiments were performed in 1981-1982 at the University of British Columbia to study these three interrelationships. The first of them involved twenty-four pianists (professionals and pre-professionals) who had earned the musical respect of their peers and the community. Twelve of them had absolute pitch and the remainder had good, if not "perfect," pitch discrimination. Each was asked to perform from memory a rapidly-moving work of five to ten minutes duration which was in his current repertoire *without auditory feedback*. The equipment used for the experiment, which included a Baldwin Electropiano, a tape recorder, industrial-type ear shields, E. A. R. ear plugs, and a vacuum sweeper, was brought together to assure that they would be unable to gather auditory information exteriorly. (The high-decibel-producing vacuum sweeper was used to mask any remaining sound left over from the attenuation procedures.) The "deaf" performance was followed by a second performance *with* auditory feedback; both performances were recorded through the electronic system, internally.

All of the performances were later evaluated for note and rhythm flaws by a panel of knowledgable musicians using the tape recordings. No significant differences could be detected between the two performances by the players with absolute pitch (beyond deviations one might normally expect). None of the pianists without absolute pitch had great difficulty in performing the well-rehearsed piece, although some slight faults were noted in terms of memory and control in the "deaf" performances.[12]

As a second part of the first experiment subjects were asked, without prior warning, to play a work from memory, without auditory feedback, which they had not played or practiced for over a year. Again, the pianists with absolute pitch experienced no particular difficulty — *especially those who had reported prolonged experience in extempore playing*. Quite independently, two members of this group volunteered the invaluable observation that, while playing the unpracticed piece, they were caused to listen more intently than usual to the music "in their heads," whereas in the first piece they had relied more heavily upon "finger memory." Only one of the twelve pianists without absolute pitch was able to play more than the first phrase or two of the unpracticed work, and he, significantly, was a highly-competent extempore player who, as he volunteered, was also able to play the music he heard "in his head."

For the second experiment I was interested in studying sensory priorities in pianists with and without absolute pitch. If possible I wanted to answer such questions as: Which of the two primary sensory systems lead in the learning process? Can pianists internalize pitches from the music notation (i.e., from visual information), or from information gathered through the haptic senses? Can either of these operations be fulfilled without auditory feedback and with only a minimum length of time to accomplish it?

Six short piano pieces were composed, coinciding in length (27 measures) and exterior form. They were identical in rhythm and texture, differing only in various degrees of pitch inflection. All began and ended with the same tonal centre, had quite similar incipits and final cadences. The compositional style was predominantly contrapuntal, the harmonic character (between pieces) ranging from extremely florid chromaticism to ersatz atonality.[13]

Twenty university piano majors took part in the experiment, ten with absolute pitch and ten without. All twenty of the pianists were supplied with a copy of the same piece, chosen randomly from the six which had been composed and recorded, and each was assigned a practice room furnished with a silenced piano (no auditory feedback). All were given ten minutes to practice the piece and, after approximately a five minute interval, were exposed to a tape recording of the six pieces, the object being to identify the piece they had practiced (by an assigned number). Of the ten students with absolute pitch seven made correct identifications; of those without absolute pitch only two responded correctly. Several conclusions can be reached based upon the supporting evidence:

1) Pianists with absolute pitch can internalize pitches from visual information provided by the music notation.

2) Unless provided with enough time to rationalize the music notation and to deduce its meaning from available knowledge, pianists without absolute pitch cannot internalize the pitches. Conclusion: internalization of pitches is not instantaneous, and auditory perception defers to the haptic mechanisms which are caused to act first.

3) In general, the haptic system, acting alone, does not appear to elicit pitch information in persons without absolute pitch, and perhaps does not do so in those with absolute pitch either. This would seem to be true except, perhaps, for those pianists who are practiced extempore players.

4) The experiment did not reveal information as to which sensory system functions first, only that, for the person with absolute pitch, the learning of pitches evidently begins quite early through audiation of pitch information derived from visual sources.

Many other conclusions are possible for the musician if this evidence is combined with experience. I prefer, however, to leave such speculations to the initiative of the reader.

As noted in Chapter Three, possession of absolute pitch is an obvious practical boon to the pianist playing from memory, although there is one drawback: a temptation to listen to pitches to the exclusion of the music (exemplified also in the tendency to hear pitches and not their intervallic relationships). Such a person must understand ultimately that ·there is a difference; hearing with absolute pitch is accomplished subconsciously, while listening to the music is a conscious affair that is synonymous with listening to musical values, one of the two fundamentals which should occupy conscious attention.

Irrespective of this tempting pitfall, there is no denying the advantage to confidence in an ability to internalize pitches — in being able to move almost instantaneously to the places on the keyboard which correspond to these pitches — in *knowing* that this can be done. A player is fortunate who can begin at this point.

The ability to internalize pitches need not be limited to the person with absolute pitch, however. With proper training and application the player without absolute pitch can learn also to internalize pitches through their interrelationships, and can eventually automate the process. In this case as well, locating the right notes without conscious effort is a matter of practice. The key to this capacity, for the person without absolute pitch, is to be found in extempore playing.

Pitch Perception and Extempore Playing.

The most effective way to integrate pitch perception and the haptic system has proved to be through extempore playing.[14] I know of no attempts to explain it. Obviously, "playing by ear" involves the auditory system to a high degree, but the important fact is its alliance with the haptic system. Absolute pitch is not a prerequisite, although auditory acuity is clearly indicated.

As a rule persons with absolute pitch learn to play extemporaneously. The reason is obvious: it is a natural step for this group of players to condition the haptic system to respond reflexively to internalized auditory signals.[15] For the individual without absolute pitch the haptic system must be conditioned to respond automatically to the *relationship* of present to future pitches. With this group, acquisition of the skill is not nearly so common as it might be, possibly because, as in so many instances, inherent psychological factors seem to inhibit its development. Some of these factors are explored below. Extemporaneous playing, regardless, appears to be a skill which needs its roots and early development in childhood.

The Role of the Visual System in Playing from Memory.

Much attention and credit has been given to so-called "photographic memory," and to other functions which may or may not result from the visual system. Evidently many pianists can visualize the smallest details of the printed score as they play. I, for one, am aware of which page I am on (most of the time, left or right), but otherwise I "see" no specific details; so I, personally, cannot vouch for photographic memory as a viable aid to musical memory.[16] But that so-called "photographic memory" is not musical memory anyway; it is visual memory. And as such, like playing from the score, the notation is used as a *prompt* for the auditory-haptic system.

A stronger case perhaps can be made for the role of the visual system in another capacity. As David Sudnow's analysis suggests, observation of the myriad of positions of the hands on the keyboard may be of utmost importance, at least to sighted pianists. The late Lillian Steuber often stressed the importance to memory of the "mental photographs" taken by the mind. I would not disagree. However, account must be taken of the many fine pianists (as well as of the many famous organists of the Middle Ages and Renaissance) who were born without sight. Evidently the visual system lends valuable aid to auditory-haptic memory for sighted persons, but its function is not indispensable. When it does assist, it unquestionably does so at the subconscious level, as I am sure that most pianists would find it very difficult to reflect with certainty upon the role their sight has played in performing from memory — at least from this second point of view.

A personal experience comes to mind. One evening not too long ago, just after I had begun the first work on a recital program, every light in the house went out, leaving the entire recital hall in total darkness. I was unable even to see the keyboard. As the piece I had begun was the Beethoven Rondo in C major, Op. 51 No. 1 — a not too difficult piece from the virtuosic point of view — I continued with the optimistic belief that the lights would come back on within a few seconds. But seconds became minutes, and I found myself near the end of the piece, with still no light. The only blemish in the performance was a slight "stumble" in the chromatic run near the end. (I never realized to what extent I relied upon my sight as an aid to dexterity.) I relate this story because it was obvious that I did not rely upon my sight for purposes of musical memory — only for technique. (It has occurred to me in retrospect how fortunate I was that the lights did not go off during the next work on the program: Beethoven's "Rage Over the Lost Penny.")

"Forgetting the Notes" and Losing Control.

The fear most commonly expressed by pianists playing from memory is of forgetting the notes, followed, usually, by fear of losing control. If one reasons it out, of course, it becomes obvious that the two fears are fundamentally interrelated and inseparable. However, for the sake of clarity, I pursue one of these fears at a time.

What is the anatomy of "forgetting the notes?" The answer should be obvious from the foregoing: forgetting the notes is the common result of an attempt to make conscious a function that is best left in the subconscious domain. Note location/recall (even "chunk location/recall") is such a function. Remembering notes involves bringing to awareness the *names* or *representations* of sounds rather than the sounds themselves. This is not musical memory at all. It is a conscious intellectual process of a type best excluded from any performance. For the properly prepared pianist note location/recall, which is concerned solely with sound, pitches and sonorities, is left at the subconscious level.

One of the ramifications of control loss, or fear of it, is often sudden concern for note memory. That is why I observed them as interrelated fears. And, vice versa, fear of forgetting the notes often triggers fear of losing control. The reader should have gathered by now that the only way to break up such a feedback loop, after one has learned to side-step the ego, is by securing the technique to its maximum, and by laying the groundwork for memory which retains note location/recall at the subconscious level, free from conscious intervention.

NOTES AND REFERENCES

1. Arnold Schultz's perceptive analysis of these outside-of-awareness phenomena should not be overlooked, especially as they can relate to musical performance. Arnold Schultz, A Theory of Consciousness (N. Y.: Philosophical Library, 1973), chapter 3.
2. Henry F. Ellenberger, The Discovery of the Unconscious. The History and Evolution of Dynamic Psychiatry (N. Y.: Basic Books, 1970), pp. 359f; Ernest R. Hilgard, "Neodissociation Theory of Multiple Cognitive Control Systems," in Gary E. Schwartz and David Shapiro (eds.). Consciousness and Self-Regulation, Vol. 1 (New York: Plenum Press, 1976), pp. 138f.
3. The works of Sigmund Freud; C. G. Jung, The Archetypes and the Collective Unconscious. Trans. R. F. C. Hull, second edition (N. Y.: Princeton University Press, 1968).

4. Barbara Brown uses the word "unconscious" to include the out-of-awareness processes which I have called "subconscious." Barbara B. Brown, Supermind. The Ultimate Energy (N. Y.: Harper and Row, 1980).

5. Charles T. Tart, States of Consciousness (N. Y.: E. P. Dutton, 1975), p. 110.

6. The pianist in Chapter Three, footnote eight, was also performing without conscious intervention.

7. I use the word "haptic" from this point onward because it includes perception by both the tactile and kinesthetic mechanisms. See S. H. Bartley, "What is Perception?" in Daniel Goleman and Richard J. Davidson (eds.), Consciousness: Brain, States of Awareness, and Mysticism (N. Y.:Harper and Row, 1979), pp. 35-39.

8. I use the designation "note location/recall" to indicate the simultaneous and integrated act of remembering and physically locating notes on the keyboard.

9. Julian Jaynes, The Origin of Consciousness in the Breakdown of the Bicameral Mind (Boston: Houghton Mifflin Co., 1976), p. 26.

10. David Sudnow, Ways of the Hand (N. Y.: Bantam Books, 1978); Talk's Body (N. Y.: Alfred A. Knopf, 1979).

11. See Robert L. Solso, Cognitive Psychology (N. Y.: Harcourt Brace Jovanovich, Inc., 1979), pp. 178ff.

12. It is interesting to note that, apparently, some pianists without absolute pitch rely very heavily upon auditory feedback, while others depend largely upon haptic memory, so that the latter, when deprived of auditory feedback, experience no significant difficulties in playing a well-rehearsed piece from memory when there is no auditory feedback.

13. One of the "Inventions" was published in the West Coast Review (17/2, June 1982), 6-7.

14. This has been noted by William S. Newman, The Pianist's Problems (N. Y.: Harper and Row, revised 1956), and by Abby Whiteside, Indispensables of Piano Technique (N. Y.: Coleman-Ross, 2nd edition, 1961), among others.

15. Eighty percent of the experienced pianists I polled who had absolute pitch were adept improvisers. Perhaps significantly, only twenty percent of those without it had developed the skill.

16. In my youth the result of my visualizations was more vivid than it is today. Perhaps, as someone has said, "I ran out of film."

Chapter 5
PRACTICE AND STUDY

As I noted in Chapter Two, the most careful and intelligent preparation may not insure the pianist totally against performance anxiety. Other factors are obviously involved. But, on the other hand, there is no defense against anxiety without adequate preparation, no matter what other steps have been taken to establish psychological equilibrium. If one goes into a performance with an insecure auditory-haptic memory, with technical problems unresolved, or with gross musical ambivalence, anxiety is to be expected. Of course experienced performers know that there is the element of risk even in the best-prepared performance, but if the program has been thoroughly prepared, and most other anxiety-inducers have been brought under control, the odds are at least in the performer's favor.

Advice on practice methods is cheap and plentiful. Much of it is good, once it is stripped of its proselytistic rhetoric. A great deal is sheer nonsense that could work only because of irrational belief in it (which does not make it a panacea for every other pianist). In truth, with a few guidelines, a little good judgment, and considerable self-discipline, most young pianists can work out their own practice procedures — methods which will work well for them regardless of their musical goals. That which follows is an attempt to clarify some of these guidelines.

INITIAL IMPRESSIONS:
SONOROUS AND HAPTIC IMAGES

Do it Right the First Time.

The motto for every pianist during each practice period should be, "Do it right the first time"— not the second, third, fourth, or fifth, but the *first time*.

Although this motto is intended as a guiding principle for all drills and repetitions, it holds equally for first encounters with new repertoire. I am certainly not the only writer to emphasize the importance of accurate first impressions.[1] The first auditory and haptic impressions unquestionably register somewhere in long-term memory, and if they are correct registrations, they can be an advantage to memory in performances for years to come. This is as true of auditory memory as it is of haptic memory (even though, as noted above, these two senses may function independently in the early stages). When succeeded by contradictory stimuli, these first stimuli still adhere tenaciously to their places in long-term memory, albeit at the subconscious level.

The greater the pitch or haptic sensitivity, the more crucial that first encounter seems to be. Pianists with high auditory acuity may carry the initial impression with them for many years. I have known pianists with acute haptic sensitivity whose "fingers" never seem to forget the music.

Such acuity can also work to the pianist's disadvantage, of course. Careless initial practice is often the cause of false impressions among students and professionals alike. And everyone knows how difficult it is to get rid of wrong notes that have been worked in after a careless first reading — errors which can surface again years later during a moment of inattention.

Eating the Cake before it is Baked.

There is something to be said for getting an "overview" of a new work — for seeing "the forest" before "the trees." Fast readers frequently do their first readings in tempo, not worrying too much about notes that may be missed along the way. This practice seems to work well for such pianists, in spite of the risk of registering wrong notes in memory. For most people, however, reading through at a tempo that insures maximum accuracy is clearly the best policy (whatever tempo that may be). Playing under the tempo need not interfere with acquiring an overview. So long as the reading goes beyond the mere kinesthetic experience, and includes concentrated listening as well, a slow tempo can be as effective as a fast one for conceptualizing the whole. Whether or not one needs to go to the extremes advocated by

James Ching[2] would depend upon the level of pianistic talent, obviously. The important thing to remember is to *do it accurately the first time*. I believe that should be the common denominator for all first encounters, the native endowments of the pianist notwithstanding.

Maintaining vigilance over accuracy in practice requires unwavering conscious attention — concentration which takes much stamina and self-discipline. There is a great temptation to "taste the cake before it is baked" — to play the music before all of the subconscious functions have been automatized — to revel in the music at the intuitive level, prematurely abandoning all conscious control. It is a temptation which we have all experienced; a mark of maturity is implicit in the ability to resist. Fatigue can contribute to a lowered resistance to the temptation, it is true. However, one needs continually to be reminded that premature release from conscious vigilance is usually responsible for an increase in errors with wasted practice time as the result.

Years ago, while listening to students practice, I came to the conclusion that probably more time was wasted in the name of practice than upon any other human activity. Much of that waste is due to the lowering of vigilance manifest in premature "cake tasting." Perhaps it is as Newman says, "It seems . . . that the most important mission of the piano teacher is to guide the practice toward the day when the student can become his own teacher."[3] I have also always believed that, if I could teach the student how to make the best use of his practice time, I would have won half the battle. "Doing it right the first time" is the first lesson the student must learn.

Internalizing the Music.

Many famous pianists and teachers have advocated study of the score away from the piano (Leschetizky, among many others). If one internalizes the music from what he sees on the printed page it is a splendid way to get familiar with a work auditorily before engaging the haptic senses. Nothing is gained, however, if notes on the page remain mere symbols of the music, with no musical internalization taking place. Visual thinking simply takes the place of aural imagery to the ultimate disadvantage of musical understanding and memory.

I have known a number of fine pianists who have learned entire scores from memory before working them out at the keyboard.[4] It is an excellent way of idealizing the music. In my experience haptic memory lags behind auditory memory, which was the main drawback for me. It is apparently not so for everybody.

Lilias MacKinnon regretted the demise of the dumb piano for practice. She believed that one could benefit from practicing on a silent keyboard, suggesting (correctly, in many cases) that it would encourage internalization of the music while engaging the haptic senses.[5] Again fine, as long as one is assured that the one who is practicing hears what he is practicing. Actually, the dumb piano is still used occasionally. A few years ago a friend of mine committed himself to a performance of a new piano concerto. It did not bother him in the least that he would be on a long ocean voyage, away from a piano of any kind for three to four weeks prior to the first rehearsal. He merely took along a portable practice keyboard and learned the concerto on that.[6] Such a practice would be utterly useless without the ability to internalize the music, obviously. Pianists with absolute pitch can do it, naturally, but the ability is not limited to them. Any good musician with above average pitch acuity can do the same thing, even if not with the same facility.

The point here is that the ability to internalize the music of the printed score should be cultivated by everyone, and these are two good ways of encouraging the practice. There is no question but that the ability to internalize pitches is important if not critical to musical memory. Without this ability one must memorize without recourse to the auditory system.[7]

Keyboard Analysis.

I observed in Chapter Three that at least one corner of a pianist's conscious attention must be reserved for the musical gestalt. Knowing where one is in the musical structure at all times with reference to the whole is essential, but presupposes an understanding of the total structure as well as of the structure's microcosm. The structural microcosm must be understood consciously before taking its place in the subconscious — the only position from which it can function effectively in performance.[8] The pianist's conscious awareness of his position within the structural macrocosm depends, to a large extent, upon this having taken place. When accomplished, not only is the performer provided with an intelligible structural orientation, but he has, as well, a secure foundation upon which to build a coherent musical conception, and an important key to musical values. Put another way, it is imperative for the pianist to know not only what is in the music and why, but it is important for him to comprehend it both consciously and, for those structural functions which pass too quickly to monitor consciously, at the subconscious level.

One of the most important steps a pianist can take prior to committing a work to memory is to filter all of its structural underpinnings through the intellect, experiencing them auditorily while allowing them to mingle freely with his intuitive faculties. Without this filtering process, the memorized musical fabric by-passes the intellect almost entirely, and rests uncomfortably and sometimes awkwardly upon pure subconscious whimsy. Fine, as long as no questions are asked about the Whys of the performance during the performance, and as long as one is not concerned about the musical gestalt. Another benefit from keyboard analysis is obviously the gain in stylistic insight, not only for the work in hand, but for all subsequent works to be studied, making each in turn more accessible.

ESTABLISHING AUDITORY AND HAPTIC MEMORY

Practicing Mistakes.

It goes without saying that fewer repetitions are needed for some pianists to secure musical memory than for others. To a great extent individual differences may rest with acuity of pitch and haptic sensitivity. One pianist may require only five accurate repetitions of a pattern to absorb a musical pattern while someone else may need eight or ten. The key word, of course, is "accurate." How frequently I hear pianists practice a passage once with an error, repeat the passage with the same error, repeat it again with the same mistake, repeat it once more without the mistake, miraculously, then go on to the next passage which they practice in the same way. Obviously, they are practicing mistakes.[9] It does not take much imagination to realize that the more repetitions that seem to be required to establish a given musical segment in haptic and auditory memory, the more important it is to make each repetition count. It is senseless to spend precious hours grinding in wrong notes and rhythms, but that is precisely what happens when they are practiced more times than the correct ones.

Practicing mistakes is clearly not what the young pianist intends; the tendency to do so is easy to understand. Practice requires undivided attention and vigilance, together with a certain objectivity that precludes "dream-world cake-tasting." As with first readings, the pianist must have the maturity to resist the temptation to play through before he is reasonably assured that he is ready to do so; i.e., when playing through assumes a tempo for which his automatic processes are not yet prepared.[10] If one simply remembers "to do it accurately the first time" the problem is usually avoided, since both concentrated attention and a judicious tempo are presupposed.

How Slow is Slow Practice?

At one time or other, obviously, no tempo is too fast provided it is monitored with full concentration. And to the contrary, without concentration even the slowest tempo can be too fast. One of my teachers could simply not understand why anyone would need to practice slowly. She apparently did not need to, since her concentration during practice was so razor sharp, and her auditory-haptic coordination so keen, that she seldom needed to practice below tempo to assure maximum accuracy. What she did not realize was that she was somewhat extraordinary in this respect, a fact which caused her to overlook the less extraordinary skills of some of her students. Many famous artists, on the other hand, insist upon much slow practice for themselves as well as for their students.[11] How slow is "slow" is seldom defined, however. Again, the determinant must be the degree of concentration that can be brought into focus to insure that each repetition is as near to flawless as possible.

I fully recognize the necessity of playing a work through in tempo; obviously, this needs to be done many times before a performance — a performance which, itself, must be rehearsed at some point or other. Doing it right the first time still holds true, nevertheless. Practicing the performance even the first time should not be done without a reasonable assurance that it can be done with as few mistakes as possible. Nothing is gained by a first play-through which, by virtue of previous flawed repetitions, has no chance of proceeding without mishap.

The excuse, often given by students, that a piece can only be played in a fast tempo (with all the attendant errors) cannot be countenanced. What this says is that the student has learned the piece without conscious attention and that his memory hangs by a slender subconscious thread that has bypassed the intellect. Obviously, this is a dangerous way to proceed since most if not all subconscious functions must be filtered through consciousness in practice if they are to be secure or musically meaningful. Knowing the music only "accidentally" is not to know it, really, even though knowing it consciously is insufficient too until many of those functions discussed above have become automatic.

How slow is slow practice? The answer is, As fast as you may wish *without errors*.

Haptic without Auditory Practice.

For pianists who question the reliability of their auditory-haptic coordination, many hours are often spent solely for the purpose of securing haptic memory. Since they do not trust their auditory capacity or, as a consequence, their ability to retain auditory stimuli, they try to compensate for it by "grinding in" haptic memory. In the process hours upon end are spent at the piano rarely listening to what comes out of it. Instead of listening to the music they may only "hear" it on the fringe of awareness, their conscious experience of the music coming to them solely by way of kinesthetic sensation. As stated in Chapter Three, many pianists who believe they are listening to the music are really only experiencing it haptically.

Whereas these pianists are usually "flying deaf" without realizing it, they do derive a fringe benefit: a more secure haptic memory. And, while in the process of confirming haptic memory, they often develop excellent key control — a control which, if they learn to listen, enables them to produce an excellent range of tone color (assuming other favorable musical attributes are at their disposal). In other words, the added keyboard contact resulting from the effort to establish haptic memory may provide them with greater technical skill and potential. If such a person never learns to listen, of course, the consequences can often be quite sad.

Fingering and Haptic Memory.

Fingering is obviously as important to haptic memory as it is to considerations of nuance, phrasing and articulation. For the pianist who relies heavily upon haptic memory, the distance between notes must be felt in the hand and arms before it feels secure in the memory. Repetition with the same fingerings establishes these intervallic relationships haptically. As Pavlov showed (in another context), the automaticity that results when identical stimuli act repeatedly upon the haptic system is analagous to repeated stimuli acting upon any of the senses.

When automaticity is achieved through haptic memory, and is coordinated with auditory memory of the same musical material, a cross-confirmation results which is of great comfort to the player when playing from memory.

The pianist for whom fingering is not important is usually one with absolute pitch and attendant extempore skills. Hearing a combination of notes irrespective of their intervallic relationships, he will be tempted to use any combination of fingers that are available and convenient, since he has learned that he need not rely upon kinesthetic/intervallic relationships to sustain his memory. This, as I will point out several times in these pages, can be a hindrance as well as a blessing if it causes him to ignore the importance of fingering for musical reasons. As noted in Chapter Four, kinesthetic awareness (of which fingering forms a part) is as important as auditory awareness in the total musical experience. Neglect of this consideration can and does lead to that "something missing" in the musical result, even when memory is apparently secure.

The pianist who must rely upon fingering to help sustain his memory usually works at it rather carefully (although the young student usually has to be taught to choose wisely). The danger to him is in a tendency to rely upon it to the exclusion of auditory memory. I need not mention the problems to which this can lead at this point. If a person's ear leads his fingers, the problem of "careless sounds" which result from poor choices of fingerings can be reconciled by giving attention to more favorable choices of fingerings. If a pianist does not learn to ally good fingerings confidently with auditory discernment, he is bound for trouble.

Rhythm in Practice.

There is some reason to believe that rhythmic responsiveness can be cultivated by most people — that it is generally latent in each individual.[12] One cannot expect good rhythm in the performance, however, unless it has been experienced, habitually, in the body. It must be experienced kinesthetically, therefore, during every moment of practice. Abby Whiteside certainly subscribes to this point of view,[13] as do most other pedagogues (who may not make such an issue of it as she does). To be aware of the rhythmic implications of every phrase, every nuance, every temporal spacing, is to be aware of nearly everything. Even shading must be gauged from the rhythmic point of view. The life's breath of the music is determined by it. Rhythm must be the final arbiter in both conception and realization.[14]

As stated above, playing in time is not the same as playing rhythmically, although, obviously, it would be impossible for one to play rhythmically if he could not play in time. Newman wants the player to go to incredible lengths to interrelate pulse and "the pattern of notes that is superimposed on that pulse," counting and using the metronome during most of the time that a piece is being studied.[15] He cites the late Arthur Loesser as a performer whose playing was infused with great rhythmic vitality. I certainly concur in his judgment; nonetheless, I cannot agree entirely with Newman's regimen of endless practice to the beat of the inexorable metronome as a way of achieving this. I have never found the metronome a very effective tool for establishing a sense of pulse. It can indicate pulse regularity, true, but, unless the perception of that pulse is felt in the body, with all of the subtle and minute deviations from it that befit an "all-encompassing" rhythm,[16] not too much is gained. Often a great deal can be lost if the student does not learn to appreciate the fact that breathing takes time. For anyone who had the pleasure of hearing Arthur Loesser, that necessity was unmistakable. He certainly would have agreed that the metronome, though a very convenient tool for certain purposes, is hardly a substitute for a pulse that is felt in the body.

It has been my experience that practicing with a strong sense of rhythmic involvement, no matter what the tempo, lends incredible excitement and meaning to the practice — that solutions to most problems one is attempting to overcome are to be found in it — that potential anxiety can be converted to excitement through it, in performance as well as in practice.

SOLVING MUSICAL PROBLEMS

Hearing What One Expects to Hear.

As observed, many pianists are inclined not to listen to what they play; not because they do not choose to, but because they do not realize that they are not. The problem results usually from one of two quite disparate tendencies. One is often evinced in the student with high pitch acuity (usually with absolute pitch) and the other in the student who does not trust his aural perception (usually with auditory faculties he has decided are unreliable). Both tendencies lead, ultimately, to self-deception about what is being played; neither pianist "hears" what he thinks he is hearing; both players perceive only what they expect to hear.

As observed in Chapter Three, the temptation for many pianists with absolute pitch is to listen to pitches and their interrelationships without reference to the musical statement. It is easy to understand this misplaced attention, since concern for "remembering the notes" takes precedence, at times, over all other concerns when performance anxiety threatens. If one is playing from memory and is concerned about forgetting the notes, the natural thing to do is to take refuge in absolute pitch as an "insurance policy," if it is there to use. It would be foolish not to do so. But frequently, as a result, concentration focused upon hearing and playing all of the notes overrides purely musical values so that the latter are never heard. Subtleties of nuance, phrasing and articulation go unnoticed.

A teacher who is alert to this problem can frequently offset the tendency by throwing greater emphasis upon musical details while de-emphasizing other matters. Ultimately, the problem may be solved by reordering the student's priorities, both for the performance and the practice session. A student with absolute pitch is no different from any other when it comes to applying less than full concentrated attention to practice. And, in fact, he is even more likely to indulge in "wool gathering" than the student with less pitch acuity, since, when the threat of anxiety is absent, even recalling notes may not command his attention. Unless musical values are given a high priority by the teacher and these students, they may never receive the attention they deserve in practice, with a result that they will be even less likely to be within the "circle of attention" during performance.

The result for the pianist who is aurally insecure is essentially the same: other matters distract him from the musical values. Usually, at least, this person engages one-half of himself — the kinesthetic half — even if he does not involve his auditory faculties in the musical experience. In fact, his total experience is often kinesthetic and, as observed in Chapter Three, this half of himself becomes the "proxy" for the other half.

It is interesting to listen to this hypothetical person practice. He is totally involved, kinesthetically. He has convinced himself that he must practice the way he does in order to secure himself technically. That he does, although most often his great determination manifests itself in an inordinate amount of physical tension — physical tension which substitutes for the musical intensity that he does not hear. The real reason for his practice, in the end, is to secure his haptic memory, inasmuch as he is afraid to rely upon his auditory memory. He seldom realizes this, of course. He will often practice for long periods of time and cover a relatively small amount of repertoire. He, too, seldom hears musical values even though he may grasp the kinesthetic parts of the total experience in isolation.

The obvious prescription for this problem is to help the student achieve confidence in his auditory faculties. This is more easily said than done. It is self-evident that the student must achieve such confidence in time, but it is a long and difficult road to traverse if secure foundations have not been built in early experience. Some ways of filling in this void will be discussed in Chapter Seven. Naturally, a change of practice habits is clearly indicated. As with the student who has absolute pitch, if auditorily-experienced musical values are emphasized, that is the surest way of drawing them into the "circle of attention."

The Person and What He Hears.

Assuming that we, as teachers, are able to get the student to listen to what he plays, what is that student going to hear? Are we going to assume that, since he is going to hear what he expects to hear, it is going to be as it should be? Even if we are on the right track, we obviously cannot assume that. All we can assume is that he may hear what he wants to hear, and is capable of hearing. The rest is up to his person: everything that he has become as a human being either through inheritance or by environment.

When someone asks me what I teach, I like to say, half facetiously, that I teach people. For if beauty is in the eye of the beholder, it is likewise in the ear of the listener. As Carl Rogers has observed, the measure of the amount of learning that has taken place in an individual is a measure of the degree to which that person has changed.[17] The teacher's objective, I believe, is to help the student in the changing process — toward self-actualization — toward becoming the kind of human being he is capable of becoming. I believe that is what education should be all about. The answer to the question concerning what the student will hear is clearly to be found in what kind of person he is — what kind of person he has become. What he hears will change as he himself changes. His entire experience, musically and otherwise, will contribute to that change, hopefully always salutarily. The music he plays, the music he listens to, will all leave their mark and alter his way of hearing, seeing and feeling.

In the process the truly musical human being will be gratifying aesthetic needs, higher needs which for him are also basic — needs which are his motivation. Their gratification will lead him on toward self-actualization.[18] Why discuss this at this point? For the simple reason that what one hears must be at the center of practice; and if what one hears depends upon one's person, well . . . .

RECONCILING CONCEPTION AND REALIZATION.

Technical Strategy.

In the last chapter I noted that some hands, arms, etc., seem to be made for playing the piano, and that fine coordination is also a product of inheritance. Pianists with both these assets are rare, and when one is born who also has all of the predispositions for music making, it is cause for celebration. It is these pianists and their teachers who most often advocate a strictly empirical approach to piano technique: any means are desirable that achieve the musical ends. Generally they are fortunate in that they have few technical problems of a mechanical nature.[19]

The empirical approach to solving technical problems is undoubtedly the best for anyone who can accomplish musical realization in this way. Ideally, musical conception and realization should always be one and the same act. In many instances it can be. Wherever mechanical and technical capabilities already exceed the demands of the musical conception, no special attention needs to be directed to the solution of executionary problems; nevertheless, almost everyone encounters an occasional obstacle which requires special planning in order to overcome the problem. Some pianists — particularly inexperienced students, or those who are less fortunate in physical and coordinative endowments — may encounter these obstacles at every turn. In this case, time spent in practice on the reconciliation of conception and realization is an obvious necessity.

This is not the place to discuss technique in any detail. A great deal more will be encountered in Chapter Eight where the relationship of relaxation to technique is given considerable attention. For now it is sufficient to point out that concern for the wisest "logistics" should always be at the center of technical practice. As most experienced pianists know, weak or poorly-coordinated muscles may not always be the cause of a technical obstacle. One of the best ways to conserve practice time is to consider the technical options that might be useful in overcoming a difficulty. Occasionally, for instance, the solution of a technical problem might be simply a change of fingering. At other times it may be in the re-positioning the hand or arm, etc.

Many hours are often wasted in repetitions for the sole purpose of building up muscle when lack of strength is not the problem at all. To "choreograph" one's movements at the keyboard is to plan movements for their maximum efficiency — to achieve the desired musical result without compromise, with less physical exertion and, as a usual corollary, more grace.

Practice and the Total Person.

Practice, then, must involve the total person, consciously and subconsciously, auditorily and kinesthetically. Consciousness and subconsciousness must, of necessity, interrelate differently during practice than during the performance; that has been observed on many occasions by performing artists (e.g., Anton Kuerti, above), as well as by numerous pedagogues. That is also my fundamental point in Chapters Three and Four of this book.

Very little should escape conscious attention in practice; full conscious awareness must be restricted to its assigned role in performance. A major function of consciousness in practice is to prepare the subconscious which must carry out most of the routine assignments in the performance (note location/recall and technique).

In the practice session as well as in the performance every aspect of the music must be experienced both auditorily and kinesthetically, with neither functioning to the exclusion of the other. I have already discussed the difficulties encountered when the kinesthetic experience is substituted for auditory awareness. At no time in either practice or performance should conscious attention to the auditory stimuli defer completely to kinesthetic stimuli. On the contrary, auditory awareness should constantly monitor the musical products that result from kinesthetic responses. The *mechanics* of piano playing could conceivably exclude auditory confirmation of kinesthetic action; *technique* could not, as it must evolve from a subtly-balanced auditory-kinesthetic alliance.

The opposite condition is also to be avoided. Although not nearly so common, it is possible to practice and perform with too little kinesthetic involvement. This sometimes happens with those otherwise-so-fortunate pianists who have absolute pitch and who improvise readily. Often they are inclined to defer almost everything to their auditory systems to the virtual exclusion of the kinesthetic experience. As they rely very heavily upon auditory memory, it is quite easy for them to neglect the kind of key contact which is at the foundation of haptic memory. That is, they are often tempted to abridge practice time. As an example, one of my former students told me recently that, when he was young, he would often put on a recording of a new work I had assigned him and learn it for his next lesson while working on his math and English assigments. After several evenings of this kind of "practice" he would have the work memorized for his next lesson. I could not understand in those days why I had such difficulty getting him to produce the right kind of tone. One lives and learns. So did he.

NOTES AND REFERENCES

1. For example: James Ching, *Piano Playing; a Practical Method* (London: Bosworth and Co., Ltd., 1946); Lilias MacKinnon, *Music by Heart* (London: Oxford University Press, 1926); William S. Newman, *The Pianist's Problems* (N. Y.: Harper and Row, 1956).
2. Ching, *op. cit.*, pp. 307f.
3. Newman, *op. cit.*, p. 72.
4. The exploits of the late Walter Gieseking are often recounted. Surprisingly, however, such achievements as his are not so uncommon as one might suppose.
5. MacKinnon, *op. cit.*, p. 107.
6. There's also the account of Rachmaninoff's preparing himself for an American performance of one of his concerti by practicing on a dummy keyboard while sailing across the Atlantic.
7. Matthay speaks of *pre-hearing*, believing too that it must be cultivated. Tobias Matthay, *Musical Interpretation* (Boston: The Boston Music Co., 1913), p. 10.
8. Micro-structural units must be intellectualized, automatized and given over to the subconscious where, as with notes and their locations, recall will function out of awareness.
9. The young woman Newman describes is typical rather than exceptional. Newman, *op. cit.*, pp. 105f.
10. This too is a variable. What is slow enough for one person may not be slow enough for another.

11. Among them is Vladimir Horowitz who said in a radio interview that he practices slowly most of the time. There is also the story of a visitor to Rachmaninoff who, arriving at his house, was just about to ring the doorbell when he heard Rachmaninoff practicing his double-thirds Etude. It was played so very slowly that the caller felt Rachmaninoff would never get through the piece.

12. Maslow sees the tendency to purposeful spontaneity, and the "letting go" that is explicit in dancing, as a natural expression of the human being. The tendency is frequently inhibited by a desire for control. Abraham Maslow, *Motivation and Personality*, second edition (N. Y.: Harper and Row, second edition, 1970), pp. 133f. The integration of dance and movement in musical study and performance is beautifully discussed by Eloise Ristad, *A Soprano on Her Head* (Moab, Utah: Real People Press, 1982), pp. 23-34.

13. Abby Whiteside, *Indispensables of Piano Technique*, second edition (N. Y.: Coleman-Ross, 1961).

14. Matthay believed that unrhythmical playing indicated inattention. *Op. cit.*, p. 24

15. Newman, *op. cit.*, pp. 83ff.

16. Whiteside, *op. cit.*

17. Carl R. Rogers, *Freedom to Learn* (Columbus, Ohio: Charles E. Merrill, 1969).

18. Maslow, *op. cit.*, p. 51.

19. The distinction between "mechanics" and "technique" made by Vladimir Horowitz is convenient here, technique implying musical realization and mechanics the physical means only. See Glenn Plaskin, *Horowitz* (London: Macdonald and Co. Ltd., 1983), p. 237.

Chapter 6

HEREDITY/ENVIRONMENT
AND THE
PERFORMING PIANIST

In this chapter I wish to consider some of the hereditary and environmental factors which contribute to making the pianist who he is, musically and personally, psychologically and somatically. My specific intentions, naturally, are to consider those factors that weigh heavily in determining the extent to which, ultimately, the pianist may be affected by anxiety in performance. That these factors include the popular notions of innate talent, plus the personal qualities which contribute to ease and self-control while performing, would seem self-evident. But while talent, traits of personality, and physical endowments assume genetic origins, how these characteristics are manifest depends upon how they are nurtured. What kind of person a human being becomes is determined by environmental factors (which need have nothing to do with music) acting upon his "givens": intellectual, psychological, and physical. How he responds to the environment, and what kind of human being he becomes, will ultimately determine his susceptibility to performance anxiety.

Musical *talent* has yet to be satisfactorily defined. The atomistic tendencies of researchers have invariably led to a segmented view of the whole that is both incomplete and, at times, out of perspective. The reason, it would seem, is that there is something more involved in musical talent than pitch perception, tonal memory, "feeling for tonal center," harmony and polyphony, appreciation, rhythmic abilities, and kinesthetic perception.[1] Those are aspects of musical *ability* that have been endlessly explored. While dedicated researchers must be commended for their noble efforts to analyze and test the many components which musical talent must certainly include, one should not be surprised if some of its most critical elements have eluded notice or measurement.[2] It would certainly be very presumptuous of me to attempt to fill the void that yet remains after so much serious research, and I would not try. Nonetheless, I believe I can state categorically that, of the many facets that comprise the musical talent, the two factors which must be considered fundamental are a genetic predisposition to auditory stimuli, and what Maslow would call an "aesthetic need." More about this in due course.

An artistic person who has anxiety under control, however, needs more than just musical talent. Genetic factors which determine the way in which he will respond to *other than* auditory stimuli, and that contribute to the formation of his personality and character are considerations of supreme importance as well, not only as determinants in his ability to cope with performance anxiety, but as determinants in his artistic development in general. As Howard Gardner notes:

> Even the combination of native talent, appropriate pedagogy, and high skill does not suffice to yield the creative [or re-creative] artist. The competent craftsman, yes — the innovative master, no.
>
> It is here, I believe, that traits of personality and character come into play. One bent on achieving artistic greatness must harbor a heightened motivation to excel, to distinguish himself. Possessed of a powerful vision, he must feel compelled to express that vision, over and over again, within the symbolic medium of his choice. He must be willing to live with uncertainty,[3] to risk failure and opprobrium, to return time and again to his project until he satisfies his own exacting standards, while speaking with potency to others.[4]

I would prefer not to join the continuing debate over which human qualities are inherited and which are products of the environment.[5] It should be enough for my purposes to recognize the obvious: that there are great individual differences among human beings and that some arrive for their first piano lessons with physical and personal characteristics that are advantageous to their development as performing pianists, and some do not. However, I am understandably concerned about which of these endowments might be influenced environmentally, i.e., which can be awakened or modified by appropriate stimuli acting upon them after birth (a natural concern of any teacher). If a human characteristic is genetically predetermined one must surmise that it is unalterable, a "given," within whose boundaries both teacher and student must work. This is most assuredly a fact where physical characteristics are concerned, except as nature allows for development of the skeletal muscles. I have, nevertheless, come to believe that, excepting those factors which are rooted in basic needs (physiological, safety, love/belongingness and esteem) and in qualities of temperament, most traits of human personality, character and talent are the result of *genetic predispositions* ("innate biases"[6] or "potential abilities"[7]) which have been activated and shaped by environmental stimuli.[8]

I have proceeded here on the assumption that there are a myriad of genetic predispositions which, as impinged upon by appropriate environmental stimuli, make the person who he is. I have also assumed at the same time that there are other genetically determined factors making up the human organism that are more-or-less impervious to the force of the environment — factors which, like the basic needs, appear to be instinctual; and physical characteristics that, except for the possibility of muscular development, are presumably immutable. I have referred to these fundamentally immutable characteristics merely as *genetic endowments*, to distinguish them from *genetic predispositions*.

"GIVENS": GENETIC ENDOWMENTS

Physical Structures.

An individual's physical structure is an obvious "given" and, as a pianist, he must contend with whatever deficits he may have inherited or, on the other hand, bless the gods for whatever attributes that may have come his way. Physical compatibility/incompatibility with respect to a particular musical instrument is an obvious, observable genetic phenomenon; and physical structure is certainly a factor to be reckoned with, especially where performance on the piano is concerned. The shape and design of the modern piano keyboard, its mechanism, and dimensions all make characteristic demands upon the performer who, if too small or weak in stature, can encounter practically insurmountable obstacles in terms of technical exigencies. While, admittedly, entirely too much attention is given today to the acquisition and administration of strength in piano playing (in needless amounts), there is no question that the repertoire for which the pianist must be responsible presupposes a body which is sufficient in weight, stature and strength to deal with the considerable demands made upon it. Additionally, the various limbs, appendages and phalanges need to be sufficiently long, and the range of movement at the joints sufficiently large (e.g., for abduction and adduction), to cope with the keyboard's design and dimensions. If the pianist inherits several structural deficits, and if he persists in making unrealistic demands upon himself in spite of them, there is every possibility that, sooner or later, he will encounter anxiety at levels too extreme for him to cope with — anxiety brought on by the resultant tension and strain — anxiety which no type of therapy can overcome.

I hasten to point out that small hands, of themselves, have not always proved to be an insurmountable impediment. There have been many instances when they have been compensated for by other attributes: unusual flexibility and range of movement at the joints, combined with excellent coordination and considerable strength in the hands.[9] It goes without saying that such compensatory attributes have usually been coupled with unusual amounts of extra-physical "talent" as well.

According to the studies by Christoph Wagner, it is apparently the amount of mechanical resistance to movement at the skeletal articulations of fingers, hands and arms that is the major cause of tension and strain in playing any instrument, particularly, one gathers, for players of the piano and strings. Wagner puts it this way:

> The mechanical and physiological state of the hand, on which the controlling impulses from the brain act, is characterised by the following three factors:
>
> 1. the shape of the hand; its size and proportions;
> 2. the quantity and nature of the muscles that are attached to the joints of the hand; and

3. the amount of mechanical resistance which every individual joint offers to movement.

The mechanical resistance arises from the geometry of the joint, the consistency of the joint capsule and ligaments, and from the extensibility of the muscles, tendons and surrounding tissues.

Each of the three components: shape, muscular strength, and joint resistance, but above all their combinations, can be a source of tension if the hand is forced to follow the demands of the instrument and the music.[10]

This is confirmed by the number of otherwise talented students one can observe who are technically limited due to the restrictions imposed by nature upon their range of movement — limitations which, presumably, can never be totally overcome by relaxation therapies or by any form of calisthenics or exercises. Unfortunately for some, this is one of those "givens" which is beyond the power of the environment to modify.

Coordination/Incoordination. I believe that no one would debate the genetic origins of physical coordination. Coordinative efficacy simply cannot be trained into anybody, even though training can improve the coordination that has been inherited. Although my coordination for playing baseball was perhaps average, it would have never been good enough to get me into major league baseball, no matter how many other qualities I may have possessed. And it was not for lack of favorable environmental factors that I failed to develop as fast as other children in that sport. I was batted and pitched to, coached, and encouraged in play almost every day that time and weather permitted during my pre-teens by a father who was an avid baseball enthusiast (as I was, and am to this day). I did turn into a pretty fair tennis player in my teens although, again, nothing to cause a Bjorn Borg or Jimmie Conners (or, more likely, a Don Budge) any alarm. As with baseball, my muscles did not function with enough efficiency, strength and control to allow me better than average amateur play. I did greatly enjoy participating in the sport over the years, even though professional status was beyond me.

Playing a musical instrument well also assumes a high degree of appropriate coordinative talent, it goes without saying, with each of the musical instruments presenting its unique challenges to coordinative skills. Of paramount importance in all cases is a basic coordination that is fluent, efficient and "easy" by nature, if any degree of competence is to be attained.

Ortmann's conclusion regarding good coordination is that it is the capacity for appropriate muscles to contract and relax at precisely the right instant, only to the degree that they should contract and relax, no more and no less.[11] The appropriate muscles, obviously, are those associated with a given movement. While that seems straightforward enough, its implications are far-reaching. For example, for many women and some men, the act of "throwing" is impossible — that is, with the "explosive" contraction and relaxation of only the muscles that are appropriate to that act. Some very excellent pianists have been technically hampered by the inability to replicate that coordination (although pianists who are talented in other ways may compensate for that inability).

For other pianists, finger dexterity is an inherent problem. Carl Friedberg once mentioned, for instance, that Percy Grainger was never able to play rapidly with any ease, but often gave the illusion of speed by means of an incredible control of rhythm and tempo (particularly in his performances of Bach). Many other cases come readily to mind from among students for whom finger coordination has been a problem.

The important observation to be made here is that want of a highly efficient coordination can be the source of technical problems that create extraordinary muscular tension which, in turn, is frequently the cause of anxiety. One can learn to make the most of that which he brought into the world with him, but short of optimum use of the coordinative talents he has, nothing can be done to fill inherent gaps.

I believe it is significant as well that rhythm (in the kinesthetic sense) is intimately allied to coordinative talent. This makes sense inasmuch as the rhythmic feeling in the body carries with it the sensation of perfectly synchronized muscular contraction and relaxation. I have never known a rhythmical player who was not also well coordinated; and I have never known a player who was poorly coordinated (again, a matter of degree) who played rhythmically.[12] I believe it is safe to assume, in the latter case, that poor coordination implies lack of rhythmic feeling rather than, merely, failure to convey rhythmic feeling through the instrument (although both may be involved). Obviously such a hypothesis is in need of systematic empirical study. Whether or not the apparent lack of coordinative/ rhythmic talent can be compensated for by early musical experiences (e.g., Dalcroze Eurhythmics) is an open question.

Body Language. Closely related to coordination is the "language" of the body, those movements of the body and characteristics of speech (as determined by the neurological/physiological structure of the vocal apparatus) which identify the person — the individual's personal style. I speak here not so much of the larger, more complex gestures with which the human being is likely to be identified, as of the myriad of small movements and nuances which constitute the larger, more noticeable idiosyncrasies. These characteristic movements are often linked to musical predilections and are often manifest in musical gestures which characterize the player. I have frequently referred to this link-up of body language and characteristic musical gesture as the pianist's musical "thumb-print." Once manifest in piano playing it is rarely completely eradicated, even when it is desirable to do so. Modifying it is tantamount to the alteration of personality, inherent tastes, and whatever natural musical inclination the person might possess. In most cases, body language must be accepted for what it is and made the best of, for better or worse. Ultimately, it is the pianist's musical personality. Attempts to alter it drastically, often can lead to very undesirable consequences, musically, physically and psychologically.[13]

Predispositions and Personality Traits.

This brings us to the aspect of humanness which I suggest is the result of the environment acting upon genetically-determined predispositions.

All the remaining components that we recognize as a person's "style" are undoubtedly products of genetically determined predispositions, as they are instinctually conditioned, and as they are acted upon by the environment. The myriad of nuances which comprise the human personality are determined by this interaction of genetic endowments, predispositions, and the force of the environment, but in what proportions no one has yet ascertained.

I wish now, by way of examples, to consider a few of the predispositions relevant to the present topic.

Self-Awareness (Self-Schema). Self-awareness is doubtless a prerequisite of all human developments in terms of personality and talent. If the world outside oneself (the non-self) cannot be distinguished from the self, how can any of the other distinguishing traits evolve that we call human? This is the genetic predisposition that is fundamental to all the others. How it develops when impinged upon by the environment is one of the basic variables of the human condition. Self-image, self-control, self-esteem, self-respect, self-dislike, etc., are qualities which are all linked to one's self-awareness.[14]

The Ratio of Rational to Intuitive Cognitive Processes. Artists must rely heavily upon intuitive cognitive processes — more so, probably, than the accountant or the engineer. That would appear axiomatic, though this is not to say that the person whose primary cognitive strategies rest with rational processes eschews intuitive insight; only a dull and ineffectual human being would be insensitive to the intuitive side of himself. Likewise, the person who is incapable of rational methods of solving problems in our world is in serious difficulties. It is all a matter of degree — a matter of ratio, and I believe it is self-evident from observation of the people we meet in everyday life that all are not born with the same ratio of intuitive to rational tendencies (in spite of our society's stress on rational processes) — that, whereas some are prone to logical, "linear" modes of thought, others lean toward intuitive, holistic methods. In any case the ratio is probably a genetic predisposition that is conditioned by the environment.

Imagery and Imagination. The capacity for imagery and, by extension, imagination would seem to be obvious variables that are dependent upon hereditary predispositions. In particular, when and if it is acted upon propitiously by the environment, the predisposition which enables the musician to image pitches (in both linear and simultaneous combinations) and timbres[15] is an indispensable tool of musicianship, which, as I will have occasion to note in more detail, is central to the auditory skills of his art.

In general, the capacity for imagery and imagination is a corollary of the intuitive-cognitive process in any art, whether musical, visual, or linguisitic — a process with which the musician, artist, or author must be able to identify with ease and naturalness.

Intellectual Capacity, Curiosity and Fleetness. The matter of intellectual capacity is continually debated. The first obstacle to agreement is lack of a mutually-acceptable definition of intelligence. We are now beginning to realize that intelligence involves somewhat more than is indicated by the traditional I. Q. tests — that there are dimensions of intelligence which no present test measures. I am thinking of the holistic, intuitive ways of knowing that are fundamental to creativity and the arts. Not, as I have indicated earlier, that the musician is entirely exempt from intellectual-rational methods! The best musicians are invariably those with a large intellectual capacity (in the rational-logistic sense), combined with natural curiosity and fleetness. They are those who have an extensive capacity for subjecting first-processes (intuitive mode) to second-process scrutiny (rational mode).

Intellectual capacity, curiosity and fleetness are all predisposed variables, as widely distributed as there are human beings, and as broadly manifest as the environment is whimsical.[16] H. J. Eysenck states his view very emphatically when he writes, "Unfortunately, the facts make it quite certain that all men are not created equal, and that heredity clearly discriminates between the bright and the dull."[17] I think, nonetheless, that it is incumbent upon psychology as well as upon education to give due credit to intuitive talent as well as to rational acuity. After all, there are many instances of intuitively-gifted people whose intellectual capacities and fleetness are not complimented by traditional measures of intelligence.

The Drive to Self-Actualization. Maslow would even include the need for self-actualization among the *basic* needs.[18] I would not call it an instinct, however, but a hereditary predisposition, since it would seem to be a need peculiar to the human species. That it would appear with varying degrees of strength among individuals would seem self-evident, I believe, and its complete manifestation is subject to its interface with the environment. The strength of the drive to self-actualization — to become what one can become — to become what one must become — would seem to be contingent upon the interaction of this variable with the forces within the environment. It would be contingent, as well, upon the relative strength of one's other drives and needs.[19] The motivation to "artistic greatness" which, according to Gardner (above), distinguishes the artist, is clearly provided by the drive to self-actualize when that drive is identified with a strong aesthetic need (discussed below). There is probably even a legitimate reason to suppose that it is *the* indispensable ingredient, inasmuch as an aesthetic need that is dissociated from a need to self-actualize through the creative or recreative act produces the *consumer* of art rather than the artist.

Aesthetic Needs. Obviously, a predisposition to aesthetic fulfillment or sensitivity to the beauties of auditory stimuli are not inherited by all human beings. It is assumed that the performer, at least, must have been born with the predisposition to respond thus, and that he learned soon after his first encounters with such stimuli that they were important to him — that he required them in order to make his life complete. Clearly, aesthetic needs and the inherent tendency to respond to sensual beauty are interdependent.

It would be hard to imagine that any pianist would spend the immense amount of time and energy it takes to achieve mastery of his art if aesthetic needs were unimportant to him and if he were impervious to the beauty of the art in which he was involved (not to undervalue esteem needs, as well, which are also prime motivations). It would seem to me that the prerequisites for the focus of attention that are so important to high-level performance must be implicit in that sensitivity and in the irrepressible urge for aesthetic fulfillment through music. Such implications seem to be born out, at least, by the accomplished performing pianists that I have known. It is self-evident that no pianist could expect to focus attention upon the music for long if the music held no particular fascination for him or if he were not motivated to gratify an aesthetic need by it.

The Ratio of Auditory to Visual Awareness. Finally I would like to consider a genetic potential which is closely related to a sonoro-aesthetic need (although independent of it): the predisposition to auditory stimuli.

I believe that evidence will eventually show that the person who develops absolute pitch is one whose auditory system has assumed an unusually high position among the senses — that, while with most people the visual sense may play a dominant role in information gathering and processing, with others, auditory awareness may be nearly equal to it. This being the case, auditory stimuli in the environment will claim a more than usual amount of attention, particularly during the formative childhood years, absolute pitch being the very likely outcome.

As Bachem concluded some years ago, "From all [of the] evidence it appears that early musical experience and *attention to pitch* [my italics] are necessities for the acquisition of genuine absolute pitch."[20] And although it is unlikely that one would be born preprogramed to the ratio of frequencies to be encountered in the musical environment (meaning equal temperament, primarily), it is more than likely that an infant may have a genetic predisposition to retain those frequencies in long-term memory once they are encountered. Much would depend upon the strength of that predisposition and would possibly take into account, as well, any inherited sonoro-aesthetic needs.

A great deal of research has been done on absolute pitch since the late nineteenth century. Most of it (to 1963) has been reviewed by W. Dixon Ward in a two-part article for *Sound.*[21] To the practical musician much of it seems singularly myopic, naive, and atomistic. A great deal of effort has been expended, for instance, 1) to determine whether absolute pitch actually exists, 2) to determine if those claiming absolute pitch somehow are "cheating" (i.e., relying upon some kind of relative pitch), 3) to determine how "absolute" it is (i.e., whether errors in pitch discrimination involving intervals smaller than a semitone negates "absoluteness"), and 4) whether or not errors involving octave transposition should count as errors. One important conclusion is that absolute pitch is more likely learned than inherited. This conclusion is also reached by R. T. C. Pratt, who reports that:

The early development of absolute pitch (in some instances by three years of age) again suggests an inborn gift, but the evidence collected by questionnaire by Sergeant and Roch (1973) argued conclusively in the opposite direction. In over a thousand professional musicians the possession of absolute pitch was related to the age at which training on a musical instrument began. Of those who began training before the age of four years 95 per cent. possessed absolute pitch, whereas of those who started training between 12 and 14 years only 5 per cent. possessed it (correlation coefficient 0.98).[22]

A similar view to mine evidently was reached very early in the present century by Abraham and Watt. Ward writes:

Considering all the factors that conspire to inhibit the development of AP, it is not unreasonable to suggest, as Abraham did, that perhaps the innate ability to develop AP is much more widespread than we think, but that it is simply trained out of many of us. Although Abraham felt that some hereditary factors must be involved (he was, after all, a possessor), so that the "potential possessors" were still in the minority, Watt in 1917 followed Abraham's line of reasoning to its logical conclusion and proposed that perhaps AP is initially universal. "In some favoured persons it is acquired early and more or less unwittingly and never lost. Perhaps these persons have some special *refinement of hearing*. . . . Or perhaps a highly favoured *auditory disposition* [all italics are mine] gives them the power to maintain their absoluteness of ear in spite of the universality of musical relativity. In that case we should all naturally possess absolute ear and then proceed to lose it or to lose the power to convert it into absolute nomenclature. In dealing with noises we all seem to retain a good deal of it, even the most unmusical of us, who recognise voices, noises, etc." Let us call this the "unlearning" theory of AP.[23]

Ward continued with this line of reasoning when he reported in 1981, "The results [of recent research] support the "unlearning" theory of Abraham and Watt: an inborn potential for developing absolute pitch is relatively common, but it tends to become atrophied or suppressed because of the far greater importance of relative pitch in our musical environment."[24] In other words, it is proposed that all or most of us are born with the capacity to develop absolute pitch (i.e., with the genetic predisposition), but that the environment, rather than being conducive to its development, thwarts its cultivation. This is an interesting hypothesis which needs further study.

Further support for the hypothesis that absolute pitch must be acquired early in life comes from Eizo Itoh, the Music Education Director for the Yamaha Music Foundation. His research has shown that the human organism is at the peak of its ability to absorb and process auditory information between the ages of three and eight, and that, after the age of eight, the ability declines.[25] His conclusions would also lend support to those by Pratt[26] and to several of the early researchers reviewed by Ward.[27] I will have more to say about this later.

ENVIRONMENTAL CONSIDERATIONS.

Hypothetically, one could speak, on the one hand, of the human being who is born with all of the predispositions and endowments described above, on the other hand, of the one born with none of them, or, obviously, of any number of others who are likely to be somewhere in between the two extremes. Whether the future pianist has all of the advantages of genetic predispositions, or whether he has only a few, the environment that acts upon him is of crucial importance. Musical and technical preparation, ultimately, will depend upon its favors, as will the ability to cope with the anxieties attendant to performance. Clearly, it would be just as ridiculous to ignore the role that "nurture" plays in the preparation for performance as it would be to disregard the role of "nature."

The two environmental milieux of most importance to the growing, maturing human being, and the ones to be explored here, are those represented by the family and by education: the environment, particularly, before the advent of public education, and the environment implicit in the educational experience. On the assumption that every human being might be born "with everything going for him," the adult (parent and teacher) whose concern it is to provide an environmental setting of advantage to the developing human being, will do well to consider the kind of experiences that the child may encounter. While genetic predispositions are impossible to assess until the environment has had time to act upon them in a meaningful way,[28] the environment can be prepared and evaluated in terms of its potentially effective interaction with the human being. The realization that this is one of his major functions, needless to say, is the mark of an effective teacher. It is a realization no less important for the successful parent.

HEALTHY ROOTS IN EARLY EXPERIENCES.

Anxiety and the Family.

As outlined in Chapter Two, it is within the family matrix that the child receives the earliest stimuli having to do with the formation of his personality (not excluding the possibility, as noted, that even earlier environmental stimuli may have played upon the organism during the prenatal period). The roots of anxiety are there along with impressions which will shape future attitudes and beliefs, and influence values, orient tastes, and stimulate intellectual/intuitive awareness. It is here, too, where the organism's innate temperament will be acted upon for the first time by the postnatal environment and its relative emotional stability decided.

Usually (if not invariably), the future pianist who is to be in control of his anxiety, will be one from a stable, self-enhancing familial environment that is supportive and encouraging without being overly protective. He will emerge from an environment in which self-reliance and self-esteem are fostered — an environment where his needs are recognized and steps taken to insure that, ultimately, they may be gratified (not, however, without learning the meaning of effort and even frustration). He will know love and be secure in it. He will learn the joy of personal achievement through conscientious and disciplined effort, and experience satisfaction in the esteem of others when those achievements have been earned.

The Auditory Environment.

An auditory environment that is filled with enchantment unquestionably supplies a basis for auditory acuity in the new human being. According to Thomas Verny, musical enchantment might even start prenatally.[29] Far be it from me to deny this possibility. My own mother said that, when she discovered she was carrying her first child, she resumed her piano study in the hopes that her child might develop into a musician. It used to be that I regarded this as a somewhat "folksy" bit of naiveté. However, I did become a musician, and Verny would claim that my mother's supposition was well founded.

Notwithstanding a possible musical influence upon the unborn child, there is little doubt but that a sonorous environment filled with warmth, delicacy and grace, must have a profound effect upon the auditory future of the young child. Delicate wind chimes, the sound of the mother's singing voice, or a music box can stimulate awareness of the world of musical sound, and start the child on the road to auditory acuity. I have known proud young mothers who have claimed that their infants enjoyed Beethoven or Mozart or Debussy. While I doubt that infants can appreciate such complex structures as these composers' works imply, I would not question their attendance to the sounds, provided they were associated with a milieu that satisfied their needs for love, belongingness, comfort, and safety. With or without an innate auditory predisposition, such an environment can awaken the new human being to a world which may later enrich his life. It is certainly very likely that it will form the foundation for pitch acuity.

When Lessons Begin.

Abraham, Watts and Ward, as noted above, could very well be right: almost everyone may be born with a predisposition to absolute pitch, but it is trained out of them by the environment. They see the prevalence of relative pitch in the environment as the factor in "de-education." That may be so, although I prefer the model of a genetic predisposition as the deciding factor: a genetically-determined neuronal connection which predisposes the individual to auditory stimuli.With or without that predisposition, however, if the early musical experience is propitiously designed, I am ready to predict that there will be a much higher incidence of pitch acuity (if not of absolute pitch) than there is at present with the "sight-centered" piano teaching which still predominates as a first experience. For, unfortunately, even in the 1980s, too much piano teaching is still consecrated to music as an art of sight, rather than as an art of sound. The musical symbol all too often represents a key to depress rather than a sound to hear, probably, I am convinced, because symbol recognition is encountered much before there has been sufficient experience with music as sound and expression: i.e., sounds and expression with which the child himself is actively involved. The preoccupation and almost irrational concern with note-reading is easy to understand, nevertheless, at least in Western society, where one of the worst things that can be said about a student (no matter how well he may play) seems to be, "But he cannot read music" — which usually means that he cannot strike keys that correspond with "blips" on the score.[30] It often does not seem to matter whether the student who can punch them more or less accurately frequently makes no music out of them; it seems not to occur to anyone that he is not in the least involved aurally.

It is significant, I believe, that two of the most progressive piano teaching methods to emerge in recent years are from one of the countries with a long aural tradition in music and music learning: Japan. The Japanese, after all, are accustomed to the notion of learning music auditorily. The vast repertoire of koto and shakahachi music, for the most part, has been passed along to the present day without notation, often by blind master teachers. The aural practices are still continuing today in the older musical traditions, with the student learning by imitation of the master.[31] So it is not surprising that the Suzuki string and piano systems, as well as the highly-developed Yamaha school, have been so successful in Japan. They are both based upon the logical premise that, since music is an auditory art, it should be experienced first aurally. It is rightly assumed that the ear should experience each new concept before the eye is involved with its symbolic representation.[32]

Both of these systems are represented in North America, of course, but they would be even more successful here, I am sure, if both the teachers and the students of our society were better prepared to accept the tenets of the systems' respective "faiths," *and could, at the same time, remain free of the prejudices which too often shake their confidence.* Unfortunately, fear of opprobrium by the musical community too often causes these teachers, students, and their parents to abandon a study based predominantly upon auditory perception and, prematurely, to focus attention upon its notation. The result, very frequently, is the same "musical deafness" which would have resulted had they begun their lessons according to traditional pedagogical methods in the first place.

Is there not something more important for the child to learn at his first lesson than what middle C looks like on the page and where it is on the keyboard?

I believe there is no question that with imaginative and vital teaching (and some help from the home environment) a child can learn, from the first lesson, to make music a spontaneous and exciting extension of himself. He can become one with the piano through creative and extempore playing, as well as through the performance of the musical creations of others. He can from the start, with little more than the minimum hereditary predispositions, learn to internalize music and can begin the process of coordinating the haptic and auditory mechanisms. And, for those who are quite anxious about such matters, he can learn — *after the bases for these other functions have been established* — to read music, better than if his values and priorities had been distorted. In short, he can make music the delight it should be for him, instead of a thankless chore that, in the end, may very likely result in defeat or in performance anxiety at intolerable levels. I am convinced that if those early musical experiences are what they should be, his anxiety will be minimized and under control. He may even discover the "excitement" of performance rather than the "anxiety."

Learning Where the Rhythm Is.

The problem of unrhythmical playing — of unrhythmical "feeling" in the body — is a major problem among many teenage and adult pianists. This need not be in the majority of cases. In my experience, failure to place rhythm in the body is usually a failure to awaken an innate and latent impulse, an awakening which is most easily accomplished during childhood. Only rarely is the innate latency totally absent (although, as stated earlier, rhythmic feeling in the body may be inextricably linked to muscular coordination: a hereditary variable). Personal inhibition is quite often linked to the failure of the impulse to manifest itself. In the adult I have found that the best way to pull it out is, by some means or other, to bring about a release from that inhibition through dance, or through any kind of vigorous and pulsating bodily movement to music. For the youngster, participation in a Dalcroze Eurhythmics program is to be highly recommended, preferably before the first piano lesson is taken, as the bodily feeling of rhythm is best released before the technical exigencies of piano playing are engaged.

Healthy Roots in Healthy Habits.

Finally, among the musically-rooted experiences which the child can acquire and carry with him into adulthood, is the habit of selective/concentrated attention, which can develop naturally if his attention is drawn irresistibly to the auditory delights which the music should hold for him; and advantageous practice habits with emphasis upon the rule of thumb, "Do it right the first time." He can also, with skillful teaching, achieve a just balance between his auditory and kinesthetic experiences, and learn to appreciate each for its role, and to ally the two modes of perception with grace. He can, in the process, achieve a judicious balance between the tension and relaxation that is essential to the realization of his musical intentions. If all of these habits have been well founded, another major step will have been taken toward control of performance anxiety in maturity.

THE EDUCATIONAL EXPERIENCE.

The future pianist has no particularly specialized needs in education other than those provided by the musical instruction itself (assuming, of course, that all of his specialized needs are provided by that instruction); at least no adjustment need be made in the educational environment other than that which might be made for the benefit of every other student as well. All students, in order to be completely aware human beings, must experience at both the intuitive ("Left hand") and rational ("Right hand") levels of their being. To be coerced into only rational modes of thought at the expense of the intuitive voice — a common tendency in Western education and society — is one of the perversions of our age. The opposite is equally bad, however: to pursue the study of an art without rational discipline. While decidedly less common in our society, in our age, this tendency is nevertheless encountered in some institutions whose sole preoccupation is with teaching the art. A usual corollary is that the art is robbed of the cultural enrichment afforded by serious inquiry in fields outside of it.

And finally, it is a mistake to think that one learns only with the mind, possibly with the assistance of either the visual or auditory system. The educational experience should include the opportunity for participation by all of the appropriate senses in every learning situation; only then can one experience fully what it is being learned. Naturally, this is of supreme importance in arts education, but its importance is not limited to the arts. Neither is its importance limited to the child.

The Care and Feeding of the "Left Hand."

For the pianist, as with anyone involved in the arts, uninhibited access to the intuitive mode of perceiving and to non-verbal modes of communication is quintessential to his development, and any educational institution which does not at least encourage exploration of these avenues of thought is not a proper place for him to be. In fact, opportunity and nourishment for the creative imagination, with both non-verbal and verbal languages, must be constantly available to him, as well as to everyone else in the on-going educational process, for to neglect them — for those artistically inclined as well as for those whose interests are not focused upon the arts — is to deprive them of "food" which contributes essentially to total growth.

This is not to say that, for the future pianist, the rational disciplines should be neglected in favor of intuitive modes of thought. Far from it. Desirably, an integration of the two modes will take place in which his intuitive products are submitted to a sympathetic but incisive rational scrutiny that is fortified by a wellspring of knowledge.

Cultural Enrichment.

No pianist, or anyone else in the arts, can afford to limit his knowledge solely to what is directly related to his art. A pianist's lack of humanity is always apparent in his musical conception, and I believe that the extent of deference to his ego is directly proportionate to the lack of breadth in his world view. The scope of his interests and intellectual involvements is invariably reflected in the depth of his musical understanding.

An essential ingredient adding depth and breadth to musical utterance is supplied by what Jerome Bruner calls the "interconnectedness" of knowledge[33] — an interconnectedness which leads ultimately to mind expansion and to human growth in the highest sense of that expression. And since, as I have insisted earlier, what one hears in music is a product of who one is as a human being, anything that contributes to greater humanness will contribute in the end to heightened perception at the strictly musical level. As in the course of all human endeavors, a restricted world view is invariably reflected in an impoverished creative or re-creative act. The things which create awe and excitement are always greatly increased in number and intensity by the extent of experience with the world outside of oneself. Nothing is more disappointing to the listener than a musical conception which is bounded by the performer's ego — which is conceived on a plane that has no horizons beyond the eighty-eight black and white keys. The pianist who is most vulnerable to an attack of extreme performance anxiety, as a matter of fact, is often one who has based his art upon just such a fragile foundation. Although other factors usually contribute as well to his discomfort, human frailty makes an unmistakable difference in his ability to resist debilitation by anxiety. The refinement of attention is directly related to one's fascination with the subject at hand, and fascination is intensified by one's growth as a human being, both intellectually and spiritually. The ability to focus attention, as we have seen, is crucial to the maintenance of psychological equilibrium in performance and, ultimately, to the control of anxiety.

Hearing, Feeling, Seeing, Thinking. In conclusion, total sensory awareness should be fostered and utilized throughout the educational process. Appeal to the delights of touch, ear, eye, even taste and smell, is often utilized in imaginative programs for young children, but once these same children have reached about the age of twelve [34], appeal to the senses is usually withheld in favor of the "formal operations" of the intellect. Even the affective elements in human motivation are ignored on the premise that, once this level of maturity is reached, the emotional response has no part in the learning process. Evidence indicates to the contrary, of course, but the popular notion that the maturing student needs to be taught to use "pure reason and logic," apart from sensory (other than visual) or emotional involvement, is one of the fallacies that continues to thwart effective teaching.[35] Efforts to integrate audio-visual techniques are all too often neglected, even when the available materials are ingeniously and imaginatively devised.

I am referring here to the education of all students, not just to the future pianist, who, as I have said, has needs in education which are different from the average student only in matters of priority. It goes without saying that, for the future pianist, auditory learning is of extreme importance. Even for him, however, it would be a mistake to assume that only the ear should be appealed to. If he is musically talented, that is what will interest him first, naturally, but he will be facilitated in learning through appeal to the other senses, as well, and through his emotional responses to them. Sensory stimulation enhances learning; sensory deprivation has been shown to inhibit it — even to reverse the process. No important learning takes place without an emotional component. Thinking is facilitated by feeling, hearing, seeing, and where appropriate, smelling and tasting. It does not go on without an affective response to the sensory stimuli associated with the thing being learned.

NOTES AND REFERENCES

1. Rosamund Shuter-Dyson, "Musical Ability." In Diana Deutsch (ed.), *The Psychology of Music* (N. Y.: Academic Press, 1982), pp. 396-404.
2. The distinction made between musical "talent" and musical "ability" by Radocy and Boyle is pertinent to the present discussion. Rudolf Radocy and J. David Boyle, *Psychological Foundations of Musical Behavior* (Springfield, Ill.: Charles C. Thomas, 1979), pp. 262f.

3. With "anxiety," as noted in Chapter One.

4. Howard Gardner, *Art, Mind, and Brain* (N. Y.: Basic Books, 1982), p. 90.

5. So far as I am concerned, it is neither heredity nor environment to the exclusion of the other, a conclusion reached also by Lumsden in his theory of *gene-culture coevolution*. See Charles J. Lumsden, "Gene-Culture Linkages and the Developing Mind." In Charles J. Brainerd (ed.), *Recent Advances in Cognitive-Developmental Theory* (N. Y.: Springer-Verlag, 1983), pp. 123- 166.

6. *Ibid.*, p. 126.

7. Philip E. Vernon's term, as quoted in Rosamund Schuter-Dyson, *op. cit.*, p. 392.

8. Abraham H. Maslow, *Motivation and Personality*. Second edition (N. Y.: Harper and Row, 1970). The line between what is inherited and what is environmentally induced has been blurred still further by the theories of Thomas Verny [discussed in Chapter Two], who postulates that many personality traits are environmentally determined during the gestation period. If true, one's hereditary and environmental categories must be extended to include the possibility of environmental influences upon the unborn. See: Thomas Verny, *The Secret Life of the Unborn Child* (Toronto: Collins, 1981). Kagan *et al.*, recognize that the "temperamental qualities" with which the child is born, along with biological maturation, explain the individual differences with which children respond to a given experience. See Jerome Kagan, Richard B. Kearsley, and Philip R. Zelazo, *Infancy. Its Place in Human Development* (Cambridge, Mass.: Harvard University Press, 1978), p. 280.

9. I once observed to Menahem Pressler that his hands appeared small, but he demonstrated to me that he could extend up to a tenth, indicating an unusually wide hand with large abduction at the hand knuckles. On the other hand, it is well known that the great pianist, Josef Hoffman, once had a piano especially built to accommodate his small hands.

10. Christoph Wagner, "The Human Hand as One of the Origins of Tension in Music Performance," Published papers, *The First International Conference on Tension in Performance* July 1982, p. 21. See also Christoph Wagner, "Die Messung rheologischer Grössen an Gelenken der menschlichen Hand in vivo." In F. Hartmann (ed.), *Biopolymere und Biomechanik von Bindegewebssystemen* (Berlin, Heidelberg, New York: Springer, 1974). Difficulties with supination in combination with movements involving fingers would seem to be the major problem for players of stringed instruments.

11. Otto Ortmann, *The Physiological Mechanics of Piano Technique* (N. Y.: E. P. Dutton, 1962; first published in 1929).

12. Although most pianists tend to avoid sports which are hazardous to hands and arms, I would be surprised if a majority of the accomplished ones would not be athletically inclined. Most of those whom I have known, and who, on occasion, have become involved in some sport or other, usually demonstrated considerable coordinative aptitude. American pianist, Russell Sherman, as a matter of fact, is not only a keen sportsman, but theorizes about the relationship of piano playing and athleticism. See: "Russell Sherman Talks to Carola Grindea," *Piano Journal, European Piano Teachers Association* (Vol. 3 No. 8, June 1982), 5-7.

13. It is sometimes easy to confuse personal style and style which has been borrowed. Assumed style obviously can be altered without jeopardy to the person's musical or personal well-being. It often results from an attempt to emulate a person who has made a strong impression upon, particularly, the young (e.g., the teacher, a peer, Vladimir Horowitz, Glenn Gould, etc.).

14. See: Ferdinand Knobloch and Jirina Knobloch, *Integrated Psychotherapy* (N. Y.: Jason Aronson, 1979), "Self-Schema," pp. 44-52.

15. Or, using Gordon's terminology, to "audiate." See E. Gordon, *Primary Measures of Music Audiation* (Chicago, Ill.: G. I. A., 1979).

16. Piaget's concern with the biological origins of intelligence are well known. Jean Piaget, *The Origins of Intelligence in Children*. Trans. Margaret Cook (N. Y.: International Universities Press, Inc., 1974; first published in 1952). See, also, Philip E. Vernon, Georgina Adamson, and Dorothy F. Vernon, *The Psychology and Education of Gifted Children* (London: Methuen and Co. Ltd., 1977), pp. 32-49.

17. H. J. Eysenck, *Sense and Nonsense in Psychology* (Middlesex, England: Penguin Books, 1957), p. 14.

18. Maslow, *op. cit.*, pp. 46f.

19. The drive to self-actualize runs like a *leitmotif* through nearly all of Maslow's books. See: A. H. Maslow, *op. cit.*; *The Farther Reaches of Human Nature* (Middlesex, England: Penguin Books, 1971); *Toward a Psychology of Being*, second edition (N. Y.: D. Van Nostrand, 1968); and *Religions, Values, and Peak-Experiences* (Middlesex, England: Penguin Books, 1970, first published in 1964). His point of view is shared by Carl Rogers, *On Becoming a Person* (Boston: Houghton Mifflin, 1961).

20. W. Dixon Ward, "Absolute Pitch," *Sound* (Part I, Vol. 2, No. 3, May-

June 1963, 14-21; Part II, Vol. 2, No. 4, July-August 1963, 33-41), Part I, p. 17. See also W. Dixon Ward and Edward M. Burns, "Absolute Pitch," in Diana Deutsch, *op. cit.*, pp. 431-452.

21. *Ibid*, Part I, p. 17.
22. R. T. C. Pratt, "The Inheritance of Musicality." In M. Critchley and R. A. Henson (eds.), *Music and the Brain* (London: William Heinemann Medical Books, Ltd., 1977), p. 29.
23. Ward, *op. cit.*, Part I, p. 15. It is interesting to note that pianist David Burge insists that absolute pitch can be developed at any time by anyone who is an astute listener. He has given a number of workshops for this purpose. David L. Burge, *Perfect Pitch: Color Hearing for Expanded Musical Awareness* (Wilmington, Delaware: Innersphere Music Studio, 1983); David L. Burge, *The Perfect Pitch Workshop* (Wilmington, Delaware: American Educational Music Publications, 1983); David L. Burge, *The Perfect Pitch Master Class* (Wilmington, Delaware: American Educational Music Publications, 1983).
24. W. Dixon Ward, "Absolute Tonality and Absolute Pitch," *Journal of the Acoustical Society of America* (Suppl. 1, Vol. 70, Fall 1981), S24.
25. Personal communication.
26. Pratt, *op. cit.*
27. Ward, *op. cit.* (1963).
28. Predictions are nearly always presumptuous. Playing god is not a particularly attractive role for anyone, in spite of frequent attempts to do so.
29. Verny, *op. cit.*
30. Musical literacy is all too often measured in terms of the ability to understand musical symbols and by the ability to execute the notes which correspond to those symbols. However, some of the most musically-illiterate people I have known have been ones who could "read" music.
31. The composer, Elliot Weisgarber, during the 1960s and '70s, spent many hours learning the classical repertoire of the shakahachi this way.
32. Eizo Itoh informs me that 85% of the children who go through the Yamaha program in Japan develop absolute pitch. Recent demonstrations at a conference of *The European Piano Teachers Association* (Kingston upon Thames, England, July 28-30, 1983) have shown that the need for a rich auditory experience in early music study is very clearly recognized in both France and England. The work of Jacques Chapuis and his colleagues, which skilfully blends the techniques of French *solfège* with the Dalcroze system, and of Lettice Stuart and her

associates at the Trinity College of Music (who implement an analogous system), speak well for more forward looking pedagogical trends in those countries.

33. Jerome Bruner, *On Knowing. Essays for the Left Hand.* Expanded edition (Cambridge, Mass.: Harvard University Press, 1979).
34. Jean Piaget, *The Child and Reality.* Trans. Arnold Rosin (N. Y.: Penguin Books, 1976), pp. 24ff.
35. A fallacy also noted by Aldous Huxley, who wrote eloquently on the subject. See Aldous Huxley, *The Doors of Perception* and *Heaven and Hell* (London: Atriad Panther Book, 1960), 60ff.

Chapter 7

REORDERING
SENSORY PRIORITIES

Filling in Experiential Gaps.

If performance anxiety has already become an untenably radical problem, what steps can be taken to alleviate it? Must one be resigned to what has sometimes been said about performing talent: "you either can or you can't"? I am not prepared to accept such a cynical view. Aside from the fact that it is not a valid judgment, to embrace such a view is to callously "write off" the many wonderfully talented people in this world who, musically, have much to say and who, by taking appropriate therapeutic steps, could very well say it.

While it is true that the ultimate solution to some problems of performance anxiety might require the professional assistance of a therapist or teacher, it is wisest to begin the therapeutic process by asking what one might do for *oneself.* The best place for a person to begin is by asking, "Is there something lacking in my musical experience or piano technique which makes me especially susceptible to out-of-control performance anxiety?" If the answer is yes, and the deficits can be identified, the next question should be, "What can be done to alleviate these difficulties?" If there are such recognizable deficits, obviously the gaps must be filled, and most importantly, the filling in must be accompanied, ultimately, by faith that they have been filled.

I must point out at the outset that, although questions about the objects occupying focal consciousness could very well be at the root of the problem (as outlined in Chapter Three), perhaps most frequently the deficits needing attention will be found among subconscious functions that are somehow deficient or absent; and while conscious attention will have to be brought to bear upon the development of new capacities, there can never be total confidence in these new capacities until they have proven their efficacy at the subconscious, intuitive level. Until there is confidence in them at that level, excessive anxiety may well remain just outside the door. If and when faith in these new capacities has been earned, the reward could likely be a reduction in performance anxiety.

Technical Deficits: the Falsely Accused?

The majority of pianists who are prone to excessive anxiety in performance seek relief through extending their technical capabilities. Such pianists probably practice more than any others, seeing want of technique as the villain behind their suffering — a villain who can be driven away only by endless drill and repetition. While it is true that a technical weakness often tends to shake one's faith in his capacity to perform well, it is not always the want of technique itself that causes the trouble, but rather other insecurities which cause anxiety which leads to the loss of technical control. In other words, when a problematical passage arrives — one that has been practiced a thousand times — a difficulty may very well arise because the technical problem has not yet been solved, but the technical insecurity may also be due to a general anxiety brought on by lack of faith in note location/recall, for instance. This, in turn, makes one doubt his faith in technical preparation. While it is not my intention to undervalue the importance of technical preparation,[1] I believe that the sources of performance anxiety can be sought, as often as not, in insecurities that are musical rather than technical, and while it is usual to cast blame upon technical insecurity for performance anxiety, even technical insecurity may be a result rather than the cause of the problem.

Reinforcing the Auditory Experience.

Keyboard Harmony. How sad it is when a teacher has occasion to refer to the harmonic "underpinning" of a passage, to a phrase's harmonic progression, or to the tonal center through which a piece of music is momentarily passing, only to be met with a look of total confusion and dismay. It is equally disturbing for the teacher when it becomes apparent that the student, whose memory has faltered, has not the foggiest notion of the music's harmonic foundation, auditorily/haptically (subconsciously), or even intellectually (consciously). I stress auditorily, haptically and intellectually because at one time or another all of these cognitive channels must be open, notwithstanding that, at the time of performance, harmonic function must rest comfortably at the subconscious level, long since freed from conscious intervention.

But most students in our day go from recital to recital, from competition to competition, or from examination to examination, without ever submitting themselves to the disciplined practice of keyboard harmony — a discipline which could and would place harmonic function at the subconscious level of their musical perception, forever placing what they play upon a secure harmonic-syntactic foundation. The resultant dilemma can be compared to that of the non-English speaking person who, after reading (phonetically) and memorizing a dozen or so English poems, attempts to recite one of the poems he has memorized with the comprehension, nuance and authority that the work implies. A person attempting such a performance would be understandably insecure, and the artistic result (notwithstanding expert coaching) would be correspondingly naive.[2]

A very obvious source of performance anxiety is discernible in such neglect, I believe. Failure to incorporate at least basic harmonic vocabulary within one's auditory-haptic coordination is tantamount to "functional illiteracy" in musical performance — "functional illiteracy" which is at the very root of musical insecurity and, ultimately, of performance anxiety. As noted in the previous chapter, it matters little in terms of musical practice whether a pianist has studied musical theory or not if steps are not taken to ally rational understanding with his auditory-haptic functions at the subconscious level (i.e., with the automated side of his performance). The study and practice of keyboard harmony is one of the means by which such an alliance is achieved.

The kind of keyboard harmony study I have in mind is not represented by the usual practice in playing from a figured bass, as handy a skill as that may be.[3] Rather, it involves the practice of cadences, common syntactical progressions,[4] characteristic approaches to cadences, and the resolution of all of the standard dissonant harmonies.[5] These should be practiced for the most part with the right hand playing the harmonies (the left hand playing them at a later time), using all of the "tops," with the left hand playing the bass. Obviously, all appropriate inversions should be included, with all progressions being played in the major and minor modes of all keys.[6]

A word of caution must be issued in the study of keyboard harmony: perception must go on at the auditory as well as the kinesthetic levels if the study is to achieve its purpose; conscious note-naming and chord-calling achieve nothing of value unless what is played is "listened to." Although the kinesthetic mode of perceiving can be assumed in any case (subconsciously experienced), conscious attention to what is played cannot be assumed unless, ultimately, the focus is upon the purely auditory experience of sonorous structures — structures, both sequential and simultaneous, which emerge gradually but inevitably as interacting entities that are perceived apart from their nominally-identified successions and components. Unthinking, auditorily insensitive kinesthetic "baths" in the name of practice accomplish nothing.

Playing by Ear. With the pianist who plays by ear the auditory system *directs* the haptic system, while with the pianist who does not, if the auditory system is engaged at all, it generally only *monitors what has already been executed* by the haptic system. The advantages to playing from memory with the kind of auditory-haptic coordination that extempore playing entails, therefore, are reasons enough for the pianist to cultivate that performance skill. Any number of modern pedagogues have noted this correlation between playing by ear and playing from memory. Newman observes, for instance:

> Almost invariably, the student who cannot play by ear memorizes slowly or insecurely. Secondly, playing by ear contributes to that elusive quality of good piano playing, fluency. It does this both because it leads to the kind of harmonic grasp that perceives notes in intelligible groups ["chunking"; see above,

Chapter Four] rather than one at a time and because it provides a variety of practical experiences. Finally, by translating to the piano a mental concept that comes via the ear, rather than a printed page that comes via the eye, the student takes active steps to heighten his harmonic, melodic, and rhythmic acuity.[7]

Newman also quotes Arthur Loesser:

Check and double check to everything you say about playing by ear. But what will you do with the earnest soul who cannot even get started at it? There are ever so many students, alas, to whom the keyboard is a completely lifeless mechanism, who cannot mentally associate a key with a tone until after they have struck it. Oh, yes, they can learn to play a Chopin Etude sometimes, but they cannot find the "Star-Spangled Banner" in E-flat. What medicine for them?[8]

But where does one begin in the practice of playing by ear, improvisation, extempore playing, or whatever one chooses to call it? It is certainly not easy for one who has never done it. Newman proposes some first steps.[9] Ultimately, of course, what must be attained is a confidence in uninhibited playing from the intuitive side of one's being — playing which links the haptic with the auditory faculties. This does not mean that it can start without conscious effort, nor can it start overburdened with fear of failure.

For some students even playing a familiar melody by ear, without accompaniment, is a feat requiring great courage. That is certainly the place to start; playing familiar tunes (ones that can be remembered from beginning to end) with one hand or the other, in any or all keys. For most novices in such practices, fear of playing the wrong notes — or the frustration in finding the right ones — is the inhibiting factor. That is why I say that the first step is to lose the inhibition, or the fear, associated with playing extemporaneously. The ultimate objective is to learn to transmit nerve impulses to the hands and fingers that come directly from the aural mechanism, doing so confidently without fear of wrong notes that might creep in — doing so finally without conscious effort. Once familiar melodies have been auditorily and haptically linked, other sonorous features can be added: the supporting harmonies that seem right, simple accompaniments and, eventually, more complex texturally-enriching devices.[10]

As Newman points out, the study of basic keyboard harmony will prove to be the best place to start for most people before attempting to provide accompaniments for the melodies that one can play. As I said above (note 6), improvisation often seems to be the natural extension of keyboard harmony practice anyway; the two practices inevitably complement one another.

Free Improvisation and Creativity. Many of the more innovative piano methods for beginners start either with playing-by-ear techniques, or with musical materials for creative exploration through improvisation.[11] This is obviously a healthy approach to early musical study — one that, unfortunately, is not yet widespread and one which is rarely carried into adulthood except by those with an irrepressible creative urge (e.g., potential composers).[12] Its advantages are numerous: encouragement in the exercise of curiosity about unstereotypical musical sounds; the encouragement it lends to an uninhibited, *self-transcendent* response to auditory-haptic stimuli; and facilitation of auditory-haptic coordination. The result of such an approach, aside from the stimulation that it gives to the potential composer, is a sense of aesthetic/creative fulfillment, a greatly increased awareness of the sound that results directly from technical manipulation and the kinesthetic experience, and the increased fluency which is a by-product of all extempore playing (as noted above by Newman). Unless started during childhood, however, facility and freedom in this kind of extemporaneous playing is hard to acquire. As in all such music-making, apparently, inhibitions are the main deterrent. If one can break through them, and can begin to explore the sounds of the instrument with a genuine aesthetic appreciation based upon what is heard as related to what is felt kinesthetically, the rewards can be great.

Transposition. Practicing transposition is an excellent way to establish a high level of auditory awareness *provided one listens* to what is being transposed. However, it is quite possible and common for one to transpose purely by interval — note by note or chord by chord — without ever engaging the auditory senses: a "mechanical" technique which has nothing to do with auditory perception. This method of transposition, of course, leads to nothing of lasting value. If the ear is utilized in at least a confirmatory capacity (i.e., to detect errors that have been made) one might hope that something is gained; nevertheless, there can never be more than minimal rewards in terms of heightened auditory awareness until such time as the ear, the eye and the haptic mechanisms are fully engaged and allied as cognitive controls in the exercise.

This is not to say, of course, that the first efforts in transposition will not start with some kind of mechanical note-by-note, chord-by-chord technique of getting all of the correct notes at the right pitch level. As with all such experiences, if they are new, one must start somewhere. Such things as C-clef transposition are used throughout the world as aids to rapid transposition, among players of transposing orchestral instruments (e.g., the French horn) as well as among accompanists. More often than not, however, such methods are means to ends, and they are of little value to the performer insofar as increased auditory awareness is concerned until such time as he brings all of the appropriate senses into play — a point in his development when, should he choose, he can usually leave all methods behind.

Learning Works by Ear. I can remember a time when, if someone suggested learning a work "sight unseen" from a phonograph recording, I would have considered it some kind of mortal sin that was unbecoming a "real musician." Nonetheless, time passes, we all learn and, during the course of my long teaching career, I eventually realized that it is by just such a method that a pianist can learn to *really listen*, if he has not already — that it is by just such a method that he can shift his habits of perception from what he sees to what he hears. This is precisely what the little Suzuki children do, of course, and it undoubtedly accounts for the extraordinarily high incidence of pitch acuity among them. Why not also the adult pianist (or almost anyone beyond the age of eight or nine)? Even though it is unlikely that anything like absolute pitch will develop, there is no question that sensory priorities can be altered, and that music will be perceived as it should be perceived: with the ear rather than with the eye.

A project centered on such a pedagogical technique is not always easy to implement. The first obstacle is always the student's fundamental fear of launching out in a direction which, for whatever reason, he has taught himself to avoid in the first place. The basis of resistance is primarily the same as that which is encountered in other efforts to stimulate reliance upon auditory processes: a fear and distrust of aural means and the feeling of security and well-being found in visual methods. Challenge the ear of such a person and he will make almost frantic efforts to substitute what he can see for what he has heard.

The method I propose does work. The teacher can search out recordings of works for which music is not readily available and arrange them in systematic order from the easiest to most difficult. He can play such pieces to the student, having the student respond at a second piano, without *seeing* what the teacher has done. Or, better, he can make cassette tape recordings of such material for the use of students who need this type of work. The exercise should begin with the very easiest things — nothing but melodies at first — progressing through simple accompaniments into more complex textures. The selections should be rather short, at least at first, so that stylistic diversity can be attained in the number of works that are assigned. There is no reason why one or two such pieces cannot be assigned at each lesson, along with the studies, technique and other repertoire to be practiced. Appropriate pieces can be selected and tailored to the level and age of the student. In most cases it is not long before the ear is awakened and a noticeable transformation takes place in the student's orientation to the music he plays. As in most such efforts perseverance is a necessary but often difficult quality to sustain; nevertheless, doing so will reap rewards that make the effort worthwhile.

Retrieving Old Repertoire from Memory without Score. Similar rewards can be forthcoming from attempts to retrieve old repertoire from memory without recourse to the score. I recall, years ago, when Lillian Steuber, just a day before one of my recitals, asked me about the encores I had prepared. I named them and, in her estimation, all were unsuitable. She then asked me to name other works from my repertoire that might be appropriate. As I did, I mentioned the first *Valse oubliée* of Liszt, which she found just right; however, I had not played the piece for at least ten years. She asked me to play it anyway. I protested that I simply could not, but she said, "Just turn off your brain and play." I took courage, did, and after some momentary faltering, the piece came out almost as if I had practiced it within the week. From that time onward I found that I could indeed entrust recall to my auditory-haptic coordination much more than I thought I could. The resultant confidence has been immeasurable. Such recall is easier for the person who has absolute pitch, naturally, especially if he is accomplished in extempore playing;[13] but it is not impossible for the pianist who does not have these attributes. It is certainly an excellent method for awakening the auditory process. Again, overcoming the fear and frustration inevitably produces its rewards.

Practicing on a Silent Piano. Although I have not had an occasion to test it, pedagogically, I cannot help but think that practicing on a silent piano, as MacKinnon observed (above, Chapter Five), might be another effective way of awakening auditory awareness and confidence. The pitfalls are obvious, of course. If practice is mechanical, and the "listening" efforts do not keep pace with the kinesthetics of the exercise, not much is gained. I am sure that it would take a considerable amount of self-discipline to persevere in listening for something beyond the sound of the noisy action that is characteristic of most silent keyboards. Theoretically, at least, it should work and undoubtedly deserves a try. A certain maturity is assumed, I believe. Internalizing the music under such conditions would be beyond the capacity of any but the most exceptional child, I am sure.

Playing Accompaniments and Ensemble Music. In the long run one of the most gratifying ways of establishing a symbiotic relationship between one's auditory and haptic senses is by performing music with others. It may be a longer, more subtle process, and one which may prove unsuccessful if unadulterated listening does not play a central role, but it is one which offers perhaps the greatest of all musical rewards if all the relevant senses are functioning and cooper-

ating the way they should. The fact is, of course, that if the auditory
and haptic systems are not integrated and involved as they should be,
the enterprise is not likely to be a success. For inasmuch as the
auditory system will be assisted by playing accompaniments and by
playing ensemble music, characteristically, these exercises usually
indicate very forcibly what is missing before they even begin; because
the prerequisite for good ensemble performance is, in the first place,
the habit of active listening. If, however, "necessity is" truly "the
mother of invention," then ensemble playing will, ultimately, ally the
senses effectively. It is certainly an essential experience for every
pianist, regardless of his musical and professional objectives — one
that cannot afford to be missed.

Another study must be done on the subject of the relationship of
memory and the visual cues represented by the musical score. I would
postulate here that any performance with score that is well prepared
(and even one that is not) assumes that a great deal of what is done
is drawn from the memory storehouse (i.e., haptic or auditory). In
stating this I am obviously basing my conclusion upon the assumption
(as enunciated throughout this book) that most of what is remembered in a performance is drawn from auditory-haptic memory at the
subconscious level, and that, whether one plays with or without the
score on the music rack, the performer requires a prompt mechanism
to "jog" those subconscious memory patterns. When one is performing without score, it is largely conscious attention to the musical
gestalt and to musical values which prompts the memory. When
playing with the score, the memory is cued by the symbols on the
page. In other words, the two modes of performance differ only in
their prompting mechanisms. In both cases the performance proceeds
on the assumption that the "road" has been traversed before, and that
the prompting mechanisms merely indicate where "the turns" are to
be made. Again, I note one of David Sudnow's observations:

> Here, as in the situation of sight-reading music that is
> nearly memorized, the sights no longer serve as instructions so
> much as reflections of my own voice. Though the look remains
> narrowly confined to the scope of the fingers' movements, I no
> longer see the text as a strict succession of places to be tran-

sported. I experience the guidance of the action being motivated
from within, and looking serves only to keep me on the track.[14]

So using the score in ensemble playing does not negate its relevance to playing from memory. The two modes of performance involve the same things: auditory and haptic acuity. The ensemble
experience, of necessity, calls auditory awareness to the fore in a way
which solo performance seldom does. For that reason alone, the
pianist should never fail to accept an opportunity of making music at
a high artistic level with another person, singer, instrumentalist, or a
small group of performers, as the experience is indispensable to his
development. Among many other values, it will add that additional
measure of musical substantiality and poise which can help fortify
him against excessive performance anxiety.

Reinforcing Awareness of the Musical Gestalt.

In addition to sharpening auditory awareness, many pianists
need to bring their awareness of the musical gestalt into sharper
focus: "Where am I within the musical 'organism'?" "How does
where I am at the present moment relate to what has gone on before
and to what is comparable in the future of the work?" "What is the
unique character of this motive in comparison with others of the
work?" "What is the role of this motive with respect to the whole?"
Awareness of the answers to all of these questions can be heightened
by appropriate experiences in the process of sensory awakening and
priority reordering, with a result that still another question mark can
be erased — another doubt eliminated that has left the performer
open to excessive anxiety.

Keyboard Harmony and Improvisation.

Another benefit obtained from the practice of keyboard harmony and improvisation is increased awareness of the music's Gestalt: keyboard harmony in a way that enhances "here-and-now"
awareness as well as awareness of larger structural relationships
(from the phrase on upward); improvisation (once "here-and-now"
structures have been automatized) as it heightens awareness of
phrase and period structures.

Once basic progressions have been "practiced in," and a certain
freedom has manifested itself in the idiomatic handling of these

progressions, practice should continue either in playing longer melodies by ear (period structures or larger), or in freely improvising phrases, periods, and larger forms. By so doing the "long line" will soon become apparent, especially when it evolves from the creative impulse. The resultant awareness will add immeasurably, thereafter, to the awareness of musical gestalt in everything that is played.

I fully recognize what all of this entails in terms of personal and musical discipline — a tall order for anyone who has allowed important early years of experience to slip by. It *is* possible, nevertheless, and the benefits are considerable. Most college and university courses in keyboard harmony and improvisation are intended as spurs to these practices, since the benefits of which I speak are well known. If they do not always work, it may be because they are either poorly taught, or are taught by teachers who cannot adapt to the extremely varied needs and capabilities of the students who take them. This in no way discounts the importance of the exercise. Eventually, of course, it has to be an individually-motivated effort. Guidance can help but, unless the student is willing and able to submit himself to the effort, without fear of failure, and with self-disciplined perseverance along with totally-committed musical faculties, not much will be gained.

Keyboard Analysis.

Matthay devotes considerable space to the subject of analysis in practice.[15] One certainly cannot argue with him. All intuitive responses in music, ultimately, must be subjected to analysis. However, the kind of analysis of which Matthay speaks could go on irrespective of a rational/intellectual foundation, and could be called "intuitive analysis" — a kind of analysis which, in the end, is based upon "gut instinct" (and which assumes, in turn, that the individual making the judgment has the enlightened musical endowments for such a judgment). While I believe that the validity of the judgments to which Matthay alludes must be based upon just such a foundation, there is something more that the performer needs in terms of analysis: analysis based upon the rational/intellectual processes, upon learning, and upon the auditory-haptic processes founded upon that learning. The "keyboard analysis" of which I speak is based upon a rational/

auditory-haptic awareness that has grown out of intellectual curiosity and involvement.

The purpose of this kind of analysis (which is *in addition to* that described by Matthay) is to establish a firm foundation for gestalt-like awareness — a practical analysis which will indicate to the pianist, at every moment, "where he is" in terms of the larger structural matrix, and what the relationship is of the "here-and-now" to that whole.

What is intellectually, auditorily and kinesthetically self-evident to the pianist in terms of harmonic "skeleton" will, of course, depend upon the amount of his experience. The practice of "blocking out" or "skeletonizing" passages (with the keyboard techniques described above), a procedure which I emphasize in teaching and practicing, obviously needs not be done when the harmonic vocabulary is already very familiar. For the young player, however, even music which is involved with nothing more than tonic and dominant oscillations may be harmonically "unconditioned," and would be blocked out to good advantage. For the more experienced player, music built upon any progression that is not in the performer's everyday "auditory-haptic repertoire" should be skeletonized (particularly sequences of various kinds). Doing so will establish the essential "ground" for the "figure," and will make the student aware of the harmonic tensions-relaxations which might otherwise escape his notice.

Heightening Awareness of Structural Units.

I recall a particular piano lesson when I was still a teenager when, after experiencing memory difficulties in a Bach fugue, my teacher asked me to start playing the fugue from the beginning, to stop playing at the first structural cadence while continuing to internalize the music (with hands in my lap), to resume playing after the next cadence, etc., all without breaking rhythm or tempo. Once I was able to accomplish what he asked without incident, I never "got lost" in that fugue again. I have used that technique many times in teaching as well as in my own practice and have never found a better technique for heightening awareness of the music's structural units and articulations — a reinforced awareness of the musical gestalt. The technique is particularly useful for helping to identify in memory those sections of a multisectional work (such as a sonata) which, while similar, pursue divergent consequents. It also encourages one's use of auditory imagery, a capacity which generally is in need of reinforcement.

*   *   *   *   *   *   *

These are a few of the means that I have found to be effective in strengthening both auditory awareness and awareness of the musical gestalt in piano playing. The reader might well find and explore other techniques for accomplishing these ends. Certainly, such objectives cannot be neglected. Doing so will only sustain the dominant position of threat as it is perceived by the performing musician. Filling in the voids, where they are evident, is the first step to be taken in the task of learning to control performance anxiety. For I must emphasize again that, no matter what therapies are pursued to reduce anxiety in the person, unless the person's musicianship and technique are organized around a strong auditory-haptic coordination in which there is great confidence, and around a confident grasp of those subjects which must engage his conscious attention in performance, there are bound to be recurrences of the anxiety which besiege him.

NOTES AND REFERENCES

1. I concur in what has been said that, "The three most important essentials in piano playing are technique, technique and more technique."
2. This often happens with singers, of course — a situation usually made less noticeable by the fact of musical/vocal preoccupations.
3. Figured bass should be practiced sooner or later, nevertheless.
4. Ultimately, one must accept the fact of statistically confirmable stereotypes where such progressions are concerned, and not be put off course by the acknowledged "exceptions" that occur throughout the literature (until much later, at least).
5. Newman describes the beginnings of such a study in *The Pianist's Problems*. Revised edition (N. Y.: Harper and Row, 1956), pp. 8ff.

Innumerable keyboard harmony texts are on the market, many of them designed for undergraduate music programs.

7. Newman, *op. cit.*, pp. 6f.
8. *Ibid.*, p. 8
9. *Ibid.*, pp. 10ff.
10. Once again I call attention to David Sudnow's efforts as he learned to improvise jazz. See especially: David Sudnow, *Ways of the Hand* (N. Y.: Bantam edition, 1979; first published in 1978).
11. For example, Lynn Freeman Olson, Louise Bianchi, and Marvin Blickenstaff, *Music Pathways*; *A Course for Piano Study* (N. Y.: Carl Fischer, 1974).
12. It is by now generally overlooked that, until about 1850, nearly all performers were composers, and that, in most cases, composition reflected playing styles. This is particularly obvious in the works of Chopin, I believe, and is also evident in the works of such composers as Rachmaninoff and Debussy (among others who were known for their extempore playing) composed during the early part of the present century.
13. As note the experiments referred to in Chapter Four.
14. David Sudnow, *Talk's Body* (N. Y.: Alfred A. Knopf, 1979), p. 95.
15. Tobias Matthay, *Musical Interpretation* (Boston: Boston Music Co., 1913).

Chapter 8

PIANO TECHNIQUE
AND RELAXATION

It is important to learn how to turn strenuous movements
into good ones — that is, into movements that are first of all
effective but also smooth and easy. Moshe Feldenkrais[1]

Is That Tension Necessary?

I once knew an outstandingly gifted student whose muscular
tension was so extreme that it prevented her from realizing anything
beyond slow-moving, relatively simple textures. Everyone recognized
her musical sensitivity but she had no fluency whatsoever. Her musical feeling was intense and compelling to the extreme. Intensity,
however, was part of her problem, not so much for itself, but because
of its alliance with her kinesthetic awareness — an alliance which
defeated her, ultimately, in almost every musical achievement she
sought — an affiliation which "paralyzed" her, technically, blocking
even partial fulfillment of her potential.

While it is true that her hands were not particularly well suited
for playing the piano, I am convinced that her real problem was with
the inseparable alliance she had formed between her muscles and her
musical feeling — from an unwavering conviction that musical intensity must be identified with physical tension. Under such radical
circumstances, of course, almost anything is an "unrealistic challenge" precluding the possibility of realization.

This is an extreme example, of course, but similar ones are not
uncommon — cases where a misplaced emphasis upon the kinesthetic experience deludes the player, convincing him that he must be

137

muscularly *tense* if he is to be musically *intense*. The results are always muscular contractions (tensions) far in excess of what is necessary to accomplish desirable musical ends; and signals from the straining muscles form a feedback loop with the central and autonomic nervous systems to create and sustain performance anxiety that is often out of control.

I have already given considerable space to the question of kinesthetic dominance in performance, but I believe the problem needs to be stressed again here. As I have noted, it is very easy for a pianist who distrusts his auditory processes to lean, instead, upon the kinesthetic experience as a gauge of his musical feelings and as a "guidance system" for his performance. The kinesthetic measure of musical reality, nevertheless, is misleading if divorced from the auditory experience. Alone, it is not completely trustworthy in note location/recall. Neither is it a faithful mirror of musical "reality"; and when one adds the tendency to confuse muscular tension and musical intensity to these nebulous perceptual states, high levels of performance anxiety are practically inevitable.

Although technical theory is beyond the scope of this book, several axioms having to do with muscular tension/relaxation in piano technique may be mentioned:[2]

1. It is impossible to play even a single note on the piano without some expenditure of muscular energy. Therefore, to play a work of even moderate difficulty involves a large number of muscular contractions (i.e., a considerable amount of muscular tension).
2. A coordinated movement presupposes the precise timing of both contraction and relaxation of appropriate muscles, and the precise degree of contraction necessary to fulfill the function of the movement that permits no musical compromise.
3. Contraction and relaxation of muscles are both essential components of coordinated movements. "The readiness with which relaxation sets in between movements . . . is a fair index of kinesthetic talent as applied to the piano."[3]
4. The point is not whether one can be relaxed while playing a passage but whether one is maximally relaxed under the circumstances, given the musical/technical demands of the passage plus the player's size, weight and reserve of muscular strength.

5. Incoordination is indicated 1) when muscle tension (contraction) exceeds that which is necessary to fulfill a musical objective, or 2) when musical fulfillment is thwarted by too much relaxation at the wrong time.
6. A muscle functions at maximum efficiency at about one-half the limit of its strength.

Stated simply, then, any muscular tension which is essential to the fulfillment of desired musical ends must be considered acceptable. Any that is not essential is unacceptable. The ideal condition is when muscular tension and relaxation fulfill the needs of the musical conception exactly. So long as the amount of muscular tension called for is within the efficient range of the player's resources, performance anxiety is less likely to result; if more muscular tension is called for than is within the effective range of the player's capacity, performance anxiety is very likely to be triggered.

"Consonance" and "Dissonance" in Muscular Contraction.

It is helpful to think of the fluctuations of tension and relaxation in technique in terms similar to the dissonance and consonance fluctuations in the music itself. This is not to say that they necessarily correspond or synchronize, but the fact of these inevitable oscillations is worth noting. One-hundred-percent muscular relaxation is impossible at anything like one-hundred-percent of the time, and music which is only consonant would be intolerably dull ("consonance" being a relative quality in both cases, obviously). On the other hand, unrelieved tension, both musically and physically, is intolerable, in spite of the efforts of some composers and some performers to achieve it.[4]

Muscular tension, of course, is often relative to the "residual tension" carried by the player;[5] and for the skilled pianist, coordination is also dependent upon his ability to employ "differential relaxation."[6] The amount of muscular tension that is necessary for the fulfillment of any given musical objective is also dependent upon the strength of the muscles involved. These three observations need some explanation.

First, "residual tension" is present, to one degree or another, in almost everyone, and it is this tension which relaxation techniques seek to minimize or eliminate.[7] Residual tension is muscular contraction in excess of muscle tone (or tonus) that usually goes unperceived even when the individual is at rest. It naturally varies widely among people. Neurotic individuals carry extremes of such tension with them while, on the other hand, many psychologically healthy people maintain none or, at most, very low levels.

The important concept here is that, whatever muscular tension is necessary to execute a given passage of music on the piano, is frequently *added to the residual tension already present in the player*. The ramifications insofar as the hypertense person is concerned should be obvious.

Second, coordination in piano playing is measured in terms of the total expenditure of muscular energy as counterbalanced by total relaxation. As an example, if musical fulfillment can be achieved by the contraction of muscle A alone, but muscles B, C, D, or E contract as well, there is obvious waste of physiological energy, and the action is therefore incoordinated. A coordinated movement, to the contrary, depends upon the individual's ability to employ "differential relaxation," i.e., the ability to relax those muscles which are not needed in the achievement of a desired musical result.[8]

Last, a muscle whose capacity is 20, which is required to contract to a degree of 15, is nearer to the point of "stress" (i.e., excessive tension) than the same muscle when it has a capacity of 30. The argument in favor of strong fingers and hands is, therefore, that they should be prepared to meet the maximum demands made upon them without recourse to undue tension, since tension is the absence of relaxation and relaxation is the absence of tension, and maximum efficiency is manifest (as noted) at about one-half the capacity of the muscles involved.

Almost every pianist, at one time or another, has encountered a passage which seemed at first to be well nigh impossible and, after careful and diligent practice, have the passage seem not difficult at all. What happens? In most cases, at the moment when the passage seems to come off effortlessly, it is because the appropriate muscles are strong enough to function without strain, they contract and relax at precisely the right moment to the degree that they should contract/relax, and note location/recall has entered the subconscious where it functions unassisted (i.e., the player has become coordinated to the passage). When that time arrives, one often wonders why there was so much difficulty in the first place. Unless all of the prerequisites were in place (muscle strength, the ability to differentially relax, subconscious note location/recall, etc.), most likely the passage would still be difficult, if not impossible, to play rapidly. More than a few cases of performance anxiety have been caused by failure to bring a passage to this stage of mastery before a performance.

The role that an "all-encompassing rhythm" plays in determining appropriate contraction/relaxation should not be overlooked. Without ever saying so, I am sure that Abby Whiteside was aware of just such a role, even though she has stated it much differently than I have.[9] Her emphasis upon an "all-encompassing rhythm" would indicate that she was very much aware of rhythm as the coordinating agent by which musical and attendant technical problems are solved simultaneously. My observation that good rhythm and good coordination seem to be embodied in the same person would point to the same conclusion: that the tension and relaxation of muscles is part of a total rhythmic "package" that centers in the body.

Muscular Tension and Anxiety.

The tendency for skeletal muscles to contract due to perceived threat or stress is well known; it is a manifestation of the "fight-or-flight" reaction built into everyone. The opposite happens as well: muscular tension elicits anxiety. This was noted many years ago (at least as early as 1929) by Edmund Jacobson[10] and, more recently, recognition of this reverse trend has been partly responsible for the burgeoning literature on psychosomatic and somato-psychic illness and therapy.[11] Holistic medicine has arisen as a viable medical practice in recognition of the unity of mind and body, of muscular tensions which arise from stress,[12] as well as of neuroses which stem from large amounts of residual tension. As I have already noted, the feedback loop which forms between unduly tense muscles, the brain and the endocrine system, causes and sustains anxiety just as surely as anxiety causes and sustains muscular tension. So, as is discussed in Chapter Nine, anxiety might be modified, in some cases, by releasing residual tension; in others, minimization of residual tension may result indirectly from a direct attack upon the manifestation of anxiety itself.

For the moment I must point out what should be obvious: that habits of piano technique which sustain inordinate levels of muscular tension cannot help but promote anxiety. Instances in which this happens are commonplace. The feedback loop linking high muscular tension/high performance anxiety, musical intensity-muscular tension/high anxiety can be seen almost every day among some of our most talented student performers. It can be seen, as well, unravelling a great deal of otherwise good teaching among quite young students who, even before playing in their first recital, become overly-involved muscularly.

If for no other reason than avoidance of excessive performance anxiety, the teacher should keep careful watch for overly-tense, incoordinated technical striving and try to prevent its becoming an established pattern of behavior in a student's development.[13] If one has already established such a pattern, steps obviously must be taken to correct it. It is not easy to do, but it can be done with critical self-appraisal, concentrated attention, and appropriate therapeutic techniques. I need not add to the often-repeated advice that one must seek technical solutions that emphasize the minimum waste of physiological energy in pursuit of the musical ideal. The repertoire for the piano demands enough of our muscular resources without adding to it unnecessarily.

Physical Incompatibility and Relaxation.

The factors of physical compatibility/incompatibility and of coordination need to be brought up here once more. As has been pointed out, incoordination as well as physical incompatibility, both products of heredity, are frequent causes of muscular strain. Clearly inordinate amounts of tension will not be a particular problem so long as challenges that are accepted do not exceed inherited capacities. Many fine performers have chosen repertoire which was within their means, avoiding such works that presented unrealistic challenges to their physical capabilities (except, perhaps, for practice). Some have had fine careers in spite of limitations when their limitations were outweighed by other qualities (provided the deficits were not too extreme, of course).[14] With the vast and rich literature available to the pianist there is almost no end to the repertoire that can be studied and performed without the strain and anxiety a great deal of it can generate. One should pick and choose, that is all, making "discretion the better part of valor."

The teacher, especially, must be extremely judicious in the challenges, technical as well as musical, which he sets before the student. One sure way to induce an anxious situation is to cause the student to accept challenges which are far in excess of his capacities and experience. I am not referring to challenges which are only *just* beyond his capabilities at the moment; these are necessary for growth. I am referring to technical demands, in terms of speed, strength or manual extensions, which are not only unrealistic at the moment, but which are likely always to be insurmountable obstacles. The resultant strain and frustration will almost invariably lead to debilitating anxiety.

I am of the opinion that one barometer of coordinative talent in piano playing (which is implied in Ortmann's observation, noted above) is the ability to "throw"; i.e., to propel a playing unit (arm, hand, or finger) by means of an appropriate muscular contraction, followed by its relaxation an instant later.[15] Weight can be "thrown" from the key surface, so I am not referring to the so-called "percussive attack," necessarily. Throwing a playing unit which is subsequently acted upon by gravity is a coordination that maximizes the muscle-relaxation phase of a movement. (Professional baseball pitchers and tennis players are models of efficiency in such movements.) The inability to "throw" is invariably characterized by playing which is stiff and labored, especially when speed and force are concomitant technical needs. The reason is that, instead of relaxing, the instant inertia has been overcome and gravity takes over, the muscles used to overcome inertia initially continue to contract to the end of the movement. Obviously, by definition, such movements are incoordinated, inasmuch as the opportunities for muscles to relax are not utilized, resulting in physiological waste. A coordinated movement is extremely difficult if not impossible to teach to someone who does not do it naturally. At least I have had very little success helping students to experience it.[16] An inability to maximize use of the kinetic energy implicit in "throwing" invariably inhibits velocity and power in piano playing with results that frequently lead to frustration and anxiety in performance. It is one of the most important facets of the coordinative system as related to piano playing.

On Fooling Oneself.

Excess muscular tension in playing the piano is seldom a problem in isolation; in most cases it is contingent upon one or more of at least three other factors which are often interrelated: how well the individual has been able to handle whatever stresses he has encountered in life (i.e., to what extent stress has manifested itself in residual tension), his body "use" in general (i.e., habits of posture and movement), and his musical predispositions (i.e., his musical intensity and whether or not he has allied it with muscular tension). I have discussed the last of these variables already. Stress in modern society, however, and the struggle to handle it, is a problem we all face; and its effect upon piano technique is comparable to the effect of "pervasive anxiety" upon musical performance anxiety as discussed in Chapter Two. Body "use" is interrelated with one's psychological makeup as well as with the ability to handle the stresses attendant to one's existence as a social animal.

In general, few people, including pianists, realize to what extent residual tension is interfering with effective functioning. For example, on a hypothetical scale of from 1 to 20 (totally relaxed to maximally contracted), an individual might carry muscular "loads" in some parts of his body at levels of up to 4 or 5 *when at rest*. If he is a performing pianist just about to go on stage, his "at-rest" residual tension might even be higher (if he is extremely apprehensive), still higher if he has had a "near miss" with his car on the way to the hall, and higher yet if there has been a death in the family during the past week or so. Continuing hypothetically, if the maximum effort from his muscles is 20, and the most athletically difficult work on the program necessitates muscle contraction as high as 8, and he begins his program with residual tension at 5, he will be forced to use his muscles beyond their most efficient range. The technical results will undoubtedly be incoordinated, with muscular tension significantly higher than should be sustained. He might have solved the problem in one of several ways (perhaps combining two or more of the means): by reducing his residual tension to a point as near 0 as possible (if only to 2), by strengthening his muscles so that their capacity is greater than 20, or by finding musically uncompromised solutions to the athletic difficulties of the piece which would require less than 8 from his muscles. I would leave the reader to ponder his choice. Under certain circumstances I could see where recourse to all three methods might be indicated.

Another source of residual tension in piano playing is in what Wilfred Barlow calls "mis-use" — "mis-use" not only in the total sense to which he refers, but in the specific sense of piano technique, as well;[17] and although the posture and balance of the body as a whole must be considered (and will be in Chapter Nine), the specific sense to which I refer here has to do with the positions of greatest mechanical advantage to the playing units: fingers, hands and arms as they interact with the rest of the body.

A great deal of nonsense has been advocated over the past two centuries or so concerning hand position. There is no telling how much unnecessary residual tension has been generated by the "penny-on-the-back-of-the-hand" approach to piano technique, for instance — an approach which is typical of those that were contrived in the past for the sake of appearance rather than for mechanical/musical purposes. While many of the curved-finger-low-wrist positions, and high-finger movements may have appeared neat and efficient, they usually fostered great tension at the expense of mechanical advantage. The more enlightened pianist of today allows "use" to determine position irrespective of appearances. "Use" and the greatest mechanical advantage, after all, promote maximum physiological ease which, as I have pointed out, is one of the measures of a well-coordinated movement.

While, as we shall see in Chapter Nine, gravity is one of the chief considerations governing proper "use" of the body as a whole, gravity is of somewhat less importance in determining the best use of the playing units (although, obviously, it is of some consequence). Of greater importance, where the positions of arms, hands and fingers are concerned, is leverage — leverage which varies according to the length of the various bones and the relative strength of the muscles that create movement at their articulations (joints). It stands to reason, therefore, that a stereotypical model for position of the playing units is not very useful (and can even be hazardous), inasmuch as there are too many human variables involved in terms of the relevant physiological structures.

As Barlow has pointed out, posturing is very often borrowed from a person one admires: a dominant parent or someone that is highly regarded for their achievements.[18] This is certainly true, I believe, where postures and positions are concerned at the piano. How often the physical attitudes of a revered artist or teacher are subconsciously emulated by the impressionable admirer; and how often, as a result, these assumed attitudes, being incompatible with one's physical uniqueness, generate tensions through the imbalances they achieve. It is in this regard, particularly, that the teacher should help the student search out his own balance and mechanical advantages, rather than force him into a mold that is inappropriate for him. It is with this in mind, as well, that each person who is trying to uncover the source of his residual tensions, should take a good look at his own technical "use."[19] There are many self-help therapies of proven efficacy which will help to relieve residual tension, temporarily, at least. Some of these will be taken up in the next chapter. It should be pointed out here, however, that no kind of relaxation therapy can be effective permanently so long as habits of performance which are founded upon unnecessary tensions persist. One must decondition "mis-use" and habituate good "use" before relaxation therapy can produce anything more than momentary relief from anxiety-inducing residual tensions.

In addition to the serious consideration of tension-reduction in one's piano technique, and to techniques for the alleviation of residual tension as discussed in the next chapter, one can spend some time each day to great advantage with certain calisthenics that have been devised, specifically, to free and strengthen the muscles of the playing units. Some of the best that I have seen and used are those formulated by the Hungarian pedagogue, József Gát.[20] A few moments each day spent on these exercises promise a salutary effect upon the playing apparatus. If one can couple these with some of those concerned with the whole body, valuable steps will have been taken to alleviate the anxiety attendant to residual tension.

NOTES AND REFERENCES

1. Moshe Feldenkrais, *Awareness Through Movement* (N. Y.: Harper and Row, 1977), pp. 86f.
2. See Otto Ortmann, *The Physiological Mechanics of Piano Technique* (N. Y.: E. P. Dutton, 1962; first published in 1929); Arnold Schultz, *The Riddle of the Pianist's Finger* (N. Y.: Carl Fischer, 1936); Reginald R. Gerig, *Famous Pianists and Their Technique* (Washington and N. Y.: Robert B. Luce, 1974).
3. Ortmann, *op. cit.*, p. 120.
4. Again, musical consonance and dissonance are relative terms as indicated by the saying, "Yesterday's dissonance is tomorrow's consonance."
5. Edmund Jacobson, *Progressive Relaxation; a Physical and Clinical Investigation of Muscular States and Their Significance in Psychology and Medical Practice.* Second edition (Chicago: Midway Reprint, 1974; first published in 1938), pp. 29-30.
6. *Ibid*, pp. 81-100.
7. Compare this observation with the one made in Chapter Two with reference to "pervasive anxiety."
8. The inability to differentially relax during the early stages of learning a new passage is a condition that is well known (that which is new being determined by the extent of one's experience). It is at these times that differential relaxation must be kept constantly in mind in practice so that the ideal coordination will be learned as the music is learned.
9. Abby Whiteside, *Indispensables of Piano Playing* (N. Y.: Coleman-Ross, 1955).
10. Jacobson, *op. cit.*
11. For instance, Kenneth R. Pelletier, *Holistic Medicine* (N. Y.: Delta, 1979); and *Mind as Healer, Mind as Slayer* (N. Y.: Delta, 1977).

12. Hans Selye, *The Stress of Life*. Revised edition (N. Y.: McGraw-Hill, 1978).

13. I emphasize the words, "overly-tense," because of the era now passed which stressed relaxation at any cost, resulting in a great deal of flaccid, unexciting piano playing due to inadequately prepared muscles.

14. It is entirely too easy to "play god" in these matters, of course. The capacity of the human spirit is impossible to predict, especially where artistic achievement is concerned. Often what has seemed to be an unrealistic challenge for someone has turned out not to be unrealistic at all. One can only predict likelihoods in these matters, basing one's judgment upon "observable-measurable" factors (a rather "uncertain" premise even for physics, as one may note).

15. I recall my frustration years ago in trying to teach a fellow tennis enthusiast how to get greater power in her service. I never succeeded. In retrospect I realize that she simply was not coordinated to the "throwing" movement and there was evidently nothing anyone could do about it.

16. The all but impossible task of conveying a coordinated feeling to someone else by verbal means has been noted by almost everyone who has ever tried.

17. Wilfred Barlow, *The Alexander Technique* (N. Y.: Warner Books, 1980; first published in 1973).

18. *Ibid.*, pp. 50f.

19. I have been caused to speculate recently upon whether "mis-use" might have contributed to the early demise of Glenn Gould. Although his arms and hands always appeared maximally coordinated, his very poor posture, which undoubtedly contributed to the high level of tension in his upper body, must have exacted a severe toll from his health over the years.

20. Many of these gymnastic exercises are founded upon the yogic principle of muscle-stretching to enhance relaxation. In the case of the hands, the muscles that are stretched are the interossei and lumbricals. See József Gát, *The Technique of Piano Playing*. Trans. Istvan Kleszky. Fourth edition (London, Wellingborough: Collet's, 1974), pp. 249-265.

Chapter 9

SOMATO-PSYCHIC AND PSYCHOPHYSICAL TECHNIQUES FOR SELF-IMPROVEMENT

The psychotherapist says, "You will only get rid of your unwanted behavior in a satisfactory way when your mental attitudes have been sorted out." The Alexander Principle says, "It will be impossible to sort out your mental attitudes in a satisfactory way as long as you persist with that faulty manner of use." Wilfred Barlow[1]

The practice of Yoga over the past fifteen years has convinced me that most of our fundamental attitudes to life have their physical counterparts in the body. Yehudi Menuhin[2]

As we begin to consider therapeutic measures it would be helpful, I am sure, to reassess our objectives. What is it that we wish to accomplish? Essentially, we want to bring performance anxiety under control and abolish it at extremes that are debilitating. This means, fundamentally, that the cognitive, behavioral and physiological components of anxiety will be brought within manageable limits and kept there in the face of stress. In terms of performance mentation it implies an unrestricted capacity for focal concentration upon "task-relevant" objects within one's "circle of attention," a posture which is mutually dependent upon homeostatic equilibrium as well as upon a skeletal musculature that is free of residual tension. Psychological equilibrium cannot exist more than momentarily apart from physiological balance.

In essence, the pianist playing from memory should achieve a focused "passive" concentration (attention),[3] with calm vigilance, a

Taoist mood of doing-without-trying, allowing and guiding without dictating, and a consciousness that functions apart from the ego.[4] In this ideally balanced state he can focus attention upon those facets of his performance which he considers essential, while observing the subconscious functions of his playing without conscious intervention. Such mentation is interdependent with a somatic condition that is at a low level of arousal, meaning a state of muscular relaxed-alertness with minimized residual tension, and homeostatic equilibrium that is not jeopardized by excessive adrenal secretion.

The first step in one's deliberations must be to assure that one's piano playing, preparation and sensory priorities are in order. Possibly there is no need to emphasize that, for unless these factors are in a state of good "health," no therapy, either somato-psychic, psychophysical, behavioral, cognitive, or psychoanalytic can be more than a "band-aid" on one's problem. One therapeutic measure or another may produce momentary relief, but the problem will not be eliminated entirely unless one is completely "ready." There are simply no substitutes for thorough preparation and a judicious ratio of auditory to kinesthetic awareness.

If all of the preparatory steps have been looked after but, as often happens, anxiety continues to bedevil one's performances, the next step is to pursue one or more of the several self-improvement strategies that are now to be discussed. In most cases these are strategies which are very helpful in the alleviation of stress-related "free-floating" anxieties and anxiety brought on by whatever musical/technical insecurity that may continue to reside in one's performing. The cost of professional behavioral and psychotherapy can be expensive, after all, and consuming of time and energy. If, as is often the case, just-a-little-too-much anxiety can be eliminated by self-administered therapies, it is worth a try. In most cases the assistance of a counsellor, teacher, or specialist is to be recommended, even when the day-to-day routines are to be carried out at home without supervision. The many popular do-it-yourself books on the shelves of bookstores seldom do more than indicate the directions one should take under proper guidance and supervision. Some of these books make valuable adjuncts to professional assistance; others are quite worthless.

Often it will be helpful to combine more than one of these strategies. I will indicate those which seem to complement one another most effectively in due course. The most important thing is to be consistent with whatever one does. Avoid jumping from one to another of the various routines indiscriminately. Be conscientious and systematic, have faith, and give whatever you choose to do a fair trial.

To facilitate discussion of the many therapies that one can self-administer, I have chosen to classify them under the two headings, somato-psychic (body-mind), and psychophysical (mind-body). Although, in reality, mind and body work together as one, it is easier for some people to think in terms of an approach that is either by-way-of the body or by-way-of the mind. We will consider first the somato-psychic approaches: those therapies whose ultimate purpose is to lower arousal of the skeletal muscles and, in turn, the autonomic nervous system with which they form a feedback loop.

SOMATO-PSYCHIC STRATEGIES

Muscle Stretching/Relaxation.

Yogic Exercise and Posturing. Whether or not one pursues the meditative disciplines of which yogic exercises and posturing form a part, the daily practice of yoga can place the skeletal muscles of the body in an optimum state of health. The emphasis in yoga is upon stretching of the muscles which span each joint, contributing a wider range of movement to the joint as it promotes relaxation of the muscles involved. A muscle stretched, after all, is a muscle that is relaxed, inasmuch as the opposite of contraction (tension) is extension (relaxation). Muscles that are routinely extended to their maximum become conditioned to a state of relaxation, a state that is more easily replicated thereafter during one's day-to-day activities. Rosemary Feitis observes:

> Hatha (gathustha) yoga is the yoga of the body; it has as its premise that work with the body will improve not only the physical but the emotional and spiritual life of the individual as

well. In physical terms, the principal aim of yoga asanas is to increase the space at bony interfaces (joints). That is to say, the assumption of yoga is that bodies need to lengthen, and the means by which this length is achieved are positions in which opposing body parts pull or twist each other.[5]

While the aims of yoga also include "firming up" many of the muscles of the body which are essential to the maintenance of proper posture, muscles are seldom contracted without their being subsequently extended or stretched, with the result that there is a gain in muscular pliability and ability to relax, together with a corresponding improvement in muscle tone.

There are usually a number of excellent hatha yoga instructors in most cities. In addition to instruction by private teachers, many colleges, universities, community centers, and other public educational and recreational organizations offer classes in hatha or Iyengar yoga.

I have found the adaptations of hatha yoga by B. K. S. Iyengar particularly fine in their special concern for spinal alignment. Iyengar is the distinguished yogi with whom Yehudi Menuhin made contact in India years ago. Menuhin subsequently invited him to England where Iyengar spent a number of years as his instructor while establishing yogic practices in that country. This particular "brand" of yoga is now widely taught in North America as are the more traditional forms of hatha yoga. The book by Iyengar, *Light on Yoga*, is valuable as a guide to yogic practice, with over 600 plates picturing the various postures, accompanied by detailed instructions.[6] The American, Richard Hittleman, has done a great deal to popularize yoga as an exercise in North America. In addition to televised instruction, he has published several worthwhile books which can be used advantageously along with professional guidance.[7]

Arica Psychocalisthenics. Arica psychocalisthenics has much in common with yoga but borrows from other physical disciplines, as well, including kinesthetic awareness (bioenergetics) and dance. Its objectives are also similar to yoga with heavy emphasis upon the role of the breath. Oscar Ichazo, originator of the Arica concept and founder of the Arica Institute (with centers in several of the larger cities of North America), conceived the program with a view to its greater appropriateness to Western culture and life-styles. As with yoga, the calisthenics are intended as a corollary to mental and spiritual discipline.[8] Whether or not one follows the total program, which includes meditation, the exercises are excellent. In addition to stretching and conditioning the musculature, a great deal of attention is given to posture and balance. It is a highly structured regimen, well organized and tested. There is much to recommend in it; many people find it an excellent alternative to yoga. Ichazo's book, *Arica Psychocalisthenics*, is a clear and concise manual of instruction for use at home.[9]

Respiration and Relaxation. Concentration upon the breath and breathing occupies a central position in nearly all of the physical disciplines, whether the primary focus of the discipline is upon muscle stretching (lengthening), muscular exercise (contracting/strengthening), or posturing. Breathing and the lungs govern the levels of oxygen in the bloodstream, a critical determinant in stress and anxiety. If for no other reason breathing habits and techniques deserve our attention here. Many of the practices being considered include separate exercises in breathing (e.g., yoga,[10] Tai-Chi,[11] Feldenkrais[12], and bioenergetics[13]). Nearly all integrate techniques with their particular systems of exercise or posturing. Special breathing exercises are prescribed to promote relaxation and stress reduction, in some instances, apart from routines involving the skeletal musculature.[14]

Whether one accepts the yogic view that the breath "connotes the soul as opposed to the body,"[15] whether one sees it as the essential link between the mind and body, as the biologic integrator, as the focal point of meditative attention, or as merely the supplier of life-giving, energy-sustaining oxygen, it is obviously an important function to consider no matter what the endeavor. It is neglected as often as not to the detriment of energy, concentration, posture and general well-being. If one is looking for an immediate source of anxiety, one should look first, perhaps, to one's breathing habits. And if one is in need of quick, momentary relief from tension, full and rapid exhalations for purposes of relaxation can often fulfill that need. I am sure that I am not the only one to have employed that technique even in the *midst* of a performance.

Posture, Balance and Gravity.

Moshe Feldenkrais,[16] as well as advocates of the Alexander Principle[17] and of Rolfing,[18] tell us that no state of relaxation can ever be more than temporary so long as body posture, balance and "use" are poor. Their arguments are convincing, and I am thoroughly persuaded they are right.[19]

Our bodies must continually withstand the force of gravity acting upon them throughout our lives. Whether standing, sitting, lying, walking, or running, the body's skeleton and musculature must counteract gravity's pull in order to maintain its position. If properly balanced and aligned vertically, the bones absorb most of the pressure, the skeletal muscles contracting only enough to maintain posture and create movement. As Feldenkrais observes:

> The nervous system and the frame develop together under the influence of gravity in such a way that the skeleton will hold up the body without expending energy despite the pull of gravity. If, on the other hand, the muscles have to carry out the job of the skeleton, not only do they use energy needlessly, but they are then prevented from carrying out their main function of changing the position of the body, that is, of movement.[20]

Indeed, most of us do not maintain anything like an ideal posture or balance, with the result that the muscles normally used to maintain posture are overly contracted, and, in addition, other muscles are used to maintain posture that were not intended for that purpose. The result is muscular contraction added to whatever residual tension we may have acquired from life's "stressors." As with residual tension, we become conditioned to the superabundance of muscular tension that results from poor "use" (dystonia) and might never notice it before a psychological or physiological pathology occurs. Barlow calls this "defective awareness," and notes, in addition:

> Our whole nature is bound up with the substratum of muscle tone that underlies our USE, and a sense of the space coordi-

nation of our postural system pervades all our behavior. We *are* our posture.

The moment we try to carry out a basic re-education of USE, we very rapidly run up against our attachment to the old feeling of ourselves.[21]

Postural faults and imbalances result not solely from gravity acting upon the body, as Feldenkrais and Rolf[22] suggest, but are also products of learning, much as many of the psychological factors leading to neurotic anxiety are learned from social matrices. Wilfred Barlow notes:

> The child at this age [two and a half or three years] will have adopted many of the tempos and tensions of the parents. The family mood — or the mood of one dominant parent — will be inducing its associated posture in the child. This process will continue with us for all of our lives, since if we are to share the constructions that people we admire put on things, we are eventually forced to share something of their manner of USE — a "posture-swapping," in which they may also adopt something of our posture. We imitate the attitudes of those we admire in order to make contact easier: it is through USE that we construe our surroundings, and since a major part of our connecting up with other people consists of an attempt to share the construction they put on things, we have to adapt our USE to theirs. In a situation in which we are dominant, they will adapt their USE to ours: "posture-swapping" is rarely fifty-fifty; it tends to favor the dominant person.
>
> The outcome of this projective posture-swapping will be a personally idiosyncratic mixture of tensions and predispositions of structures and potential attitudes, an amalgam of nature and not so much nurture as selective preference on the part of the *child* as he brings up his parents as best he can![23]

Most postural problems, whether one is in motion or at rest, involve unnatural alignments of the spine (especially the neck and head); most imbalances result from the tilting of the pelvis, the shoulders and/or the rib cage (among the larger structural components).

The Alexander Principle. All of the therapies and disciplines under survey have their own ways of correcting these problems. The

Alexander technique achieves it by the "de-education" of postural "mis-use" and the substitution of proper alignments and balances, in stationary positions as well as in movement — by lengthening muscles that, in mis-use, have been allowed to remain shortened (contracted). As Barlow observes, "The lengthening of anatomical muscles can be brought about not simply by stopping off the activity which originally made that muscle contract, *but by learning voluntarily to lengthen muscles until they achieve a better resting length.*"[24] The technique requires a well-trained teacher who has undergone a long apprenticeship — one who has an acute eye for the critical misalignments, imbalances and mis-uses, and who has the training in appropriate therapeutic measures to correct them. The Alexander principle involves "doing," on the part of the one learning the technique, rather than massage or manipulations (as does Rolfing). A great deal of self-discipline is presupposed, together with a great deal of conscious effort. The technique has a huge following in Great Britain and a growing number of advocates in North America. Among those of renown who have given testimony to it are John Dewey, George Bernard Shaw and Aldous Huxley, as well as Hollywood stars Paul Newman, Joanne Woodward and Nina Foch. An increasing number of prominent teachers of piano, voice, violin and other instruments are incorporating it in their pedagogy. Some of its principles have been embodied in other somatic-improvement approaches (e.g., Samama[25] and, to a certain extent, Feldenkrais[26]). The Alexander technique is the oldest of the *modern western* procedures concerned with posture and balance and, as of the present time, still remains the most popular.

There are many books on Alexander. Some are aggravatingly simplistic and devoid of information other than that given to the story of F. Matthias Alexander, himself, and to the evolution of the technique. Many pages have been filled with laudatory comments about it and what it promises to do for one, sometimes with hints that there may be something esoteric and supernatural involved. For a while I had the distinct impression that the only way I would find out anything about the principle would be to take the lessons — and that was what I was told I should do on several occasions. I did, nevertheless, locate the excellent books by Wilfred Barlow, *The Alexander Technique*, and *More Talk of Alexander*[27], and the handy little volume by Sarah Barker, called also, *The Alexander Technique.*[28] Both are highly recommended although, to be sure, not much of therapeutic value is to be gained from the books alone; lessons are essential. Barlow is editor of the *Alexander Journal*. The technique is taught by qualified teachers in many centers throughout North America.

Feldenkrais. Posture and the structural integration of the skeletal/muscular systems probably have their most eloquent spokesman in Moshe Feldenkrais. His apparently consummate knowledge of the body's skeleton and musculature, and of the mechanics involved in its posture and movement, together with his ability to discuss the complex issues involved lucidly and succinctly, lend credence to his point of view and attractiveness to his methods. Nor does he stop only with somatic considerations; his discussion of posture and movement as it relates to awareness offers, as well, an appealing model of mind/body integration.

Feldenkrais's rationale is very similar to that of the advocates of the Alexander Technique and Rolfing although, as might be expected, his methods for correcting postural defects are different from the others. His thorough-going analysis, as noted, is the clearest that I have found; and the exercises he has devised for remedial work appear to be very well conceived, mechanically, to accomplish what he sets out to do. His book, *Awareness Through Movement*, is available in most bookstores. The method is widely taught throughout North America.

Rolfing. As a doctor friend said to me, "If one has slightly masochistic leanings, Rolfing is great, and it is certainly effective." My understanding of this approach to structural integration from the Rolfian point of view, admittedly, is purely theoretical (which Rolf would undoubtedly say is not to understand it at all). I have had no occasion to experience the treatments first hand.[29] What I have learned has been largely from one book, *Ida Rolf Talks about Rolfing and Physical Reality*, edited by one of her students, Rosemary Feitis.[30]

In principle, Rolf and her protégés reorganize the posture and structural interrelationship of the skeleton by manipulation of the myofascia. As Rolf says:

> In Rolfing, we work in terms of alignment. We align the
> myofascial structure, which is the connective tissue system.
> Fascial connective tissue is the organ of structure. Fascial layers
> comprise the organ of structure, the organ that holds the body
> appropriately in the three-dimensional material world. . . . This
> organ of structure is a very resilient, elastic, plastic medium. It
> can be changed. It can be changed by adding energy. In Rolfing,
> one of the ways we add energy is by pressure. The practitioner
> deliberately contributes energy to the person with whom he is
> working. This is not energy in the sense in which the meta-
> physicians throw the word around. This is energy as they talk
> about it in a physics laboratory. When you press on a given
> point, you literally are adding energy to structures under that
> point.
>   You can change human beings. You can change their struc-
> ture, and in changing their structure you are able to change their
> function. Structure determines function to a very great degree
> and to a degree which we can utilize. The basic law of Rolfing is
> that you add structure to the body.[31]

Structural integration is achieved, normally, in ten sessions.
Essentially, the treatment achieves much the same thing as do the
Alexander and Feldenkrais techniques, but in quite a different way.
As with all of the therapies and exercises for physical integration and
conditioning, psychological improvement is claimed as a result of the
structural improvement — a claim that is not difficult to believe.[32]

Bioenergetics. The therapy known as "bioenergetics," formulated by psychiatrist Alexander Lowen, is based upon the concept of
psychotherapy through body awareness. Built upon the teachings of
his mentor, Wilhelm Reich, it owes a great deal, as well, to Eastern
disciplines. Lowen makes the distinction, however, "In yoga the direction is inward, toward spiritual development; in Reichian therapy
it is outward, toward creativity and joy."[33] He has devised a number
of physical exercises over the years to promote his psychotherapeutic
aims, some of them borrowed from Tai-Chi Chuan and yoga. They
are mostly oriented toward postural improvement and structural integration, with heavy emphasis upon breathing. He observes:

> [Bioenergetic exercises] represent an integration of both and Eastern and Western attitudes. Like the Eastern disciplines, they eschew power and control in favor of grace, coordination and the spirituality of the body. But they also aim to promote self-expression and sexuality. Thus, they serve to open up the inner life of the body, as well as to aid the extension of that life into the world.[34]

Lowen synthesizes his formulations as follows:

> Only through your body do you experience your life and your being in the world. But it is not enough to get in touch with the body. A person must also keep in touch, and that means a commitment to the life of the body. Such a commitment does not exclude the mind, but it does exclude a commitment to a dissociated intellect, a mind that is not mindful of the body.[35]

Lowen is executive director of the Institute of Bioenergetic Analysis. His book, *Bioenergetics*, is readily available.[36] Not only is this form of therapy widely practiced by many psychotherpists, but bioenergetic clinics and workshops are common in many North American cities.

Muscle Control for Musicians. Physiotherapist, Ans Samama, mentioned earlier, has spent many years working specifically upon musicians' muscular problems. Her book, *Muscle Control for Musicians*, is especially useful in that it is designed as a practical self-help manual.[37] Although, as she points out, it is always preferable to have the supervision of a professional, it is not always possible. For that reason she has prepared her book with maximum clarity, organized it logically, and accompanied the excellent illustrations with carefully detailed instructions. It would be hard to go wrong. All it takes, as usual, is self-discipline and perseverance.

Samama has done a great deal of work with students in various music schools on the European continent and in England, where she has worked at the Menuhin School.[38] She believes, as does Barlow,[39] that attention should be given to matters of posture and muscular control/relaxation in all educational institutions — in her case, specifically, in all schools of music. Samama's work is frankly based upon the Mensendieck System which she adapts, as well, to the specific problems presented by performance on the various musical instruments. Although some of the exercises and poses remind one of those found in other techniques (including yoga and Feldenkrais), the total repertoire addresses more varied physical concerns: relaxation (lengthening/extending), strengthening (shortening/contracting) of "balancing" muscles, as well as postural improvement. Integrated breathing is also given considerable attention.

* * * * * * * *

It is obvious that these disciplines and systems share much in common. They all recognize, albeit tacitly in some cases, that the common enemy of the skeleton and its musculature is gravity — that failure to maintain a properly integrated posture against the force of gravity leads to muscular contraction (tension) in excess of muscle tone. Their are two alternatives, in this event: strengthen those muscles which poor posture necessitates so that the limits of their capacity are not encroached upon, or "de-educate" the mis-use which requires the useless muscular tension.[40] In the first case, no amount of yoga or any kind of muscle-lengthening/relaxing exercise can be permanently effective, inasmuch as gravity acting upon poor physical "use" will soon re-activate those muscles to their original level of tension. While muscle stretching/lengthening may give momentary release from tension and anxiety, ultimately it will return. The second alternative, on the other hand, offers hope of a permanent solution to the problem. If, while learning to maximally relax and extend the muscles needed for postural support (thus eliminating residual tension), the mis-use which caused the unnecessary muscular tension is "de-educated," efforts toward alleviation of wasted muscular effort can have some hope of permanency, with a result that the anxiety which that tension provokes and sustains can also be reduced.

The various systems or techniques also commonly recognize the unity of mind and body. All of them have as their aim the improvement of psychological health by way of somatic improvement. The Eastern disciplines of the body, Tai-Chi Chuan and yoga, are in fact essential adjuncts to spiritual and psychological discipline. They, as well as Arica calisthenics, were not formulated for themselves but for the greater purpose of achieving enlightenment through meditation and other forms of spiritual exercise. This does not devaluate the effectiveness of the exercises themselves, of course; if one does not wish to pursue spiritual enlightenment by these means, the physical exercises are nevertheless extremely effective. Psychological benefits will no doubt accrue anyway.

Without exception, all of these systems likewise recognize the role of the breath in the promotion of physical and mental health. For the yogi and for the adept in Tai-Chi Chuan the breath takes on spiritual significance (reminding one of the healthful practices that have emerged, symbolically at least, as spiritual tenets in many religious practices). Whether for spiritual reasons or merely for somato-psychic health, one's breathing habits should not be overlooked. They clearly have an important role to play in the control of performance anxiety via physical health, balance and wise use of the skeletal musculature.

Muscle Strengthening and Physical Fitness.

I am sure no one would argue that physical fitness is a great asset, regardless of one's interests in life, whether for specific purposes of promoting maximum effectiveness in one's profession, or, in general, to maximize one's chances of functioning fully as a human being. The sheer number of joggers one sees at their rituals on the parkways and medians, the hundreds that can be seen riding their bicycles, swimming, playing tennis and racketball, or the thousands that are enrolled and participating in exercise classes, attest to current public awareness of physical fitness as an important, if not essential, part of living.

Such activities of course take time and energy; and for this reason, many musicians fail to keep pace. The number of hours needed for practice and rehearsals, taking into account the limited number of hours in the day, too often cause him to ignore his need for fitness and to lapse into a sedentary existence, much to his eventual disadvantage. The amount of physical, nervous and intellectual energy that is required to sustain a career is too often mustered by way of determination that is manifest in tension and anxiety — a way of determination that is manifest in tension and anxiety — a way of life which usually results in counterproductivity. So, in reality, the musician needs physical fitness almost more than anyone else, inasmuch as he must function as a total person in pursuit of his art:mind *and* body. The adverse effect upon the mind notwithstanding, if the body breaks down it will not function effectively as an interface with the instrument; coordination and muscular capacity will suffer, and damage to the total person will ensue due to muscular tension that is beyond the capacity of human endurance.

The physical exercises I am now considering emphasize muscle shortening (contraction) rather than lengthening and, in addition, aerobic conditioning: i.e., they involve the cardiovascular system in sustained and vigorous (but controlled) exercise. I am excluding those athletic forms which emphasize muscular strength without the corresponding cardiovascular effect (e.g., weight-lifting, wrestling, gymnastics, etc.) because, if for no other reason, they are unsuitable for players of musical instruments for reasons of the emphasis put upon the prolonged tetanic state of large muscle groups — a practice which conditions these muscles to react in a way that is at variance with the technical needs of piano, string and most woodwind playing. While it is true that many sports that offer excellent opportunities for aerobic conditioning can also cause the undesirable "locking" of large to small muscle groups (e.g., in tennis), the fact that, in addition, the cardiovascular system receives the workout it needs can make it an acceptable activity for some musicians. The musician has to decide on a basis of his own tolerance level and upon whether or not the activity involves critical muscles disadvantageously. For example, though I loved tennis with a passion, I found, as I grew older, that the muscles of my right arm and hand took too long to recover from the continuous "locking" that was encouraged by stroking the ball. Eventually, I was forced to give it up.

Logically, the emphasis upon muscle shortening by any means would seem to be counterproductive where muscular relaxation is concerned. It is much less likely to be a problem than one might think, however. If a muscle works most efficiently at about one-half its capacity, then, theoretically at least, the stronger the muscle, the more work it is capable of doing without exceeding its most effective range (i.e., the stronger the muscle the nearer it will be to relaxation by the fact that less of its capacity is utilized for work). A muscle which stays well within its most effective range is less tense (even when at work) than one which is continually working above its middle range. It follows, therefore, that muscular strength can contribute to muscular relaxation. This is not to say that muscular strength will result unfailingly in muscular relaxation; one still must often *learn* to relax. Nevertheless, logically at least, strong muscles have a greater capacity for relaxation inasmuch as they are placed under less strain to start with by the activities of everyday living and — for the musician in particular — working.

Kenneth Cooper, the leading spokesman for aerobics, explains the principle as follows:

> The main objective of an aerobic exercise program is to increase the maximum amount of oxygen that the body can process within a given time. This is called your *aerobic capacity*. It is dependent upon an ability to 1) rapidly breathe large amounts of air, 2) forcefully deliver large volumes of blood and 3) effectively deliver oxygen to all parts of the body. In short, it depends upon efficient lungs, a powerful heart, and a good vascular system. Because it reflects the condition of these vital organs, the aerobic capacity is the best index of overall physical fitness.
>
> Collectively, the changes induced by exercise in the various systems and organs of the body are called the *training effect*. Unless the exercise is of sufficient intensity and duration, it will not produce a training effect and cannot be classified as an aerobic exercise.[41]

It is for these reasons that sports activities such as weight lifting and and wrestling, together with the kind of hard work that involves lifting or similar muscular application, do not satisfy all of the requirements of the aerobic principle: they do not sufficiently involve the cardiovascular system as outlined. The training effect produced by aerobic exercise increases the capacity to utilize oxygen in the following ways according to Cooper:

1. It strengthens the muscles of respiration and tends to reduce the resistance of air flow, ultimately facilitating the rapid flow of air in and out of the lungs.
2. It improves the strength and pumping efficiency of the heart, enabling more blood to be pumped with each stroke. This improves the ability to more rapidly transport life-sustaining oxygen from the lungs to the heart and ultimately to all parts of the body.
3. It tones up muscles throughout the body, thereby improving the general circulation, at times lowering blood pressure and reducing the work on the heart.
4. It causes an increase in the total amount of blood circulation through the body and increases the number of red blood cells and the amount of hemoglobin, making the blood a more efficient oxygen carrier.[42]

As a practitioner of the aerobics principle for many years I can vouch for the salutary effect it has upon overall physical fitness, especially if it is coupled with judicious dietary practices. As stated before, however, for purposes of lowering residual tension in the skeletal muscles it is still necessary, for most people, at least, to apply some form of auto-therapy for purposes of relaxation. One of the muscle stretching/lengthening practices, together with postural considerations serve this purpose quite well. There are also other effective methods.

PSYCHOPHYSICAL STRATEGIES

Only within the past fifty to sixty years has western science begun to realize the power of the human mind to control functions within the body that were formerly thought to be beyond its control. Practitioners of the eastern psychologies have known it for centuries, but until quite recently, it has been popular for westerners to regard the demonstration by a yogi of his skill at autonomic control as some sort of freakish "side-show" spectacle which was either a trick, on the one hand, or an esoteric-supernatural feat, on the other. An eastern adept's ability to slow his heart rate, change his blood pressure, or alter his body temperature was regarded, at best, with suspicion. By now, however, western man has accepted the fact that he too can monitor and regulate many of his autonomic processes and that the power is not in the least esoteric. Such controls, in fact, are now being exercised every day as adjuncts to treatment in the behavior/cognitive psychologies as well as in psychotherapy. There is, furthermore, a veritable glut of research under way to determine precisely what is happening and the extent of its possible applications.

Muscle Relaxation.

Progressive Relaxation. The earliest western scientific publication that I know of to postulate personal control over autonomic processes was the work by Edmund Jacobson, *Progressive Relaxation* (1929).[43] Jacobson demonstrated, empirically, that man can not only govern the amount of residual tension in the larger muscle groups, but can also regulate tension in very small groups of muscles — muscles which, normally, are beyond his control — muscles which can be controlled only by the subtlest attentional means. By learning to experience true muscular contraction (as distinct from awareness of the feeling in the skeletal articulations), at smaller and smaller levels, he can learn to release whatever tension that remains in a given muscle or muscle group. It is an educational process requiring time and great concentration, but it works extremely well.

Roughly speaking, the procedure is this. The subject is asked to recline, comfortably, with eyes closed, his legs uncrossed and arms resting at his sides. After a period of time when he has had a chance to survey the tension in his body (insofar as he is able to experience it), he is asked to contract, forcibly, one or more of the large muscle groups (e.g., flexor muscles in the forearms), to experience the tension in those muscle groups in the extreme and then, by stages, to relax the same muscles, experiencing the difference as they are progressively relaxed (e.g., by one-half, then one-half, etc.). When the individual believes he has fully relaxed, he is asked to cut the remaining tension in half, etc. Generally, he is then asked to repeat the same process, with the same muscle groups, endeavoring to reach lower and lower levels of tension each time. The procedure is repeated for each of the larger muscle groups of the body until all have been relaxed as fully as possible, after which (days, weeks, or even months later) he proceeds to the control of relaxation in smaller and smaller muscle groups. As noted, the technique is widely used clinically by psychotherapists. Popular versions of it are available in book form[44] and on cassette tapes (available even in some supermarkets) and can be practiced sometimes with salutary effect on one's own, without professional guidance. On several occasions I have advocated use of one or another of these popular versions to students with beneficial results. Even at this level of application it can give momentary relief from the ravages of uncontrolled anxiety. It is logical to predict even greater, longer-lasting benefits when the technique is administered by an experienced therapist.

Biofeedback Relaxation. Since the 1960's there has been a growing interest in a new technique for controlling autonomic and out-of-awareness phenomena within the body. The technique is bio-feedback: a procedure utilizing devices (some of them electronic) which enable the practitioner to monitor such things as the levels of his muscular tension, skin temperature, skin conductance, and even brain waves. If one is able to accurately monitor the first three of these, particularly, he can learn to control the levels of tension in the skeletal muscles — muscles, in some cases, he may not have even realized he had. I will consider monitoring of brain waves further on.

The literature on biofeedback has become immense — even those for more-or-less popular consumption.[45] So has empirical experimentation and its literature. Biofeedback training, in fact, has become faddish to the point where, apparently, some of its most serious supporters have become a bit alarmed, and have drawn back to take another long look at the technique, its instrumentation and its potentials. Although the potentials are evidently still enormous, many of biofeedback's staunchest advocates have now taken a more conservative view of the procedure and what it will accomplish, some (unfortunately, I believe) abandoning the procedures in favor of more conventional methods. Some people will invariably "throw the baby out with the bath water." The scattered ambivalence notwithstanding, biofeedback continues to hold a huge amount of interest, and it is still being used widely with much success — if not always by itself, at least as an adjunct to other techniques.

There are several kinds of muscle-relaxation biofeedback which the reader will find quite successful: electromyograph (EMG), temperature, and electrodermal (EDG). Temperature biofeedback is perhaps the simplest, inasmuch as the necessary equipment is uncomplicated and inexpensive. The idea is to monitor skin temperature, particularly in the hands, with the aid of a skin thermometer, or thermistor.[46] Relaxation of the hands and arms can be achieved by monitoring temperature and, through visualization (using progressive relaxation or a number of other techniques), raising the temperature of the skin. Since increased blood flow (a measure of muscular relaxation) produces warmth, one is able to achieve relaxation by increasing the warmth of the skin. The opportunity to monitor one's progress through the biofeedback is the key to success of the technique.

Also very excellent are EMG and EDG techniques. With EMG the actual muscular contraction is monitored with electrodes affixed (as for an EKG) at a position on the skin nearest to the muscle group that is to be monitored. Relaxation is accomplished by monitoring the changes in bioelectric potential, measured by the EMG, which are turned into either auditory or visual signals. The procedure is similar for EDG biofeedback where, instead, changes in galvanic skin resistance are measured and monitored.[47]

Some of the EMG biofeedback equipment has, by now, become so compact that it can be used during piano practice for the purpose of learning to relax. The equipment, as such, does not hamper mobility and is comfortable enough that it can soon be ignored except for the biofeedback signals. A great deal of experimentation is now in progress which capitalizes on this convenience.

The only drawback to biofeedback, one might assume, is the cost of electronic equipment for home use. Some alternatives to the purchase of expensive hardware are given in Peper and Williams, however,[48] and I can personally recommend the Biodots mentioned in note 46. The training is best learned in the laboratory from a professional therapist with high-quality equipment.

Closely related to these muscular relaxation techniques is "autogenic training." However, due to its resemblance to other "mind-over-matter" techniques that are discussed below, I have chosen to defer its consideration until then.

Disciplining the Mind

Meditation. In Chapter Three I implied that, when a pianist is at his best, he is in a conscious state which, if not an "altered state of consciousness," is something quite near it — that the experience of meditation is not new to the pianist who has repeatedly enjoyed "peak experiences" in performance. I now return to that theme.

I believe, for at least two reasons, that the practice of meditation is quite important for the pianist, especially if he has trouble with performance anxiety and with the frequent loss of concentration that accompanies it. The principal reasons are these:

1) *Concentrated attention and the passive mood are critical determinants in meditation.* The narrowing of awareness to, and the complete absorption with, a single object with which one ultimately forms a unity in meditation is nearly identical with the mentation in performance; the escape from ego-consciousness and the feeling of oneness with the universe is identical with the performer's experience of self-forget-fulness and of being one with the music, the instrument and the audience. As Claudio Naranjo writes, "In general, a meditator is one who has acquired the ability to control inner states — not in the sense of filtering-suppressing control, but in that of being able to *create* his mental states."[49] This is precisely the ability that the accomplished pianist must have in pursuit of his art: an ability *to be*, to be aware, and *to allow*, in the Taoistic sense, without coercion. In addition, it would seem self-evident that, if one has learned to give un-wavering attention to one's breath, a candle, a mantra, or a koan for twenty minutes, he should encounter no difficulty in giving undivided attention to musical values for the same length of time. As a matter of fact, I am convinced that such absorption by the accomplished pianist *is a form of medita-tion in its own right*[50] — a mindful attitude which is different from the esoteric practices of the East only in that which occupies the focus of attention.

2) *One of the most important achievements of meditation is the relaxation response.* As Kenneth Pelletier notes, "The abil-

ity of a trained meditator to induce a state which is the exact physiological and psychological opposite of the "fight-or-flight" response is clearly a very beneficial kind of adaptation."[51] According to Pelletier, reporting upon the research of Benson, Beary, and Carol, meditation activates the "relaxation response," a response involving the trophotropic system of the brain's hypothalamus, that is the exact opposite of the "fight/flight" or ergotrophic response, also a neurophysiologically identifiable system.[52]

So while psychological quiescence attends meditation, the balanced posture of traditional poses minimize the contraction of the body's supporting muscles, and the total effect is of psychophysiological relaxation via the brain's trophotropic system. Can one speak of performance anxiety under such conditions? Hardly, since the meditative state and anxiety are mutually exclusive conditions.

But will the practice of meditation (as distinct from the performance itself) help to lower the levels of performance anxiety during a performance; i.e., will the psychophysiologic conditions which meditation brings about carry over into the "real life" situation of concert giving? The evidence seems to indicate that the practiced meditator is, during normal everyday pursuits, much more relaxed, both physiologically and psychologically, than the non-meditator. As Pelletier observes in *Mind as Healer, Mind as Slayer*:

> There is considerable evidence to indicate that there are positive long-term changes which take place due to the practice of meditation itself. Studies which have used longitudinal designs and pre- and post-test designs have found significant decreases in anxiety measures in functions which are considered to be constant over the life of the individual.[53]

He notes further:

> Research evidence indicates that . . . the effects of the meditation carry over and transform the individual in a more permanent way, [and] it is more likely to be of value in the clinical management of stress and stress-related disorders. . . . One of the reasons why meditation produces this carry-over effect is that it helps an individual learn to maintain [a] low

arousal state of neurophysiological functioning. This may be used in response to stressful situations to minimize stress reactivity.[54]

So the only question that remains is not whether the practice of meditation is beneficial as a means of controlling anxiety, but what kind of meditation should be practiced. In my opinion, it really doesn't matter. There are many, and apparently any one of them will provide the therapeutic results that are "fringe benefits" of the practice: yoga, vipassana, transcendental (TM),[55] Tai Chi, Zen, or a host of other eastern disciplines, along with western forms like Arica. One more bit of advice should be offered, nevertheless. In the words of Kenneth Pelletier:

> Meditation that has the stated goal of stress reduction is no longer meditation, which properly has no goals. Perhaps stress reduction, or relaxation response induction, is a good initial impetus, but it too can become another "you must relax" situation unless one remembers the second condition, that of a passive attitude, of not trying or striving to attain anything.[56]

For best results one should seek the help of a teacher in one of the meditative disciplines (of whom there are many in almost every city), although many excellent books are available in the bookstores. Some of these books provide a great deal of insight into their respective practices. It is suggested that a little reading be done before one chooses the form that is to be followed. The reference notes at the end of this chapter are rich in recommended reading material.

EEG Biofeedback. Closely related to meditation is EEG biofeedback, which has been called "electronic yoga." As I am not convinced that the reader will run right out and take training in EEG biofeedback and buy equipment for home use, I am limiting my discussion to this very interesting, if questionably useful form of relaxation therapy — questionable, at least, for present purposes. There is a plethora of literature on electroencephalographic (or "alpha") biofeedback, and I refer the reader to it for further information.[57]

In principal, similar objectives are obtainable with EEG biofeedback as with meditation. In the relaxed state (trophotropic response) that is achieved with meditation, brainwaves form a characteristic alpha rhythm; i.e., the brain's activity, as indicated by the electrical potentials of its complex neuronal interconnections, forms a pattern which differentiates it from the other characteristic rhythms: beta (state of wakefulness), theta (hypnogogic, or state of sleep onset), and delta (state of deep sleep). With the EEG, the brain's electrical activity is monitored, and when the information is fed back to the subject via lights or an auditory signal, he can learn to duplicate the feelings that go along with the state of deep relaxation. One does not train to produce alpha waves; one trains his awareness of the subjective state which duplicates that of a relaxed state. "It is a matter of passive concentration and increased awareness. Once your awareness is increased, the responsibility for letting go of tension is yours and yours alone."[58] Often these subjective states are promoted by meditation itself or by autogenic training (discussed below).

Technically, EEG training involves affixing electrodes to appropriate positions on the scalp where they can pick up the delicate signals from the brain. Although there is absolutely no danger involved, it is generally advised, for satisfactory results, that the training be pursued with professional assistance. There are usually places in all of the larger cities where EEG biofeedback can be learned.[59]

Self-Hypnosis. The control of performance anxiety by hypnosis has been the topic of only one study that I know of.[60] Although that one study is hardly sufficient to regard the subject as fully explored, there is every reason to believe that, practiced with expertise and judgment, self-hypnosis could indeed prove to be a viable aid in the control of performance anxiety. Advocates certainly make extravagant claims for it as a strategy for stress management; if it is as they say, there is no reason why it should not be applied successfully, as well, to the management of anxiety.[61] T. A. Brantigan, in his study with organ performance majors, concluded that hypnotic training was beneficial in significantly reducing performance anxiety in every one of his subjects.[62]

Advocates of self-hypnosis point out that we are all hypnotized, to one extent or another, almost every day of our lives. When we become entirely absorbed with an idea, an activity, or an object, we are hypnotized. They tell us that even day-dreaming is a form of self-hypnosis. Obviously no one is afraid of these day-to-day states of mind, even though the popular image of the hypnotist and his helpless subject may cause some reticence where hypnotism, in general, is concerned. What is not generally known, however, is that hypnotism is frequently used in the medical and dental professions to alleviate pain (obviously with the patient's consent, inasmuch as it is impossible to hypnotize anyone against his will), and that several of the most commonly-used techniques in psychotherapy are guided fantasy and visualization or imagery, which are nothing more than applied self-hypnosis called by other names. In fact, as will be noted in the next section, autogenic training, one of the most effective and often-used techniques in psychotherapy and stress reduction, is a "spin-off" from hypnosis.

In my limited experience with self-hypnosis, I will admit, its effects were hardly discernible from those of meditation; the relaxation response, characteristic of the meditative mood, results also from self-hypnosis. I am not an expert, however, and no doubt I have not gone deeply enough into a trance to be susceptible to the post-hypnotic suggestion for which hypnotism is known (and for which meditation is not). The susceptibility to one's own post-hypnotic suggestion, in fact, is seen as its greatest value in stress and anxiety reduction. If one says to oneself while under self-hypnotic trance, "Be calm," one is likely to follow that suggestion. At least this is the assumption.

Even behavior-cognitive therapists are aware of the possibilities of self-hypnosis in clinical practice. I once asked psychologist, Margaret Kendrick (whose work is discussed below), if she had ever thought of combining self-hypnosis with her cognitive restructuring techniques (which involves the alteration of self-talk in the face of anxiety), and she said that very definitely she had but, at that time (1981), she had not yet had an opportunity to explore its possibilities, clinically. It had occurred to us both, independently, that if one could change, "I know I'm going to fall flat on my face when I get in the middle of my recital," to, "I know that I am going to enjoy sharing the music on my program with my audience," and *believe it*, he should expect to have no problem with performance anxiety.

There are a number of good popular books on self-hypnosis as well as a number of cassette tapes on the market. One of the best books I have read is Roger A. Straus's *Strategic Self-Hypnosis*.[63] It is very well written, conscientiously and intelligently conceived, and obviously based upon profound experience in the field — a "how-to-do-it" book of the best kind. There are other good ones by Leslie LeCron, Freda Morris,[64] and others, but of those for popular consumption, Straus's work has impressed me the most. More technical works by specialists Milton Erickson, Erika Fromm and Ronald E. Shor, Ernest R. Hilgard, T. X. Barber *et al.*, are noted in the bibliography.

Autogenic Therapy. One of the most effective techniques for the relief of stress and anxiety is autogenic therapy. Training in autogenics is employed not only for itself, but as one of the most commonly-used adjunctive techniques, equaled in frequency only by progressive relaxation. I could add hypnosis and meditation, as well, among the methods that are associated with other psychotherapeutic techniques, but, as a matter of fact, autogenic therapy *is* a form of self-hypnosis (as mentioned above) and, in its more advanced stages, also utilizes a kind of meditation. I have prescribed the training for anxious students who have pursued it with salutary results.

Sometimes referred to as "western yoga," the therapy was developed by the German psychiatrist, Johannes H. Schultz in the 1930's.[65] Schultz's associate, Wolfgang Luthe, has become the system's leading exponent in North America. The total program is profound and very powerful; and, although the trainee is expected to practice a great deal on his own, training under the supervision of a professional is assumed. Some of the first steps might be practiced on one's own but, beyond these, an experienced therapist should be sought for guidance.

Pelletier observes:

> Persons who, for whatever reason, are not inclined to engage in any of the Eastern meditative techniques . . . might do well to consider autogenic training. It is a remarkably thorough and systematically designed practice with an end result comparable to that of diligent meditation.[66]

The complete autogenics program includes three kinds of exercises, all involving verbal formulae: 1) standard exercises with concentration upon the body, 2) meditative exercises which focus upon the mind, and 3) special exercises to alleviate specific problems. For reasons of space I have not tried to discuss all three here, but I direct the reader instead to Luthe's and Pelletier's discussions referred to in note 65. It is the first of these which I see as of major importance for present purposes, the remainder belonging more appropriately with the psychotherapeutic techniques discussed in Chapter Ten.

In the first set of exercises (standard) the focus of "passive attention" is upon heaviness and warmth in the extremities, upon the calm and regularity of the heart and respiration, warmth in the upper abdomen area, and upon coolness of the forehead. The estimated time for mastery of the six exercises is from four to ten months, taking up a new one every week or so, depending upon progress. One proceeds basically as follows:

While in a prescribed posture (of which there are three, discussed at length by Pelletier[67]), and in a mood of *passive concentration and volition*, prescribed phrases are repeated slowly which, as in the case of "My right arm is heavy," causes the muscular relaxation which produces the sensation of heaviness in the arm; and in the case of "My right arm is warm," induces vasodilation in the peripheral arteries which is perceived as warmth due to increased blood flow.

The concept of "passive attention" is of primary importance to the exercises. Pelletier points out:

> Central to the success of autogenic training is the attainment of the "paradox of self-induced passivity," which is a concept very similar to that of "passive volition," which plays such a vital role in biofeedback and meditative training. Through this process, individuals learn to abandon themselves to an ongoing organismic process rather than exercising conscious will. Once again, too strong an effort of purposive volition immediately interrupts movement toward deep relaxation.[68]
> [This should sound quite familiar by now.]

As stated, the system is used not only as an autonomous psychotherapy and as one of the most important of the relaxation and stress-reduction techniques, but is often used, as well, in conjunction with other procedures: specifically, with biofeedback[69] and with behavior therapy (discussed below, Chapter Ten).[70] The self-hypnotic nature of the practice is obvious, despite protestations to the contrary by some experienced practitioners.[71] Whether it is or is not makes no difference; there is no question but that the system provides an effective tool in the control of performance anxiety. The standard exercises, particularly, are highly recommended for present purposes.

Prescriptions.

Clearly, the individual case must determine the specific therapeutic strategies. Nonetheless, assuming that a person has enough time to pursue more than one daily routine, he would not go wrong by including up to four of those discussed in this chapter from the following categories:

A. 1. Posture/balance/structural integration (i.e., Alexander, Feldenkrais, Samama, Rolfing, or bioenergetics)
   2. Muscle stretching (i.e., yoga or AricaPsychocalisthenics)
   3. Meditation

or

B. 1. Posture/balance/structural integration
   2. Aerobic exercise
   3. Muscle relaxation (i.e., progressive relaxation, muscle biofeedback, or autogenic training)
   4. Meditation

or

C. 1. Posture/balance/body integration
   2. Muscle relaxation and breathing exercises.
   3. Meditation

I fully realize that it is difficult for a busy person to devote time to these things every day. However, if performance anxiety is a difficult problem, an hour with such self-improvement strategies may be better spent than an extra hour at one's instrument.

Anxiety and Musical Performance

NOTES AND REFERENCES

1. Wilfred Barlow, *The Alexander Techniques* (N. Y.: Warner Books, 1973), p. 135.
2. Yehudi Menuhin, *Forward* to K. S. Iyengar, *Light on Yoga*. Revised edition (N. Y.: Schocken Books, 1977), p. 11.
3. See Erik Peper, "Passive Attention: Gateway to Consciousness and Autonomic Control." In Erik Peper, Sonia Ancoli, and Michael Quinn (eds.), *Mind/Body Integration* (N. Y.: Plenum Press, 1979).
4. A state of mind that is ego free forms the crux of Arnold Schultz's *A Theory of Consciousness* (N. Y.: Philosophical Library, 1973).
5. Rosemary Feitis (ed.) *Ida Rolf Talks about Rolfing and Physical Reality* (N. Y.: Harper and Row, 1978), p. 8.
6. Iyengar. *op. cit.*
7. Richard Hittleman, *Introduction to Yoga* (N. Y.: Bantam edition, 1969); *Yoga. 28 Day Exercise Plan* (N. Y.: Bantam edition, 1969).
8. See John C. Lilly and Joseph E. Hart, "The Arica Training." In Charles T. Tart (ed.), *Transpersonal Psychologies* (N. Y.: Harper and Row, 1975).
9. Oscar Ichazo, *Arica Psychocalisthenics* (N. Y.: Simon and Schuster, 1976.).
10. Iyengar, *op. cit.*, pp. 43-45; 441-461.
11. Tsung Hwa Jou, *The Tao of Tai-Chi Chuan* (Rutland, Vermont: Charles E. Tuttle Co., 1980), pp. 116-133.
12. Feldenkrais, *op. cit.*, pp. 100-108; 162-171.
13. Alexander Lowen, *Bioenergetics* (N. Y.: Penguin Books, 1976).
14. Martha Davis, Elizabeth R. Eshelman, and Matthew McKay, *The Relaxation and Stress Reduction Workbook* (Richmond, Calif.: New Harbinger Publications, 1980), pp. 29-37.
15. Iyengar, *op. cit.*, p. 43.
16. Feldenkrais, *op. cit.*
17. See especially, Barlow, *op. cit*; and Sarah Barker, *The Alexander Technique: The Revolutionary Way to Use Your Body for Total Energy* (N. Y.: Bantam Books, 1978).
18. Feitis, *op. cit.*
19. Their insistence runs parallel to mine. While I maintain that freedom from excessive anxiety cannot be counted upon unless one's piano playing, mentation and sensory priorities are in order, they maintain that relaxation is a fiction without a more fundamental consideration of

bodily posture and use. In both cases there is a prerequisite to long-lastingly effective therapy.
20. Feldenkrais, *op. cit.*, p. 68.
21. Barlow, *op. cit.*, p. 174.
22. Feitis, *op. cit.*, p. 37.
23. Barlow, *op. cit.*, pp. 50f.
24. *Op. cit.*, p. 85.
25. Ans Samama, *Muscle Control for Musicians.* Trans. H. Nouwen and H. Graham. Second edition (Utrecht: Bohn, Scheltema and Holkema, 1981).
26. Feldenkrais, *op. cit.*
27. Barlow, *op. cit*; Wilfred Barlow (cd.), *More Talk of Alexander* (London: Victor Gollancz Ltd., 1978).
28. Barker, *op. cit.*
29. My understanding of the procedure is that it tends to be somewhat uncomfortable.
30. Feitis, *op. cit.*
31. *Op. cit.*, p. 34
32. *Op. cit.*, p. 26
33. Lowen, *op. cit.*, p. 72. It should be noted, in passing, that the concept of body awareness is common to all of the practices now under survey.
34. *Loc. cit.*
35. *Op. cit.*, p. 107.
36. *Op. cit.*
37. Samama, *op. cit.*
38. Hephzibah Menuhin has great praise for her work. See the facsimile of her letter in Samama, *op. cit.*
39. Barlow, *op. cit.*
40. Several apparatuses are presently on the market which cnable the individual to hang upside down by his feet, ankles and lower legs, thus allowing him, for whatever period of time he chooses, to counteract the normal gravitational pull upon the body. This is not a new concept, obviously. It is largely for this reason that the headstand is such an important part of the yogic regimen.
41. Kenneth H. Cooper, *The New Aerobics* (N. Y.: Bantam Book, 1970), p. 16.
42. *Loc. cit.*
43. See Edmund Jacobson, *Progressive Relaxation.* Second edition (Chicago: Midway Reprints, 1974; first published in 1938); Edmund Jacobson, *You Must Relax* (London: Unwin Paperbacks, 1980).

44. For example, Davis, Eshelman, and McKay, *op. cit*, pp. 23-27; Erik Peper and Elizabeth Ann Williams, *From the Inside Out. A Self-Teaching and Laboratory Manual for Biofeedback* (N. Y.: Plenum Press, 1981), pp. 9-12.

45. See, for example: Elmer and Alyce Green, *Beyond Biofeedback* (N. Y.: A Delta Book, 1977); Barbara B. Brown, *New Mind, New Body* (N. Y.: Bantam Books, 1974); Barbara B. Brown, *Stress and the Art of Biofeedback* (N. Y.: Bantam Books, 1977); Peper and Williams, *op. cit*; George D. Fuller, *Biofeedback: Methods and Procedures in Clinical Practice* (San Francisco: Biofeedback Press, 1977).

46. I have recently come upon a type of skin thermometer called "Biodots" (a trade name) which is excellent to use with techniques for relaxation. They are inexpensive and, when affixed to the hand, skin temperature can be monitored as outlined. They can be purchased from: Medical Device Corp., 1555 Bellefontaine St. N. Dr., Indianapolis, Indiana 46202.

47. Electrodermal activity (EDA) varies with sweat gland activity: the greater the sweat gland activity, the lower the resistance of the skin. Relaxation is therefore greatest when the sweat gland activity is lowest and skin resistance is highest. For an excellent explanation of the three procedures, in layman's language, see Peper and Williams, *op. cit.*

48. *Ibid.*, pp. 329ff.

49. Claudio Naranjo and Robert E. Ornstein, *On the Psychology of Meditation* (N. Y.: Penguin Books, 1976), p. 41.

50. An experience not unlike that of Eugen Herrigel after he had mastered the Zen art of archery. Eugen Herrigel, *Zen in the Art of Archery*. Trans. R. F. C. Hull (N. Y.: Vintage Books, 1971; first published in 1953).

51. Kenneth R. Pelletier, *Mind as Healer, Mind as Slayer* (N. Y.: A Delta Book, 1977), p. 201.

52. Kenneth R. Pelletier, *Toward a Science of Consciousness* (N. Y.: A Delta Book, 1978), p. 202.

53. Pelletier, *Mind as . . .* , *op. cit.*, p. 204.

54. *Op. cit.*, p. 200.

55. See Peter Russell, *The TM Technique* (Boston: Routledge and Kegan Paul, 1977).

56. Pelletier, *Toward . . .* , *op. cit.*, p. 204.

57. See, for example, references under notes 44 and 45 (above).

58. Davis, Eshelman and McKay, *op. cit.*, p. 168.

59. For information about training, or to find out about the latest in available biofeedback equipment, one may write The Biofeedback Society of America, 4301 Owens Street, Wheat Ridge, Colorado 80033.

60. T. A. Brantigan, "Hypnosis and the control of performance anxiety" (Unpublished D. M. A. Thesis, Northwestern University), 1975.

61. Rachmaninoff's recovery from a creative stalemate and long period of depression is attributed to the practice of auto-suggestion, prescribed for him by a Dr. Dahl, a psychiatrist to whom the composer later dedicated his Second Piano Concerto.

62. Brantigan, *op. cit.*

63. Roger A. Straus, *Strategic Self-Hypnosis* (Englewood Cliffs, N. J.: Prentice-Hall, 1982).

64. See Leslie LeCron, *Self-Hypnotism* (N. Y.: New American Library, 1970); Freda Morris, *Self-Hypnosis in Two Days* (N. Y.: E. P. Dutton, 1975).

65. Readings in autogenic therapy should begin with Wolfgang Luthe, "About the Methods of Autogenic Therapy," in Erik Peper, *et al.* (eds.), *Mind/Body Integration* (N. Y.: Plenum Press, 1979), pp. 167ff; and with Pelletier, *Mind as . . , op. cit.*, pp. 229ff. Also see Wolfgang Luthe, "Autogenic Training: Method, Research, and Application in Medicine," in Charles T. Tart (ed.), *Altered States of Consciousness* (Garden City, N. Y.: Anchor Books, 1969), pp. 316ff. The primary source is Wolfgang Luthe (ed.), *Autogenic Therapy*. Six vols. (N. Y.: Grune and Stratton, 1969).

66. Pelletier, *Mind as . . , op. cit*, p. 229.

67. *Ibid.*, pp. 233-238.

68. *Ibid.*, pp. 230f.

69. See Johann Stoyva and Thomas Budzynski, "Cultivated Low Arousal — An Antistress Response?" In Peper *et al.*, *op cit.*, pp. 411ff; Green and Green, *op. cit.*, pp. 21ff; and Luthe, "About the Methods of Autogenic Therapy," *op cit.*, p. 179.

70. See Luthe, *Ibid.*, pp. 178f.

71. Pelletier, *Mind as . . , op. cit.*, pp. 231f.

Chapter 10

PSYCHOLOGICAL AND PHARMACOLOGICAL INTERVENTIONS

While for some pianists the problem of performance anxiety may be rooted in the technical or musical aspects of their playing and whatever residual tensions that have resulted from life's stresses, others may discover that, perhaps in addition, there have been unfulfilled needs, frustrated drives, severe traumas, or other adverse psychological stimuli in their lives (factors that may be only distantly related to music-making) which are at least partially responsible for the performance anxiety that is debilitating them. In some cases the cause may be "noxious" stimuli somewhere in their past environments; in others, deep-seated psychic disturbances may be the problem — disturbances manifest in repressions and inhibitions that have blocked further humanistic growth. One can take steps on one's own to correct musical and pianistic deficiencies, and can become involved with some of the stress-management strategies discussed in the preceding chapter to achieve somato-psychic or psychophysical balance and ease; but where psychological problems are more deeply rooted, professional therapeutic guidance is essential.

The present chapter deals with some of the techniques for psychological intervention that hold promise for present purposes (some of tried and proven efficacy), and, as well, presents some of the available information on certain pharmacological discoveries of recent years which are now being used, tentatively at least, to mitigate performance anxiety when it threatens the extinction of a professional career.

As defined in Chapter One, performance anxiety is a form of neurosis. This is not to say that anyone who has a slight degree of performance apprehension is "sick"; nonetheless, even a small amount of performance anxiety is considered neurotic. Obviously there are degrees of performance anxiety just as there are degrees of every type of neurosis, and no doubt nearly all of us partake of neurotic behavior in one form or another, to some degree of another. As Hans Eysenck observes:

> There may be a continuum, ranging from the most stable to the most unstable or neurotic; there may not be an absolute point at which we may say that those to the left are 'normal' and those to the right 'neurotic'. The difficulty is precisely the same as that we would encounter if we were asked to make an absolute distinction between people who were tall and people who were short; the difference is real but any absolute cutting point is arbitrary.[1]

One does not need to delve too deeply into the psychological literature before becoming aware of the on-going debate that rages between the various psychological disciplines: between psycho-analytic and behavioristic points of view, for instance, and their multifarious subdivisions — debates and mutual disparagements which take place to the confused dismay of those who perhaps need therapy, and to the discredit of the disciplines involved.

I recommend the handy volume edited by Richie Herink, *The Psychotherapy Handbook*, for preliminary reading.[2] Following that, the specific therapies that seem promising should be studied in the greater detail covered by specific references. Then, start asking "educated" questions of people "in the know," and draw conclusions accordingly.

BEHAVIOR AND COGNITIVE THERAPY

Behavior Therapy.

The behavioral school of psychology and therapy arose during the first two decades of the present century, partly, at least, as a reaction against the alleged "excesses" of Freudian psychoanalysis. Presently it vies with psychoanalysis for preeminence on the North

American continent and it is quite strong, as well, in western Europe. It is the psychological persuasion commanding the most attention in the North American colleges and universities, largely because of its image as a scientific discipline.

As suggested in Chapter One, behavior and cognitive therapeutic approaches to intervention are, by comparison with traditional psychoanalytic methods, coolly detached, methodical, almost impersonal and self-consciously scientific.[3] I do not intend this as a criticism but, rather, as a characterization, and I must quickly point out that behavioristic methods have already demonstrated effectiveness in the treatment of many cases of performance anxiety. I will cite specific instances in due course.

It is indicative, I believe, that most behaviorists prefer the term "behavior therapy" or "cognitive-behavior therapy" to "psycho therapy." This is because they are reluctant to accept the notion of the psychic origins of "maladaptive behavior," as do the psychotherapists of the psychoanalytic persuasion. They are unconcerned about the *origin* of a maladaptive behavior except to identify the environmental stimulus or stimuli that conditioned it (thus indicating the plan of treatment). In therapy, total concentration is upon neutralizing or eliminating the symptoms associated with the undesirable behavior. Eysenck writes, in a statement resembling that of Skinner (above, Chapter One), "The symptoms are indeed the disease, and are not 'symptomatic' of anything . . . except themselves."[4]

As noted in Chapter One, behaviorists believe that, in the name of science, the only valid indices of behavior are those that can be measured: cognitive, behavioral and physiological patterns of change. Except for self-reports involving cognitive self-statements, behaviorists lend little credence to introspective reflections. Characteristically, some have even expressed concern that, in cognitive-behavior therapy, particularly, too much emphasis might be placed upon *irrational* cognitions (and "unconscious, symbolic meanings").[5]

All behaviorists recognize that anxiety, as well as other neurotic tendencies, are *learned* emotional responses (as do most psychoanalysts for that matter, as noted in Chapter Two): conditioned responses derived from the environment. They see learning theory based upon conditioning, and the failure to adapt to noxious stimuli (rooted ultimately in Pavlov's early experiments), as the explanation for all neurotic behavior.

Several basic techniques are used in behavior therapy that are of interest to us here: desensitization, flooding, behavior rehearsal, and modeling. To one degree or another each of these has played a role in studies modifying maladaptive behavior in performance (i.e., performance anxiety). One of the most important of these, where present purposes are concerned, has proved to be the first: Wolpe's "systematic desensitization."[6]

Systematic Desensitization. The method proceeds as follows: A list of threatening images is derived from interviews with the subject and arranged in a hierarchy from the least to most severe. The subject is then taught progressive relaxation (see above, Chapter Nine) and, at successive sessions, after he has reached an advanced state of relaxation, is asked to visualize one of these scenes at a time, starting with the least threatening. The object is to remain relaxed while visualizing each of the scenes, interrupting the visualization whenever anxiety begins to intrude. Extinction of the anxiety is sought in the pairing of the noxious stimulus (the visualization) with feelings of comfort (the relaxed state). When the most threatening scene can be visualized without tension, therapy is considered to be complete, with anxiety either diminished or extinguished. The procedure can also be pursued *in vivo*, i.e., overtly, under live circumstances, rather than through imagery.

At least two studies have been done on musical-performance anxiety in recent years which have utilized systematic desensitization as the primary therapeutic strategy: one by Wardle with instrumental players in a sight-reading scenario,[7] and one by Appel with solo adult pianists under public performance conditions.[8] Both studies came to essentially the same conclusion: that systematic desensitization training did indeed lower the levels of performance anxiety. Appel's study (which does not specify whether the pianists were performing without the score) pitted anxious subjects who were given training in systematic desensitization against a similar group of subjects who were given additional instruction in musical analysis and another which received no instruction at all. The first group benefitted most, followed by the group having only musical analysis.

In the Appel study the anxiety hierarchy was encountered *in vivo* rather than through imagery.

An observation made by Appel is relevant to earlier statements that I have made concerning therapy, concentration, and technical/musical preparation:

> The results of the MA [musical analysis] training procedure, although partially successful, were disappointing by comparison. Although significantly effective in reducing performance errors, the MA procedure had little effect on the reduction of cognitive or physiological anxiety indicants. . . . Further investigation is indicated, especially because of the traditional faith held by many musicians and teachers in the anxiety-reducing qualities of thorough musical analysis and improved mental concentration on the performance material. *If cognitive and physiological anxiety responses are not controlled, it may not be possible to retain mental concentration throughout a threatening solo performance* [my italics].[9]

The converse is also true. If musical/technical preparation is incomplete and mentation is confused and ill-focused, no amount of behavioral or any other kind of therapy can provide more than a fictitious, temporary relief from the performance anxiety that originates in inevitable low "expectations of self-efficacy" (i.e., confidence).

Although both Appel and Wardle used progressive relaxation as the point of departure for encounters with threatening stimuli, neither employed hypnosis conjunctly as did Wolpe on several occasions.[10] One wonders if there would be any therapeutic advantage in making one's performance-threatening imagery the more convincing by proposing them to oneself while in a light trance. It is perhaps significant, in this regard, that autogenic training has been used successfully as an alternative to progressive relaxation with various techniques of behavior therapy, including systematic desensitization.[11] This makes good sense, logically, inasmuch as autogenic therapy has components of both relaxation and self-hypnosis.

Flooding. Although the technique of flooding and implosion therapy are similar in that they are both forms of desensitization, Wilson and O'Leary make the following distinction:

> Flooding should not be confused with *implosion therapy*, a
> technique developed by Thomas Stampfl. A major difference is
> that implosion therapy involved an emphasis on psychodynamic
> themes (e.g., aggressive and sexual impulses; Oedipal conflict)
> that are assumed to play a role in the etiology and maintenance
> of neurotic disorders.[12]

The technique of flooding appears to have proven most successful *in
vivo* while implosion therapy is predominantly a visualization procedure.

Flooding is just the opposite of systematic desensitization in the
sense that, instead of visualizing scenes of adversity in a hierarchical
arrangement *while remaining calm and comfortable*, the subject is
asked to visualize or experience anxiety-inducing stimuli *in vivo* and
*sustain the full thrust of the attendant anxiety over a protracted
period of time*.[13] In this case, apparently, the length of exposure is the
critical determinant (up to two to three hours for each session). If
exposure to the dreaded stimuli is too short, the effect will be to
reinforce it (an effect called "incubation"); however, past a certain
point, anxiety begins to subside and is eventually extinguished. It
seems a rather brutal method, its effectiveness in treating agora-
phobics and obsessive-compulsives notwithstanding. Theoretically,
giving a full public recital in spite of the high anxiety would be the
equivalent, I suppose, but I am convinced that the result would be to
make matters worse unless some measure of accomplishment (and
self-efficacy) were perceived by the player in the doing. I understand
that there are some adventuresome teachers who have made use of
the *in vivo* technique while preparing their students for performance.
Obviously, it would have to be used very skillfully in order to avoid a
negative result.

A related, but more psychodynamic approach is implosion therapy. The fundamental departure from the foregoing is that, instead of
utilizing actual *in vivo* experiences, or visualizations that have
emerged from interviews with the subject, the therapist contrives
"horror" fantasies that he believes have been associated with the
anxiety-stimulus but repressed, therefore becoming part of the
unconscious (an assumption which understandably elicits raised

eyebrows in many quarters of the behaviorist community). The subject is asked to visualize these catastrophic scenes as vividly as possible, over a protracted period, feeling all of the attendant emotion that they induce. Extinction evidently occurs after a number of repetitions of such exposures. I, personally, can see where this technique might be very effective in lowering the effects of perceived threats that are the cause of advanced performance anxiety. It would not be too difficult to construct "horror" images that are far in excess of those that one would associate with the usual public performance.

Behavior Rehearsal. The technique of behavior rehearsal is somewhat akin to flooding. In fact, an *in vivo* encounter with anxiety-inducing stimuli *is* a behavior rehearsal. From Kendrick's analysis and review of the literature on behavior rehearsal[14] one can conclude that the technique is advantageous *so long as the subject perceives the experience as one of success (or, at least, of less danger to his well-being than he had supposed) — one in which the threat is viewed, both before and after the fact, as one that he can handle (and one that he does) without reinforcement of the initial response.* If, nevertheless, there is a bad experience — one that equals or exceeds his expectations, the anxiety response will be reinforced, perhaps manifesting itself more powerfully than ever.

The behavior rehearsal technique, therefore, is not new to most musicians. Nearly every pianist or teacher of piano I have ever known has advocated "try-outs" before a concert or recital. Some prefer several. For many years I have held weekly "performance classes" with my students (each meeting for two hours), at which time they not only rehearse their performances (i.e., behaviors), but lend encouraging support and constructive criticism to the others. The conditions thus replicate not only those for behavior rehearsal, but for "modeling" as well (see below), since I model the supportive, constructive attitude for the students, and the less anxious students model for those who are more anxious. The key to the success of such a class is, of course, the supportive and constructive milieu; for without a friendly, encouraging environment, nothing is gained and, in fact, a great deal of damage can be inflicted. Even when students know that they have not achieved their best under such circumstances, the threat of disapproval and of *ostracism* (the ultimate threat, I am convinced) never enters the picture.

Although the cognitive-restructuring technique Kendrick utilized proved superior to behavior rehearsal, she found that behavior rehearsal was decidedly better than no treatment at all.[15] There is, according to her dissertation, a great deal of additional research yet necessary to determine the values of the behavior rehearsal technique. Nonetheless, most musicians will continue to make use of such a technique, the paucity of clinical evidence notwithstanding. I am certain of its effectiveness (and the results of Kendrick's study would seem to so indicate), provided every measure is taken to make the experience one that at least approximates success.

Modeling. The modeling effect utilized by behavioral psychology (as well as by parents and teachers, either intentionally or unintentionally) is anything but new. The effect is present whenever one person serves as an example for another. A child "picks up" a behavior (or, as noted in Chapter Nine, a postural characteristic) from a parent, teacher, sibling, peer, or anyone with whom he might identify, as often as not without any imitative intentions. The effect is frequently and purposefully utilized in behavior therapy, most often adjunctively with one of the other methods: flooding, behavior rehearsal, or attentional training.

In behavioristic terms modeling is either *behavioral* (i.e., communicated visually) or *cognitive* (i.e., communicated verbally). It is either *covert* (i.e., modeled in the imagination) or *participant* (i.e., modeled actively). It can be used to increase behavior (*acquisition effect*), as when teaching a piano piece by rote, to encourage assertion behaviors in the face of inhibitions (*disinhibitory effect*), or to encourage socially-acceptable behaviors (*facilitation effect*). It is also used to decrease behavior (*inhibitory effect*), as when attempting to inhibit inappropriate conduct, or to promote courage in the face of perceived dangers (*incompatible behavior effect*). Although several of the techniques are commonly used in teaching, the most useful for present purposes would seem to be the *disinhibitory effect* and the *incompatible behavior effect* in tandem, for while one therapeutic objective is to shore up confidence in one's ability to perform capably and effectively, the other is to instill confidence in one's ability to rise above the performance's perceived threats. Significantly, Kendrick made use of both approaches, behaviorally as well as cognitively, in her work on attentional training in the control of performance anxiety (see below).

Modeling can be of mastery over adverse conditions or of successfully coping with them. Psychologists are finding that the latter is most effective in mitigating maladaptive behavior, calling into question the procedures used traditionally in such therapies as systematic desensitization, which asks that the subject remain relaxed while visualizing threatening scenes — a situation which assumes that mastery has been achieved rather than merely the ability to cope. Adaptations of Wolpe's original procedures are now common practice — techniques which employ coping-skill imagery rather than mastery imagery.[16] This brings us to the subject of the hybrid form of behavior therapy:

Cognitive-Behavior Modification.

During the 1970s behavioral psychologists began to accept the fact of cognitive mediation in conditioning: that the human organism, when confronted with a stimulus, responds to it according to his *cognitive view* of it. In the event the stimulus is regarded as noxious, he will respond to it either with adaptive or maladaptive behavior; and, in the future, he need only to imagine the appropriate stimulus (or, often, a factor that is only remotely connected to it) to respond in the same way; the actual stimulus need not be present at all. The situation is well known to the performance-anxious pianist who often needs only to imagine the scene of the performance or its circumstances for anxiety to be aroused — for questions of self-doubt to rise to the surface, creating all of the physiological and behavioral responses that are associated with his cognitive ruminations.

Imagery had been used in therapy for a long time, of course. Wolpe's systematic desensitization, after all, was founded upon the individual's ability to visualize adverse stimuli. Nevertheless, it was not until the 1970s that the "maverick" discipline of cognitive-behavior therapy arose as a systematic, nearly independent form of therapy, vying with traditional behavioristic methods for serious clinical consideration.[17]

Rational-Emotive Therapy. The roots of cognitive-behavior therapy are apparently in Rational-Emotive Therapy (RET). As with other cognitive-therapeutic methods, the aim of RET is semantic restructuring, on the premise that to restructure one's internal dialogue is to restructure one's thoughts.

RET, which was devised by psychologist Albert Ellis during the 1950s, began outside the acceptable parameters of behavior therapy, but when other cognitive approaches were admitted to the behavioral fraternity so was RET. As its main concern is with the irrational beliefs that one harbors about oneself within oneself, it seems particularly appropriate in dealing with such beliefs in their commonplace manifestations among performers — beliefs that arise, in most instances, in spite of otherwise skillful professional preparations.

In Albert Ellis's words:

> Rational-Emotive Therapy (RET) is a theory of personality and a method of psychotherapy; it is based on the hypothesis that an individual's irrational beliefs result in erroneous (or "crooked") and damaging self-appraisals. RET attempts to change these faulty beliefs by emphasizing cognitive restructuring (or "philosophic disputating"), in accordance with its ABC theory of emotional disturbance and of personality change. This theory holds that when a highly charged emotional Consequence (C) follows a significant Activating Experience or Activating Event (A), A may importantly contribute to but only partially "causes" C. Rational-emotive theory hypothesizes that emotional difficulties or Consequences are largely created or "caused" by B — people's Belief System about A.[18]

According to Meichenbaum:

> In order to counteract such beliefs, the rational-emotive therapist encourages, goads, challenges, educates by means of a Socratic dialogue, provides information, conducts rational analyses, assigns behavioral homework assignments, and so on, in order to have the client entertain the notion that his maladaptive behavior and emotional disturbance are a reflection of a commitment to irrational beliefs.[19]

Rational Emotive Therapy is still viewed with some misgivings by some of the more reactionary members of the behavioral-therapeutic society, inasmuch as they feel uncomfortable with the idea of treating belief systems.[20] The effectiveness of the technique in the treatment of performance anxiety has been tested experimentally only once that I know of, by Goldstein, with results which were not terribly impressive.[21] This surprises me and causes me to wonder if additional studies might not be in order.

Attentional Training (Self-Instruction). So far as I have been able to ascertain, Goldstein and Margaret Kendrick[22] were among the first clinical psychologists to apply cognitive-behavioral techniques specifically to the problems of musical-performance anxiety. One of Kendrick's experimental techniques was that of "attentional training," or "self-instruction," a technique involving alteration of the negative internal dialogue that an anxious person carries on in the face of threatening stimuli. The method entails conversion of self-deprecating, negative self-statements such as, "I'm sure I'm going to forget and make a complete fool of myself," to "I'm in full command of this music and will enjoy sharing it with my audience," *and believing it.* On the face of it, the method might seem to be just another "think good thoughts, dear" kind of routine; but it is evidently much more than that, especially under the guidance of an experienced and well-trained therapist.

Kendrick's procedure[23] was to give several extended sessions when, after assembling her subjects' negative self-statements, she taught them how to substitute corresponding positive self-statements for those that were inclined to be negative, so that when that "moment" arrived, they could successfully cope with the attendant threats in an effective, task-oriented way. Among the techniques Kendrick used for instructional purposes were, as observed earlier, cognitive and behavioral modeling. She encouraged both covert and participant modeling on the part of her subjects. Homework assignments were given for the purpose of reinforcing the subjects' coping skills. The procedure evidently works very well, to judge by the results of her study. Kendrick concludes by noting, "More surprising perhaps was the efficacy of both attentional training and behaviour rehearsal in increasing positive and decreasing negative thinking about performing."[24] Those receiving the attentional training were better prepared to cope than those who had been exposed only to behavioral rehearsals, and were decidedly at an advantage over her "waiting-list control" group, which received no therapeutic guidance at all.

Of special interest are the comments provided by Kendrick *et al.* at the end of their article:

> Music teachers could be advised that their student-rehearsal gatherings probably benefit students, provided that favorable concepts of audiences were fostered. Attentional training would complement this technique. Programs for music teachers incorporating attention-focusing therapeutic instructions and the cognitive-modeling slide-tape sequences [utilized in the study] appear to be feasible and to have cost-benefit advantages. *It certainly would be easier to teach music teachers what they need to know about attentional training than to teach psychologists what they would need to know about music!* [Italics mine.][25]

Cognitive Therapy. The cognitive therapeutic approach employed by Aaron Beck[26] varies only in the type of cognitions to be altered and in the kind of neurosis that is its target. Instead of treating anxiety, his main objective is alleviation of depression and similar psychopathologies. Beck, like Ellis and other cognitive-behavior therapists, bases his therapeutic methods on the premise that cognitions play a critical role in all neurotic disorders. His approach "is based on an underlying theoretical rationale that an individual's affect (moods, emotions) and behavior are largely determined by the way in which he construes the world; that is, how a person thinks determines how he feels and reacts. His thoughts (cognitions) are verbal or pictorial mental events in his stream of consciousness."[27] Therapy proceeds along the line of specific learning experiences, not unlike those that have been adopted by cognitive-behavioral therapists. The approach to cognitive restructuring could have considerable relevance where performance anxiety is concerned, even though anxiety is not the central target. If, for instance, one is prone to think, "If I don't play this piece perfectly all is lost," the depression attendant to such an irrational belief is very likely to lead to anxiety: a probability for the performer who is obsessed with meeting challenges (realistic or otherwise) that have been set by himself or by musical society in which he functions.

PSYCHOTHERAPEUTIC INTERVENTIONS

It is at that psychic level called the unconscious, or subconscious, that behavioral psychology and the remaining psychologies part company. As implied above, while behaviorists are willing to accept consciousness, inasmuch as self-reports of conscious cognitions can be perceived and measured, they refuse to acknowledge the presence of an intelligence below the level of awareness which they can neither observe nor weigh. This is rather unfortunate, in my estimation, since it limits the range of their vision and therapeutic potential, particularly for those individuals in the performing arts. The common rationale for disclaiming the unconscious is that, since its manifestations cannot be perceived or measured, it would be unscientific to accept hypotheses founded upon it — which, I am not the first to point out, is a rationale based upon Newtonian rather than modern scientific paradigms. (It has been suggested that the word "science" simply means "methodical or systematic knowledge."[28]) It is precisely for its preoccupation with intrapsychic, unobservable phenomena, however, that psychoanalysis is regarded by the behaviorists as unscientific. However, recognition of the unconscious makes dynamic psychology no less scientific than a physical science that recognizes the probability theory and the uncertainty principle.

Obviously, I am convinced of a dynamic psychic force below the level of awareness; and for that reason I am prone to seek the more permanent solutions to performance anxiety implicit in those therapies which take these vital psychic substrata into account. To this extent, at least, I am admittedly biased, although I nevertheless appreciate what behavior therapy can and does accomplish "with one hand tied behind its back." Whether only the symptoms are removed by behavior therapy, as psychodynamic specialists often claim, I am not equipped to say.

The Psychoanalytic Points of View.

There is a continuum in psychoanalytic psychology which runs from classical Freudian "psychodynamic" to existential-humanistic psychology. At one pole are many of today's psychiatrists who remain adherents to the psychoanalytic precepts set down and disseminated by Sigmund Freud; at the other are the humanistic psychologists (some of whom were trained as psychoanalysts, and others as clinical, even behavioral psychologists) who espouse existential-phenomenological philosophic views. In between there is a host of other points of view: neo-Freudianism, depth psychology, etc., which are further subdivided into an endless array of techniques from Gestalt Therapy, to Logotherapy, to Integrated Psychotherapy, and Transactional Analysis. For present purposes, to facilitate both writing and reading, I have chosen to separate this continuum rather arbitrarily into two segments: those whose orientations seem to be primarily toward treatment of psychopathologies, and those whose primary concerns are with Being and the facilitation of growth. There are obvious "gray areas" in and between these two segments which are beyond my capacity to discuss — areas which, even if I were competent to characterize them in detail, would carry the present volume far beyond its intended scope. I have used pre-existent terms for these two segments — terms which may not be quite accurate, but which should suffice for present purposes, nevertheless: psychodynamic and humanistic. Obviously, in many cases, elements of one are present in the other. The reader should keep this in mind.

There are two fundamental points of view in psychotherapy: 1) that of curing the patient's psychopathologies (within the general context of Freudian psychoanalysis) and 2) of facilitating the patient's natural striving for creativity and humanistic growth. The first asks, "What is the root of the disorder?" ("uncovering" analysis) the other asks, "What are this person's motivations and organismic aspirations?" ("opening up" analysis). Viewed from these points of view, the first is equivalent to traditional medicine (with an entropic or deteriorative view of man), whereas the latter is analagous to "preventive medicine" (with a morphic, evolving, or growth view of man's tendencies)[29] and is not limited in its usefulness solely to those who are psychologically sick (although it recognizes that only a "self-actualizing" person is totally "healthy"). The first is interested in causality — in the historical roots of a pathology; the second is interested in Being and Becoming, in potentials, in personality, and in motivation.

Dynamic Psychology. The fundamental tenet of dynamic psychology (i.e., traditional psychoanalysis) is that the sources of psychopathology are to be found in the repressed guilt, hostility, anxiety, and other adverse emotional reactions that have arisen from individual experience — experience which has brought together instinctual drives (the id) and unpropitious environmental circumstances. They are psychodynamic manifestations resulting from forgotten traumas that inflicted wounds of which one was not aware — wounds leading to repressions that are lodged somewhere in the dark recesses of the unconscious. The usual therapeutic objective is to uncover these repressions, bringing them to consciousness. Generally, they are assumed to have originated in the family matrix where, particularly, the parental roles are dominant. Once the repressions are made conscious, presumably the patient can begin to deal with them, thus placing him on the road to psychological health.

In the Freudian view, most of the repressions are sexually founded, the so-called Oedipus complex forming their basis.[30] Many of Freud's followers, including Carl Jung, Alfred Adler and Otto Rank, parted company with him on this issue, forming independent points of view which have led in many new directions to the present day, some of them toward humanistic psychology. This is not to say that the precepts of Freud ended with his death in 1939. Quite to the contrary, they too continue.

While I personally have difficulty with the Freudian view of sex as the source of all psychic disturbance, I can accept the possibility of a reservoir of repressed desires and adverse experiences ("hang-ups," in today's popular parlance) in something like an unconscious; and I am equally convinced that these repressions, in some cases at least, account for a great number of performance-anxiety problems. James Ching, as well as pianist Nancy Bricard and her psychiatrist husband, Sherwyn Woods, are of similar mind.[31]

In psychoanalysis, the troublesome content of the unconscious is little by little exposed to the light of day through patient and deliberate probing by the therapist. Inasmuch as, from the start, neither the therapist nor the patient knows what the source of the conflict may be (since the repression is lodged out of awareness), it is necessary to probe the unconscious by means which will expose the root of the conflict unwittingly; i.e., without the patient's conscious effort to do so. The skilled psychoanalyst searches for answers in the verbal and behavioral clues that surface during subliminal psychic experiences, as during dreams, in "slips of the tongue," during "free association," etc. Dream interpretation has been one of the most widely used of these methods, having been utilized by nearly every dynamic psychologist from Freud to the present day. Dreams, according to the psychoanalytic point of view, represent the play of the unconscious during sleep.

The classical psychoanalytic procedure sometimes takes a long time — months and even years. Nevertheless, the procedure has proven effective over the years in treatment of many severe cases of anxiety and other neuroses, and deserves serious consideration as a psychotherapeutic method.

Among the revisions of classical Freudian psychoanalysis, those by Carl Jung and Alfred Adler have been of particular interest to me in the present study. Jung's theories are well-known today, having gone through a period of great popular interest. The main concepts are, according to Daniel Goleman:

> The polarity of introversion and extraversion; the collective unconscious with its archetypes; the psyche as composed of personal (the social mask) and shadow (the person's hidden aspects), anima (the feminine in men), animus (masculine in women), and self (a person's inmost core). Whereas Freud saw his therapy as a scrubbing away of preconceptions, and thus a return to reality, Jung saw his form of therapy as "individuation," the patient changing from *identification with what he was not to what he in fact could become* [Italics mine. Jung was therefore among the early humanistic psychologists].[32]

The implications of Jung's theory of the "collective unconscious" are particularly attractive to those in the arts: that every painter, sculptor, composer, and performer may share a common store of intuitive knowledge with all of mankind from all the ages of human history.[33] Jung referred to his particular brand of psychotherapy as "Analytical Psychology," a point of view which relied very heavily upon the techniques of dream analysis and free association.[34]

With the reformulations of Alfred Adler, dynamic psychiatry moved even further in the direction of humanistic psychology. Adler held, at least in his early career, that man's feelings of inferiority in the face of a hostile environment (the famous "inferiority complex") motivates him to react compensatorily in order to maintain equilibrium and fulfill himself as a human organism. However, as Dorothy Peven observes:

> Toward the end of his career he became more concerned with observing the individual's struggle for significance or competence (later discussed by others as self-realization, self-actualization, etc.). He believed that, standing before the unknown, each person strives to become more perfect and is motivated by one dynamic force — the upward striving for completion — and all else (traits, drives, etc.) is subordinated to this one master motive. . . . [He] postulated that it is neither the individual's genetic endowment nor his social environment that determines his behavior, but that each person responds in an adaptive, creative way to the social field in which he finds himself.[35]

Adler's theoretical base was referred to as "Individual Psychology." He too lays particular emphasis upon the family as the social matrix from which disorders emerge.[36]

One contemporary psychoanalytic practice with which I have become intrigued is "Integrated Psychotherapy," a method that was first used in Czechoslovakia, but which, some years ago, was successfully transplanted to North America.[37] The originators of the practice are Ferdinand and Jirina Knobloch, husband and wife, who are both practicing psychotherapists of long experience. Their book, *Integrated Psychotherapy*, details the plan thoroughly from both the theoretical and practical standpoints.[38] I need not describe the practice theoretically here. I have seen convincing practical evidence of its effectiveness — enough to convince me, at least. The Knoblochs claim a high percentage of successful treatment: something over 80%, which, I gather, is possibly about as high a percentage as one can expect from any therapy.

The therapy is quite eclectic and its success may depend, to a large extent, upon the resourceful inventiveness, energy and experience of the Knoblochs themselves (which could probably be said of a large number of the psychotherapies, I am sure).[39] The Knoblochs' approach unfolds within the context of a social milieu on the premise that, as R. M. Yerkes has said, "One chimpanzee is no chimpanzee."[40] Their theory is that, since neuroses are born and nurtured within the social matrix, it is within such a context that the repressed conflicts upon which the neuroses are founded must be exposed and dealt with. As they point out, "The group schema is the result of social learning and it can be changed by social relearning and new learning, which is the focus of psychotherapy."[41]

The program usually takes six weeks, successful "cures" usually occurring within that time. Eighteen to twenty patients comprise the group taking part, a group which meets at the day house five days each week, from nine to four in the afternoon. It is a very powerful, comprehensive program, elaborately organized — an integrated psychotherapy in the sense that all manner of techniques are employed, from systematic desensitization to psychodrama, psychomime, psychogymnastics, fantasy games, rituals, free painting, and various other guided imagery methods, carried out in many different sociodynamic settings. From what I have learned, it is an exciting program which bears watching — a program which could very well provide the kind of therapy needed for pianists who have some kind of inner conflict that is hampering their full realization.

Humanistic Psychology and Psychotherapy.

It is at approximately this point that we encounter the psychological orientation that arose as a significant movement during the 1960s and 1970s: humanistic psychology. Although, as someone has said, all of the psychoanalysts from the Freudian school onward have considered themselves humanists, and although the movement is rooted, at least in Europe, in existential and phenomenological philosophy, it began to command attention as a movement in North America only within the last two decades. The American humanistic psychologists, in a sense, comprise a group apart from the Europeans who embrace a somewhat different perspective of their humanistic roles. The Europeans have founded their movement upon the existential philosophical views of Kierkegaard and Jean-Paul Sartre, and phenomenological views of Husserl and Heidegger, respectively. Only some of the Americans seem to owe such allegiances. The North American movement appears to break down into the Existentialist (e.g., Amedeo Giorgi, James Bugental, Rollo May, Viktor Frankl, Ira Progoff and Frederick Perls) and Humanistic or "third-force" psychologists (e.g., Abraham Maslow, Gordon Allport, Erich Fromm and Carl Rogers). One amalgamated therapeutic formulation, on the other hand, is called "Existential- Humanistic Psychotherapy."[42]

All of the humanistic psychologists start from the premise that man, his personality, motivation, and being are issues which must command the center of attention. While the movement is, in part, a reaction against the "dehumanized" behavioral sciences, it is also, as we have seen, a reaction against the Freudian psychoanalytic points of view that were already implicit in the revisionisms of Jung and Adler.[43] Although it appears to be a movement in total disarray and with considerable difference of opinion (which is characteristic of most new movements, it seems), it holds a great deal of hope, I believe, for the future of psychotherapy. As of now, much of the energy of the movement seems to be consumed in disputation and rhetoric; what unity there is, however, is being concentrated upon the following guidelines, adopted by the American Association for Humanistic Psychology in 1962:

> (1) A centering of attention on the experiencing *person* and thus a focus on experience as the primary phenomenon in the study of man. . . . (2) An emphasis on such distinctively human qualities as choice, creativity, valuation and self-realization. . . . (3) An allegiance to meaningfulness in the selection of problems for study and of research procedures, and an opposition to a primary emphasis on objectivity at the expense of significance. (4) An ultimate concern with and valuing of the dignity and worth

of man and an interest in the development of the potential inherent in every person. Central in this view is the person as he discovers his own being and relates to other persons and to social groups.[44]

The goals, predominantly, are the achievement of self-actualization (Maslow and Goldstein) or self-realization, becoming a fully-functioning creative person (Rogers), finding meaningfulness and purpose in life (Frankl), achieving total awareness (Perls), reestablishing self-esteem (Sullivan), and many other achievements that are facets of Being and Becoming. The therapeutic approaches are highly variegated and largely dependent upon the unique personal qualities of the therapist. Of the several codified systems, Frankl's Logotherapy,[45] Perls's Gestalt Therapy,[46] Rogers's Client-Centered Therapy,[47] and Progoff's Intensive Journal process,[48] to name but four, have large followings throughout North America. All told, as pointed out earlier in this chapter, the emphasis, as with current practices in preventive medicine, is upon growth and mental health rather than upon psychopathological diagnosis and treatment as an end in itself. While psychopathologies that are blocking growth and mental health cannot be ignored, the idea that their treatment is a concomitant to an initiative toward further growth is a concept which I find very attractive.[49]

Suffering in Silence.

Before bringing this section on behavior therapies and psychotherapies to a close I want to make one final point, and that is, if a pianist is well-prepared both technically and musically, and if he has taken decisive steps in stress management (as outlined in the previous chapter), but continues to suffer uncontrollable performance anxiety, a psychotherapist or behavior therapist is the answer. Such an action does not imply that he is mad or necessarily even sick; it merely indicates that his neurosis (which, according to some estimates, is sustained to one degree or another by over thirty percent of the population in our society — more undoubtedly in fields of public performance) is of sufficient intensity to cause functional impairment. Unfortunately, however, most people would prefer to hide their need for help with emotional disorders, even from themselves. This is a ridiculous but common fear, of course, but it continues to prevail, nevertheless, in spite of the fact that a larger proportion of modern society than not will suffer some sort of neurotic disorder sometime during their lifetimes. There is not even a rough estimate available of the number of potentially excellent piano performers (as well as performers upon other instruments and in other fields) who, as Eysenck says, "suffer in silence."[50]

PHARMACOLOGIC INTERVENTION: BETA BLOCKING DRUGS.

The deteriorative effect of alcohol and sedative-type drugs upon performances requiring high-level coordination and sharpness of attention are well known. Many musicians have taken one or another of these recourses to escape the ravages of performance anxiety only to find that the functional impairment which resulted, while of a different kind, was still functional impairment. Therefore, when anyone mentions the word "drugs" in connection with a musical performance, most people gasp with profound shock and disapproval. I admit, too, that the recourse to any measure outside of personal discipline and control disturbs me a great deal. It is not that I am averse to pharmacological intervention in the treatment of aches and pains, or to medical prescriptions where they are necessary and appropriate; but in an art which reflects the Person as much as does piano playing, I dislike the idea of an intrusion by something inorganic and exterior to the Person. Perhaps that is silly and old-fashioned, considering the augmenting pressures upon the concert-giver in this second half of the 20th century. Nevertheless, I suffer this prejudice, in spite of my great concern with the problems attendant to performance anxiety.

A growing number of musicians are not nearly so reticent, however, and are making tacit and tentative use of one or the other of several drugs referred to generically as "beta blockades." At this juncture, at least, I maintain that it is ill-advised; but desperation often elicits precipitate action.

These beta-blockers were cultivated, essentially, to alleviate the effects of stress upon sufferers of cardio-vascular disorders — notably, persons who had sustained a first heart attack. They have been a blessing in this capacity, I understand. The two drugs most mentioned, propranolol and oxprenolol, block the effects of adrenaline upon the heart and other organs which induce further adrenal release, thus breaking up the feedback loop which causes anxiety to "feed upon itself"[51] and, in the case of the heart-attack-prone individual, lessen the chances of a second heart attack.

Interrupting the feedback loop attendant to anxiety soon suggested its application to the conditions of musical performance. Research, which began in England in 1974, nevertheless, has been sparse. I had occasion to discuss the research with Dr. Ian James in 1981, when he gave a lecture on the effects of beta blockade upon performance anxiety at the *First International Conference on Tension in Performance*. His report at that time was that beta-blocking drugs worked well. He cautioned informally, nevertheless, that there were still things they did not know about the long-range effects when used continuously. One cause of possible concern seemed to be that a performer might become psychologically dependent upon it. As part of their experiment, however, and unknown to the chronic sufferers with whom they were working, they gradually withdrew the drug, substituting a placebo. In due time they told the musicians about the placebo, noting with them that they had been performing effectively without the drug, and from that point onward the drug was no longer requested. James notes:

> There is evidence from this study and also from subsequent clinical use that once confidence is restored the need to continue taking them diminishes. Our aim should be to re-educate the sufferer so that he learns a more appropriate response. Of course other methods have an important role to play in alleviating the miseries of stage fright as well, but we can at least buy time with beta-blockers and give the other methods a chance to be effective.[52]

Similar findings resulted from the experiment performed by Brantigan, Brantigan, and Joseph in 1979.[53] They report, "Propranolol caused a dramatic decrease in both maximum heart rate achieved by the group, and in the average heart rate during the performance."[54] Of interest to most potential users is that, "Blockade of the beta adrenergic system is carried out with such surgical precision that there is no effect on mental functioning. Some effective beta blockers don't even cross the blood brain barrier."[55] There need be no concern, therefore, about the possibility of mental impairment. They conclude, nonetheless, that "Beta blockade should find its best use as an adjunct to conservatory training rather than as a performance crutch."[56]

A note of caution is issued by Clarke C. Godfrey in his discussion of the study by Brantigan *et al.*, however — a caution which, I believe, should be given serious consideration:

> Indiscriminate and uncontrolled use by individuals within the "performance" community can be anticipated to produce potentially serious medical problems. For this reason I would emphasize, as did Dr. Brantigan and his colleagues, that any individuals who receive Beta blockade therapy for this purpose need to be carefully screened by a physician familiar with the contraindications and side effects of the various Beta blocker agents. . . . Unpredictable central nervous system side effects of propranolol therapy are now being recognized with increasing frequency and their mechanisms are poorly understood.[57]

It is on the basis of such findings that I repeat here what I wrote several years ago: "It is [to be hoped pianists] are aware that the way to solve their problems is through discipline of the mind [and body] — not by acquiescence to pharmacology."[58] I believe it is still too soon to say otherwise.

NOTES AND REFERENCES

1. H. J. Eysenck, *You and Neurosis* (Glasgow: Fontana/ Collins, 1977), p. 16.

2. Richie Herink (ed.), *The Psychotherapy Handbook* (N. Y.: The New American Library, 1980).

3. Arguments over the behaviorists' scientific pretentions continue to rage, the most damning criticism being that these pretensions are based upon scientific principles which are no longer held even by the most severely scientific discipline of them all: physics. See Arthur Koestler, *The Ghost in the Machine* (London: Pan Books, 1975; first published in 1967), pp. 3-18. Also see Gordon Allport's reserved but pointed inference in Chapter One (above).

4. Eysenck, *op. cit.*, p. 108.

5. G. Terence Wilson and K. Daniel O'Leary, *Principles of Behavior Therapy* (Englewood Cliffs, N. J.: Prentice-Hall, 1980), pp. 279f.   6. Joseph Wolpe, *Psychotherapy by Reciprocal Inhibition* (Stanford, California: Stanford University Press, 1958).

7. A. Wardle, "Behavioral Modification by Reciprocal Inhibition of Instrumental Music Performance Anxiety." In C. K. Madsen, R. D. Greer, and C. H. Madsen, Jr. (eds.), *Research in Music Behavior: Modifying Music Behavior in the Classroom* (N. Y.: Columbia University, Teachers College Press, 1975).

8. Sylvia S. Appel, "Modifying Solo Performance Anxiety in Adult Pianists," *Journal of Music Therapy* (Vol. XIII, No. 1, Spring, 1976), 2-16.

9. *Ibid*, p. 13.

10. Wolpe, *op. cit.*, pp. 143ff.

11. Wolfgang Luthe, "About the Methods of Autogenic Therapy." In Erik Peper, Sonia Ancoli, and Michael Quinn (eds.), *Mind/Body Integration* (N. Y.: Plenum Press, 1979), pp. 178f.

12. Wilson and O'Leary, *op. cit.*, p. 164n.

13. See Eysenck's explanation in *op cit.*, p. 123.

14. Margaret J. Kendrick, "Reduction of Musical Performance Anxiety by Attentional Training and Behaviour Rehearsal: An Exploration of Cognitive Mediational Processes" (Unpublished Ph. D. Dissertation, The University of British Columbia, 1979), pp. 18-23.

15. *Ibid*; and Margaret J. Kendrick, Kenneth D. Craig, David M. Lawson, and Park O. Davidson, "Cognitive and Behavioral Therapy for Musical-Performance Anxiety," *Journal of Consulting and Clinical Psychology* (Vol. 50, No. 3, 1982), 353-362.

16. Donald Meichenbaum, *Cognitive-Behavior Modification* (N. Y.: Plenum Press, 1977), pp. 118ff.

17. Some of the names and methods that are associated with the movement are: Albert Ellis (Rational-Emotive Therapy), Aaron T. Beck (Cognitive Therapy), Albert Bandura (Social Learning Theory), and Donald Meichenbaum (Self-Instructional Training). See Albert Ellis, *Reason and Emotion in Psychotherapy* (Secaucus, N. J.: Lyle Stuart, 1962); Albert Ellis and John M. Whiteley, *Theoretical and Empirical Foundations of Rational-Emotive Therapy* (Monterey, California: Brooks/Cole Publishing Co., 1979); Aaron T. Beck, *Cognitive Therapy* (N. Y.: New American Library, 1976); Albert Bandura, *Social Learning Theory* (Englewood Cliffs, N. J.: Prentice-Hall, 1977); Albert Bandura,

Principles of Behavior Modification (N. Y.: Holt, Rinehart and Winston, Inc., 1969); Meichenbaum, *op. cit.*

18. Albert Ellis, "Rational-Emotive Therapy." In Herink, *op. cit.*, p. 543.
19. Meichenbaum, *op. cit.*, p. 188.
20. See Wilson and O'Leary, *op. cit.*, pp. 251ff. Ellis attempts a valiant defense of his therapeutic methods in the face of continuing criticism in Ellis and Whitely, *op. cit.* One has the feeling that much of the criticism is petty and irrelevant.
21. Joel Goldstein, "Systematic Rational Restructuring and Systematic Desensitization as Treatments of Musical Performance Anxiety" (Unpublished master's thesis, University of Cincinnati, 1975).
22. Kendrick *et al.*, *op. cit.*
23. Kendrick, *op. cit*, p 76.
24. *Ibid.*
25. Kendrick *et al.*, pp. 360f.
26. Beck, *op cit.*
27. A. John Rush, "Cognitive Therapy." In Herink, *op. cit.*, pp. 91f.
28. Amedeo P. Giorgi, "Humanistic Psychology and Metapsychology." In Joseph R. Royce and Leendert P. Mos, *Humanistic Psychology* (N. Y.: Plenum Press, 1981), pp. 32f.
29. Carl R. Rogers, Foreward; "The Formative Tendency." In Royce and Mos, *op. cit.*, pp. viii-ix.
30. For an overview of Freud's theories, see Sigmund Freud, *Introductory Lecture on Psychoanalysis*. Trans. James Strachey (N. Y.: Pelican Books, 1976; first published in 1963); and *New Introductory Lectures on Psychoanalysis*. Trans. James Strachey (N. Y.: Pelican Books, 1976; first published in 1964).
31. James Ching, *Piano Playing. A Practical Method* (London: Bosworth and Co., Ltd., 1946), pp. 323-341; Nancy Bricard and Sherwyn M. Woods, "Memory Problems in Concert Performers," *College Music Symposium*, 18: 102-109, Fall, 1978.
32. Daniel Goleman and Kathleen Riordan Speeth (eds.), *The Essential Psychotherapies* (N. Y.: New American Library, 1982), p. 76. For an interesting comparative discussion of Freud, Adler, Jung and Rank, see Ira Progoff, *The Death and Rebirth of Psychology* (N. Y.: McGraw-Hill, 1956).
33. C. G. Jung, *The Archetypes and the Collective Unconscious*. Second edition, trans. R. F. C. Hull (N. Y.: Princeton University Press, 1980; first published in 1968).

34. C. G. Jung, *Two Essays on Analytical Psychology*. Second edition, trans. R. F. C. Hull (N. Y.: Princeton University Press, 1972; first published in 1966).
35. Dorothy E. Peven, "Adlerian Psychotherapy." In Herink, *op. cit.*, p. 10.
36. Alfred Adler, "Understanding and Treating the Patient." In Goleman and Speeth, *op. cit.*, pp. 32-48. Others who contributed much to the psychoanalytic tradition, while leading inexorably toward humanistic psychology, were Karen Horney, Otto Rank, one of Freud's students, and the American, Harry Stack Sullivan. See Karen Horney, *Neurosis and Human Growth* (N. Y.: W. W. Norton and Co., 1950); Karen Horney, *The Neurotic Personality of Our Time* (N. Y.: W. W. Norton and Co., 1964; first published in 1937); Karen Horney, *New Ways in Psychoanalysis* (N. Y.: W. W. Norton and Co., 1939); and Karen Horney, *Self-Analysis* (N. Y.: W. W. Norton and Co., 1942); Otto Rank, *Will Therapy* and *Truth and Reality* (N. Y.: Alfred A. Knopf, 1945); and Otto Rank, *Art and Artist, Creative Urge and Personality Development* (N. Y.: Alfred A. Knopf, 1932); Harry Stack Sullivan, *Conceptions of Modern Psychiatry*. Second edition (N. Y.: W. W. Norton and Co., 1947).
37. It is now practiced in Vancouver, Canada, at the University of British Columbia.
38. Ferdinand and Jirina Knobloch, *Integrated Psychotherapy* (New York: Jason Aronson, 1979).
39. Ferdinand Knobloch, who heads the Day House in Vancouver without his wife, has several trained assistants who work with him in an active therapeutic capacity.
40. Quoted in Knobloch and Knobloch, *op. cit.*, p. 20.
41. *Ibid.*, p. 71. Their point of view is similar to that of Harry Stack Sullivan. See *Ibid.*, pp. 64f.
42. See James F. T. Bugental, "Existential-Humanistic Psychotherapy." In Herink, *op. cit.*, p. 186.
43. For a recent discussion of the humanistic movement in psychology, from both the European and North American standpoints, see Joseph R. Royce and Leendert P. Mos (eds.), *Humanistic Psychology*. Concepts and Criticisms (N. Y.: Plenum Press, 1981).
44. Quoted by Amedeo P. Giorgi, "Humanistic Psychology and Metapsychology." In *Ibid.*, p. 23.
45. Viktor E. Frankl, *Psychotherapy and Existentialism* (N. Y.: Simon and Schuster, 1967).

46. Frederick Perls, Ralph F. Hefferline, and Paul Goodman, *Gestalt Therapy* (N. Y.: Bantam Books, 1977; first published in 1951).
47. Carl R. Rogers, *On Becoming a Person* (Boston: Houghton Mifflin Co., 1961)
48. Ira Progoff, *At a Journal Workshop* (N. Y.: Dialogue House Library, 1975); and *The Practice of Process Meditation* (N. Y.: Dialogue House Library, 1980).
49. Aside from the works by Maslow, May, and Rogers cited in earlier chapters, and additional works referred to in the present chapter, the following books in humanistic psychology are to be recommended: Gordon W. Allport, *Becoming* (New Haven and London: Yale University Press, 1955); J. F. T. Bugental, *The Search for Authenticity.* Enlarged Edition (N. Y.: Irvington Publishers, 1965); and Clark E. Moustakas (ed.), *The Self. Explorations in Personal Growth* (N. Y. Harper and Row, 1956).
50. Eysenck, *op. cit.*, p. 28.
51. I. M. James, "Blocking the Effects of Adrenaline — a Cure for Severe Stage Fright?" Published papers, *The First International Conference on Tension in Performance* (July 1982), 99-102.
52. *Ibid.*, p. 102. See also I. M. James, D. N. W. Griffith, R. M. Pearson, and P. Newbury, "The Effect of Oxprenolol on Stage-fright in Musicians," *The Lancet*, (*2*, 1977), 952-954.
53. Charles O. Brantigan, Thomas A. Brantigan, and Neil Joseph, "The Effect of Beta Blockade on Stage Fright," *Rocky Mountain Medical Journal* (*76*, 5, 1979), 227-232.
54. *Ibid.*, p. 228.
55. *Ibid.*, p. 230.
56. *Ibid.*, p. 232.
57. *Ibid.*, p. 233. See also C. O. Brantigan, T. A. Brantigan, and N. Joseph, "Effect of Beta Blockade and Beta Stimulation on Stage Fright," *The American Journal of Medicine* (*72*, January 1982), 88-94.
58. Dale Reubart, "Playing the Piano from Memory," Published papers, *The First International Conference on Tension in Performance* (July 1982), pp. 49-63.

AFTERWORD

I have taken the reader on a rather long and tortuous journey; but it has been necessary, I believe, if all facets of the problem were to be considered, even in survey. I am sure that the majority of performers who are relatively free of anxiety never stop to question why it is that they are so fortunate. Why should they ask themselves such questions? And most performers who are occasionally or even consistently debilitated by anxiety have no idea what to do about it, other than to work harder and develop new pre-concert rituals. Seldom, if ever, have any of either group stopped to consider what it is that occupies conscious thought during performance. In most cases, it has never occurred to the performance-anxious player that it could be his "crooked thinking" which is central to his problem. Few performers, for that matter, have given much thought to the conscious versus subconscious functions in performance — to what they would best concentrate upon and what they had best leave out of awareness. Few realize that, as Gallwey would say, nothing but grief is in store for one who allows "self 1" to dictate to "self 2"[1] — that *trust* in one's subconscious functions is central to the success of any performance, a trust which every performer, ultimately, must develop.

Why, then, is knowing all this not enough to resolve one's difficulties? It is obvious, I believe, that before adequate means can be found for the control of performance anxiety, one should understand something of what that anxiety is and how it got there in the first place. Strategies for its control are more purposeful, less indiscriminate, and less prone to the superstitious rituals that rarely achieve more than would be accomplished with a rabbit's foot.

As I have said before, the best place to start in the control of performance anxiety, if one could, would be with "an ounce of prevention." As Heinrich Neuhaus has observed:

> Before beginning to learn an instrument, the learner, whether a child, adolescent or adult, should already be spiritually in possession of some music; he should, so to speak, carry it in his mind, keep it in his heart and hear it with his mind's ear.[2]

I have given considerable space in the foregoing pages to this consideration as well as to preliminary steps that should be taken if one hopes to have anxiety function as a creative rather than as a destructive force in performance (Chapters Five and Six). I will not amplify further except to re-emphasize the importance of early musical experiences that are centered upon auditory and kinesthetic perception.

If those preliminaries have been missed (which, unfortunately, is most often the case), there are still fruitful steps that can be taken to improve one's lot, even though the way to a permanent solution to the problem may be long and, at times, arduous.

If, after musical and technical matters have been set aright, control of performance anxiety is still out of reach, the next step should be to consider those common denominators of anxiety which behavioral psychologists like to measure: the behavioral, physiological and cognitive reactions. Presumably most behavioral problems will have been taken care of through a program of musical and technical re-education and through just performing (i.e., with "behavioral rehearsals"). Afterward, the physiological reactions to anxiety often can be brought under control by addressing the reaction itself, by means of relaxation therapy, either somato-psychic or psychophysical. However, should negative self-talk be at the heart of the problem (which is very often the case), cognitive restructuring may be indicated: i.e., the renovation of one's internal dialogue. For this the assistance of a behavior-cognitive therapist is needed.

When, after all of these steps have been considered, and the problem persists, it is quite possible that there may be some intrapsychic disturbance which is at the heart of the difficulty. In that case, the assistance of a psychodynamic specialist should be sought. This does not imply lunacy, as I have said, but, most often, only the necessity for uncovering and dispelling repressions which arose from experiences "back there somewhere" in one's life — repressions which may very well be the main obstacle to "self-actualization." This kind of problem, most assuredly, is outside the capacity of amateur therapists; certainly, no piano teacher or other person lacking the specific expertise should attempt it. Professional help is usually not far away; only an educated choice of the appropriate kind needs to be made.

Recapitulating, then, the hierarchical approach which is recommended here for the solution of problems in performance anxiety is as follows:

1. Consider sensory priorities, taking steps to align and balance auditory and kinesthetic awareness.
2. Consider technical approaches, eliminating all unnecessary tension.
3. Give attention to general relaxation and physical well-being through such methods as yoga, progressive relaxation, EMG biofeedback, or the Alexander principle.
4. Learn to trigger the relaxation response through such means as meditation, self-hypnosis, or autogenic training.
5. Seek help through behavior, cognitive-behavior therapy, or some form of awareness therapy, such as Rogerian client-centered or Gestalt therapy.
6. Seek help from psychodynamic therapy, perhaps through the integrated psychotherapeutic approach mentioned in Chapter Ten (above).

There may well be a musico-pedagogical system somewhere which fulfills all or most of these needs. Perhaps it is in the very effective and elegant methods employed by Eloise Ristad.[3] Provided someone with her insight and experience (along with her personality) were in charge of its implementation, her approach might very well succeed as an alternative to numbers 1 through 5 in the hierarchy. Time and testing will tell. In the meantime, addressing various facets of the problem of performance anxiety by one or more of the various means that I have suggested above may have much to offer.

* * * * * * * *

One further problem remains after all of the foregoing has been considered: getting the performer who needs help to take whatever steps are necessary to improve his condition. This is often one of the major deterrents to a satisfactory solution to the problem of performance anxiety. There are prerequisites:

1. The performer must recognize that he has a problem but that there is a fruitful alternative to "suffering in silence."
2. He must accept the fact that the solution is not ordinarily to be found in more practice and greater determination.
3. He must care enough about performing that the prospects of therapy are less repugnant than the idea of giving up performance.

If the performer is convinced of these things, a solution to the problem of his debilitation by performance anxiety is most assuredly within his grasp.

NOTES AND REFERENCES

1. W. Timothy Gallwey, *The Inner Game of Tennis* (N. Y.: Bantam Books, 1974).
2. Heinrich Neuhaus, *The Art of Piano Playing*, trans. K. A. Leibovitch (London: Barrie and Jenkins, 1973), p. 1.
3. Ristad applies the methods of Gallwey to musical performance and its pedagogy. Eloise Ristad, *A Soprano on Her Head* (Moab, Utah: Real People Press, 1982).

BIBLIOGRAPHY

Allport, Gordon W. *Becoming: Basic Considerations for a Psychology of Personality*. New Haven and London: Yale University Press, 1955.

Allport, Gordon W. *Personality and Social Encounter*. Chicago and London: The University of Chicago Press, 1960.

Appel, Sylvia S. "Modifying Solo Performance Anxiety in Adult Pianists," *Journal of Music Therapy*. Vol. XIII, No. 1, Spring, 1976, 2-16.

Assagioli, R. *Psychosynthesis*. New York: Penguin Books, 1976 (first publ. in 1965).

Auden, W. H. *The Age of Anxiety*. A Baroque Eclogue. London: Faber and Faber Limited, 1948.

Backus, John. *The Acoustical Foundations of Music*. N. Y.: W. W. Norton and Co., 1969.

Bandura, A. *Principles of Behavior Modification*. N. Y.: Holt, Rinehart and Winston, 1969.

Bandura, A. *Social Learning Theory*. Englewood Cliffs, N. J.: Prentice-Hall, 1977.

Barber, T. X. *Hypnosis: A Scientific Approach*. Cincinnati: Van Nostrand Reinhold, 1969.

Barber, T. X., Nicholas P. Spanos, and John F. Chaves. *Hypnosis, Imagination, and Human Potentialities*. N. Y.: Pergamon Press Inc., 1974.

Barker, Sarah. *The Alexander Technique*. Toronto: Bantam Books, 1978.

Barlow, Wilfred. *The Alexander Technique*. N. Y.: Warner Books, 1973.

Barlow, Wilfred (ed.). *More Talk of Alexander*. London: Victor Gollancz Ltd., 1978.

Beck, Aaron. *Cognitive Therapy*. N. Y.: New American Library, 1976.

Berne, Eric. *Transactional Analysis in Psychotherapy*. N. Y.: Ballantine Books, 1961.

Bever, Thomas G., and Robert J. Chiarello. "Cerebral Dominance in Musicians and Nonmusicians," *Science,* 185, 1974, 537-539.

Bonpensiere, Luigi. *New Pathways to Piano Technique*. N. Y.: Philosophical Library, 1952.

Brainerd, Charles J. (ed.). *Recent Advances in Cognitive Developmental Theory*. N. Y., Heidelberg, Berlin: Springer-Verlag, 1983.

Brantigan, Charles O., Thomas A. Brantigan, and Neil Joseph. "The Effect of Beta Blockade on Stage Fright," *Rocky Mountain Medical Journal, 76* (5), 1979, 227-232.

Bricard, Nancy, and Sherwyn M. Woods. "Memory Problems in Concert Performers," *College Music Symposium*, 18, Fall 1978, 102-109.

Broadhurst, P. L. "Emotionality and the Yerkes-Dodson Law," *Journal of Experimental Psychology*, 1957, 54, 345-352.

Brown, Barbara B. *New Mind, New Body*. N. Y.: Bantam Books, 1975.

Brown, Barbara B. *Stress and the Art of Biofeedback*, N. Y.: Bantam Books, 1977.

Brown, Barbara B. *Supermind. The Ultimate Energy*. N. Y.: Harper and Row, 1980.

Bruner, Jerome S. *On Knowing. Essays for the Left Hand*. Expanded edition. Cambridge, Mass.: Harvard University Press, 1979.

Bugental, J. F. T. *The Search for Authenticity*. Enlarged Edition. N. Y.: Irvington Publishers, Inc., 1981.

Burge, David L. *Perfect Pitch: Color Hearing for Expanded Musical Awareness*. Wilmington, Delaware: Innersphere Music Studio, 1983.

Burge, David L. *The Perfect Pitch Master Class*. Wilmington, Delaware: American Educational Music Publications, 1983; and *The Perfect Pitch Workshop*. Wilmington, Delaware: American Educational Music Publications, 1983.

Capra, Fritjof. *The Tao of Physics*. N. Y.: Bantam Books, 1977.

Ching, James. *Piano Playing. A Practical Method*. London: Bosworth and Co., Ltd., 1946.

Clynes, Manfred (ed.). *Music, Mind, and Brain*. N. Y. and London: Plenum Press, 1982.

Cone, Edward T. *The Composer's Voice*. Berkeley: University of California Press, 1974.

Cooper, Kenneth H. *Aerobics*. N. Y.: M. Evans and Co., Inc., 1968.

Cooper, Kenneth H. *The New Aerobics*. N. Y.: Bantam Books, 1970.

Craske, Michelle G. "The Three-Systems Model and Self Efficacy Theory: Piano Performance Anxiety." Unpublished Master's Thesis, The University of British Columbia, 1982.

Critchley, M., and R. A. Henson. *Music and the Brain*. London: William Heinemann Medical Books, ltd., 1977.

Davis, Martha, Elizabeth R. Eshelman, and Matthew McKay. *The Relaxation and Stress Reduction Workbook*. Richmond, Calif.: New Harbinger Publ., 1980.

Deutsch, Diana (ed.). *The Psychology of Music* N. Y.: Academic Press, 1982.

Easterbrook, J. A. "The Effect of Emotion on Cue Utilization and the Organization of Behavior." *Psychological Review*, 1959, 66, 183-201.

Ellenberger, Henri F. *The Discovery of the Unconscious. The History and Evolution of Dynamic Psychiatry*. N. Y.: Basic Books, Inc., 1970.

Ellis, A. *Reason and Emotion in Psychotherapy*. N. Y.: Lyle Stuart Press, 1962.

Ellis, A., and R. A. Harper. *A New Guide to Rational Living*. Englewood Cliffs: Prentice-Hall, 1975.

Ellis, A. and John M. Whiteley (eds.). Theoretical and *Empirical Foundations of Rational-Emotive Therapy*. Monterey, Calif.: Brooks/Cole, 1979.

Eysenck, M. J. *Sense and Nonsense in Psychology*. Middlesex, England: Penguin Books, 1957.

Eysenck, M. J. *You and Neurosis*. Glasgow: Fontana/Collins, 1977.

Fagan, Joen, and Irma Lee Shepherd (eds.). *Gestalt Therapy Now*. N.Y.: Harper Colophon, 1971 (Orig. published in 1970).

Feldenkrais, Moshe. *Awareness Through Movement*. N.Y.: Harper and Row, 1972.

Ferguson,Marilyn. "Karl Pribram's Changing Reality," *Human Behavior*, May 1978, 28-33.

Feitis, Rosemary (ed.) *Ida Rolf Talks About Rolfing and Physical Reality*. N. Y.: Harper and Row, 1978.

Frankl, Viktor E. *Psychotherapy and Existentialism*. N. Y.: Simon and Schuster, 1967.

Frankl, Viktor E. *The Will to Meaning*. N. Y.: New American Library, 1969.

Freud, Sigmund. *A General Introduction to Psychoanalysis*. N. Y.: Liveright, 1968 (first published in German in 1916).

Freud, Sigmund. *Introductory Lectures on Psychoanalysis*. Trans. James Stachey. Middlesex, England: Penguin Books, 1962.

Freud, Sigmund. *New Introductory Lectures in Psychoanalysis*. Middlesex, England: Penguin Books, 1973.

Freud, Sigmund. *An Outline of Psycho-analysis*. N. Y.: W. W. Norton and Co., 1970.

Freud, Sigmund. *The Problem of Anxiety*. Trans. by H. A. Bunker. N. Y.: W. W. Norton and Co., 1964 (first published in 1927).

Fromm, Erich. *Escape from Freedom*. N. Y.: Holt, Rinehart and Winston, 1941.

Fromm, Erich. *Man for Himself*. N. Y.: Holt, Rinehart and Winston, 1947.

Fromm, Erich. *Psychoanalysis and Religion*. New Haven: Yale University Press, 1950.

Fromm, Erich. *The Sane Society*. New York: Fawcett Premier, 1955.

Fuller, George D. *Biofeedback: Methods and Procedures in Clinical Practice*. San Francisco: Biofeedback Press, 1977.

Gallwey, W. Timothy. *The Inner Game of Tennis*. N. Y.: Bantam Books, 1974.

Gardner, Howard. *Art, Mind, and Brain*. N. Y.: Basic Books, 1982.

Gardner, Howard. "What We Know (and Don't Know) About the Two Halves of the Brain," *The INS Bulletin*, December 1978, 27-31.

Gát, József. *The Technique of Piano Playing*. Tr. Istvan Kleszky. 4th edition. London and Wellingborough: Collet's, 1974.

Gates, Anne, and John L. Bradshaw. "Music perception and cerebral asymmetries," *Cortex*, 1977, Dec., Vol. 13 (4), 390-401.

Gazzaniga, Michael, and Joseph E. LeDoux. *The Integrated Mind*. N. Y.: Plenum Press, 1978.

Gerig, Reginald R. *Famous Pianists and Their Technique*. Washington-N. Y.: Robert B. Luce, Inc., 1974.

Globus, Gordon G., Grover Maxwell and Irwin Savodnik (eds.). *Consciousness and the Brain*. N. Y.: Plenum Press, 1976.

Goldstein, J. "Systematic Rational Restructuring and Systematic Desensitization as Treatments of Musical Performance Anxiety," Unpublished master's thesis, University of Cincinnati, 1975.

Goldstein, Kurt. *Human Nature in the Light of Psychopathology*. Cambridge, Mass.: Harvard University Press, 1940.

Goldstein, Kurt. *The Organism, a Holistic Approach to Biology*. N. Y.: American Book Co., 1939.

Goleman, Daniel, and Richard J. Davidson (eds.). *Consciousness: Brain, States of Awareness, and Mysticism*. N. Y.: Harper and Row, 1979.

Goleman, Daniel, and Kathleen Riordan Speeth (eds.). *The Essential Psychotherapies*. N. Y.: A Mentor Book, 1982.

Gordon, H. W. "Hemispheric Asymmetries in the Perception of Musical Chords," *Cortex*, 6, 1970, 387-398.

Gordon, H. W. "Left hemisphere dominance for rhythmic elements in dichotically-presented melodies," *Cortex*, 1978, Mar., Vol. 14 (1), 58-70.

Green, Elmer and Alyce. *Beyond Biofeedback*. N. Y.: Dell Publishing Co., 1977.

Grindea, Carola (ed.). *Tensions in the Performance of Music*. 2nd edition. London: Kahn and Averill, 1982.

Hendricks, Gay, and James Fadiman. *Transpersonal Education*. Englewood Cliffs, N. J.: Prentice-Hall, 1976.

Herink, Richie (ed.). *The Psychotherapy Handbook*. N. Y.: New American Library, 1980.

Herrigel, Eugen. *Zen In the Art of Archery*. Trans. R. F. C. Hull. N.Y.: Vintage Books, 1971 (first published in 1953).

Hilgard, Ernest R. *The Experience of Hypnosis*. A shorter version of *Hypnotic Susceptibility*. N. Y.: Harcourt Brace Jovanovich, 1968.

Hoch, Paul, and Joseph Zubin (eds.). *Anxiety*. N. Y.: Grune and Stratton, 1949.

Horney, Karen. *Neurosis and Human Growth*. N. Y.: W. W. Norton and Co., 1950.

Horney, Karen. *The Neurotic Personality of Our Time*. N. Y.: W. W. Norton and Co., 1937.

Horney, Karen. *New Ways in Psychoanalysis*. N. Y.: W. W. Norton and Co., 1939.

Horney, Karen. *Self-analysis*. N. Y.: W. W. Norton and Co., 1942.

Hutterer, Jeffrey. "A Structural Analysis of the Performance Anxiety Syndrome as Experienced among Solo Musicians." Unpublished Dissertation, City University of New York, 1980.

Huxley, Aldous. *The Doors of Perception* and *Heaven and Hell*. London: Granada, 1977 (first published in 1954 and 1956, respectively).

Ichazo, Oscar. *Psychocalisthenics*. N. Y.: Simon and Schuster, 1976.

International Conference on Tension in Performance, 1981. Publication of Conference Papers, July 1982.

Iyengar, B. K. *Light on Yoga*. Revised Edition. N. Y.: Schocken Books, 1977.

Jacobson, Edmund. *Progressive Relaxation*. Chicago: The University of Chicago Press, 2nd edition, 1938.

Jacobson, Edmund. *You Must Relax*. London: Unwin Paperbacks, 1976.

James, I. M., et al. "Effect of Oxprenolo on Stage-Fright in Musicians," *Lancet*, 8045, 1977, 952-954.

James, William. *The Principles of Psychology*. 2 vols. N. Y.: Dover Publications, 1950 (first publ. in 1890).

James, William. *The Varieties of Religious Experience*. N. Y.: Mentor Books, 1958.

Jaynes, Julian. *The Origin of Consciousness in the Breakdown of the Bicameral Mind*. Boston: Houghton Mifflin Co., 1976.

Jersild, A. T. *Child Psychology*. Rev. ed. N. Y.: Prentice-Hall, 1940.

Jou, Tsung Hwa. *The Tao of Tai-Chi Chuan*. Rutland, Vermont: Charles E. Tuttle Co., 1980.

Jung, C. G. *The Archetypes and the Collective Unconscious*. Trans. R. F. C. Hull. Princeton: Princeton University Press, 1980 (first Published in 1959).

Jung, C. G. (ed.). *Man and His Symbols*. N. Y.: Dell Publishing Co., 1968 (first published in 1964.).

Jung, C. G. *Two Essays on Analytical Psychology*. Trans. R. F. C. Hull. Princeton: Princeton University Press, 1966 (first published in 1956).

Kagan, Jerome. *The Second Year*. Cambridge, Mass.: Harvard University Press, 1981.

Kagan, Jerome, Richard Kearsley, and Philip Zelazo. *Infancy: Its Place in Human Development*. Cambridge, Mass.: Harvard University Press, 1978.

Kahneman, D. *Attention and Effort*. Englewood Cliffs, N. J.: Prentice-Hall, 1973.

Kapleau, Philip. *The Three Pillars of Zen*. Garden City, N. Y.: Anchor Books, 1980 (first published in 1965).

Kasulis, T. P. *Zen Action, Zen Person*. Honolulu: University of Hawaii Press, 1981.

Kazdin, A. E. *Behavior Modification in Applied Settings*. Homewood, Ill.: Dorsey Press, 1975.

Kellar, Lucia A., and Thomas G. Bever. "Hemispheric asymmetries in the perception of musical intervals as a function of musical experience and family handedness background," *Brain and Language*, 1980, May, Vol. 10 (1), 24-38.

Kendrick, Margaret J. "Reduction of Musical Performance Anxiety by Attentional Training and Behaviour Rehearsal: An Exploration of Cognitive Mediational Processes." Unpublished Doctoral Dissertation, The University of British Columbia, 1979.

Kendrick, Margaret J., et al. "Cognitive and Behavioral Therapy for Musical Performance Anxiety," Journal of *Consulting and Clinical Psychology*, 1982, Vol. 50, No. 3, 353-362.

Kierkegaard, Søren. *The Concept of Anxiety*. Trans. Reidar Thomte. Princeton, N. J.: Princeton University Press, 1980.

Kimura, Doreen. "Functional Asymmetry of the Brain in Dichotic Listening," *Cortex*, 3, 1967, 163-178.

Kimura, Doreen. "Right Temporal-Lobe Damage," *Archives of Neurology*, 8, 1963, 264-271.

Klinger, Eric (ed.). *Imagery*. Vol. 2. N. Y.: Plenum Press, 1981.

Knobloch, Ferdinand and Jirina. *Integrated Psychotherapy*. N. Y.: Jason Aronson, 1979.

Koestler, Arthur. *The Act of Creation*. London: Pan Books Ltd., 1964.

Koestler, Arthur. *The Ghost in the Machine*. London: Pan Books Ltd., 1975 (first published in 1967).

Kuhn, Thomas S. *The Structure of Scientific Revolutions*. Second edition. Chicago: The University of Chicago Press, 1970.

Landis, C., and W. A. Hunt. *The Startle Pattern* N. Y.: Rinehart and Co., Inc., 1939.

LeCron, Leslie M. *The Complete Guide to Hypnosis*. N. Y. Barnes and Noble Books, 1973.

Le Cron, Leslie M. *Self Hypnotism. The Technique and Its Use in Daily Living.* N. Y.: Signet, 1964.

Leglar, Mary Alice. "Measurement of Indicators of Anxiety Levels Under Varying Conditions of Musical Performance." Unpublished Dissertation, Indiana University, 1978.

LeShan, Lawrence. *Alternate Realities.* Toronto: Ballantine Books Edition, 1977 (Originally, 1976).

LeShan, Lawrence. *Clairvoyant Reality.* Wellingborough, Northamptonshire, G. B.: Turnstone Press Ltd., 1974.

Levee, John R., Michael J. Cohen, and William H. Rickles. "Electromyographic Biofeedback for Relief of Tension in the Facial and Throat Muscles of a Woodwind Musician," *Biofeedback and Self-Regulation,* Vol. 1, No. 1, 1976.

Levy, Jerre, Colwyn Trevarthen, and R. W. Sperry. "Perception of Bilateral Chimeric Figures Following Hemispheric Deconnexion," *Brain,* 95, 1972, 61-78.

Levi-Agresti, Jerre, and R. W. Sperry. "Differential Perceptual Capacities in Major and Minor Hemispheres," *Proceedings of the National Academy of Science,* Vol. 61, 1968, 1151.

Lowen, Alexander. *Bioenergetics.* N. Y.: Penguin Books, 1976.

Lund, D. R. "A Comparative Study of Three Therapeutic Techniques in the Modification of Anxiety Behavior in Instrumental Music Performance." Doctoral Dissertation, University of Utah, 1972. *Dissertation Abstracts International,* 1972, 33, 1189A (University Microfilms No. 72-23, 026).

MacKinnon, Lilias. *Music by Heart.* London: Oxford University Press, 1938.

Maslow, A. H. *The Farther Reaches of Human Nature.* N. Y.: Penguin Books, 1976 (first published in 1971).

Maslow, A. H. *Motivation and Personality.* 2nd edition. N. Y.: Harper and Row, 1970.

Maslow, A. H. *Religions, Values, and Peak-Experiences.* N. Y.: Penguin Books, 1970.

Maslow, A. H. *Toward a Psychology of Being.* 2nd edition. N. Y.: D. Van Nostrand Co., 1968.

Matthay, Tobias. *Musical Interpretation.* Fourth Edition. Boston: The Boston Music Co., 1913.

May, Rollo. *The Courage to Create.* N. Y.: Bantam Books, 1976.

May, Rollo (ed.). *Existential Psychology.* 2nd edition. N. Y.: Random House, 1960.

May, Rollo. *The Meaning of Anxiety.* Revised edition. N. Y.: Washington Square Press, 1977.

Meichenbaum, Donald. *Cognitive-Behavior Modification.* N. Y.: Plenum Press, 1977.

Meyer, Leonard B. *Emotion and Meaning in Music.* Chicago: The University of Chicago Press, 1956.

Milner, Brenda. "Interhemispheric Differences in the Localization of Psychological Processes in Man," *British Medical Bulletin,* 27, #3, 1971, 272-277.

Morasky, Robert L., Creech Reynolds, and Larry E. Sowell. "Generalization of Lowered EMG Levels During Musical Performance Following Biofeedback Training," *Biofeedback and Self-Regulation,* Vol. 8, No. 2, 1983, 207-216.

Morris, Larry W., and Robert M. Liebert. "Relationship of Cognitive and Emotional Components of Test Anxiety to Physiological Arousal and Academic Performance," *Journal of Consulting and Clinical Psychology*, 1970, (3), 332,337.

Moustakas, Clark E. (ed.). *The Self*. N. Y.: Harper Torchbooks, 1956.

Murchison, Carl (ed.). *The Foundations of Experimental Psychology*. Worcester, Mass.: Clark University Press, 1929.

Nagel, Julie, David Himle, and James Papsdorf. "A Cognitive-Behavioral Approach to Musical Performance Anxiety." Paper delivered at the *First International Conference on Tension in Performance*, September 1981.

Naranjo, Claudio, and Robert E. Ornstein. *On the Psychology of Meditation*. N. Y.: Penguin Books, 1976 (first published in 1971).

Newman, William S. *The Pianist's Problems*. Revised. N. Y.: Harper and Row, 1956.

Norman, D. *Memory and Attention*. 2nd edition. N. Y.: Wiley, 1976.

Ornstein, Robert E.(ed.). *The Nature of Human Consciousness*. San Francisco: W. H. Freeman and Co., 1973.

Ornstein, Robert E. *The Psychology of Consciousness*. N. Y.: Penguin Books, 1972.

Ortmann, Otto. *The Physiological Mechanics of Piano Technique*. N. Y.: E. P. Dutton and Co., 1962 (first published in 1929).

Ostrander, Sheila, and Lynn Schroeder. *Super-Learning*. N. Y.: Delta, 1979.

Pelletier, Kenneth R. *Holistic Medicine*. N. Y.: Delta Books, 1979.

Pelletier, Kenneth R. *Longevity*. N. Y.: Delta Books, 1981.

Pelletier, Kenneth R. *Mind as Healer, Mind as Slayer*. N. Y.: Delta Books, 1977.

Pelletier, Kenneth R. *Toward a Science of Consciousness*. N. Y.: Delta Books, 1978.

Pelletier, Kenneth R., and Charles Garfield. *Consciousness: East and West*. N. Y.: Harper and Row, 1976.

Penfield, Wilder. *The Mystery of the Mind*. Princeton: Princeton University Press, 1975.

Penfield, Wilder, and Lamar Roberts. *Speech and Brain-Mechanisms*. Princeton, N. J.: Princeton University Press, 1959.

Peper, Erik, Sonia Ancoli, and Michael Quinn (eds.). *Mind/Body Integration*. N. Y.: Plenum Press, 1979.

Peper, Erik, and Elizabeth Ann Williams. *From the Inside Out*. N. Y.: Plenum Press, 1981.

Perls, Frederick, Ralph F. Hefferline, and Paul Goodman. *Gestalt Therapy*. N. Y.: Bantam Books, 1977 (first published in 1951).

Piaget, Jean. *The Child and Reality*. Trans. Arnold Rosin. N. Y.: Penguin Books 1976.

Piaget, Jean. *The Origins of Intelligence in Children*. Trans. Margaret Cook. N. Y.: International Universities Press, Inc., 1952.

Piperek, Maximilian (Scientific Coordinator). *Stress and Music*. Vienna: Wilhelm Braumueller, 1981.

Pirsig, Robert M. *Zen and the Art of Motorcycle Maintenance*. N. Y.: Bantam Books, 1979 (first published in 1974).

Plaskin, Glenn. *Horowitz*. London and Sydney: Macdonald and Co., 1983.

Popper, Karl R., and John C. Eccles. *The Self and Its Brain*. N. Y., London, Heidelberg, and Berlin: Springer-Verlag, 1981.

Progoff, Ira. *The Death and Rebirth of Psychology*. N. Y.: McGraw-Hill, 1956.

Progoff, Ira. *The Practice of Process Meditation*. N. Y.: Dialogue House Library, 1980.

Radocy, Rudolf, and J. David Boyle. *Psychological Foundations of Musical Behavior*. Springfield, Ill.: Charles C. Thomas, Publ., 1979.

Reineke, Toni. "Simultaneous Processing of Music and Speech," *Psychomusicology*, Vol. 1, No. 1, 1981, 58-77.

Reubart, Dale. "Performance in the Academic Community: Opportunity and Dilemma," *Journal of the Canadian Association of University Schools of Music*, I (Fall, 1971), 1-8.

Reubart, Dale. "Playing the Piano from Memory," *The First International Conference on Tension in Performance*, July 1982, 49-63.

Ristad, Eloise. *A Soprano on Her Head*. Moab, Utah: Real People Press, 1982.

Rogers, Carl R. *Freedom to Learn*. Columbus, Ohio: Charles E. Merrill, 1969.

Rogers, Carl R. *On Becoming a Person*. Boston: Houghton Mifflin Co., 1961.

Royce, Joseph R., and Leendert P. Mos (eds.). *Humanistic Psychology*. N. Y.: Plenum Press, 1981.

Sagan, Carl. *The Dragons of Eden*. N. Y.: Random House, 1977.

St. James-Roberts, Ian. "Neurological Plasticity, Recovery from Brain Insult, and Child Development," *Advances in Child Development and Behavior*, Vol. 14, 1979, 253-319.

Samama, Ans. *Muscle Control for Musicians*. Trans. H. Nouwen and H. Graham. Second edition. Utrecht: Bohn, Scheltema and Holkema, 1981.

Sarason, Irwin, and Charles Spielberger (eds.). *Stress and Anxiety*. Vols. II and III. N. Y.: John Wiley and Sons, 1975, 1976.

Sartre, Jean-Paul. *Existential Psycho-Analysis*. Trans. Hazel E. Barnes. Chicago: Gateway Edition, 1962 (first published in 1953).

Schultz, Arnold. *The Riddle of the Pianist's Finger*. Boston: Carl Fischer, 1936.

Schultz, Arnold. *A Theory of Consciousness*. N. Y.: Philosophical Library, 1973.

Schwartz, Gary E., and David Shapiro (eds.). *Consciousness and Self-Regulation*. N. Y.: Plenum Press; vol. 1, 1976; vol. 2, 1978.

Scientific American, The. *The Brain*. San Francisco: W. H. Freeman and Co., 1979.

Selye, H. *The Stress of Life*. N. Y.: McGraw-Hill, 1956.

Selye, H. *Stress Without Distress*. N. Y.: New American Library, 1975.

Sherbon, James W. "The Association of Hearing Acuity, Diplacusis, and Discrimination with Music Performance," *Journal of Research in Music Education*, Vol. 23 (4), 1975, 249-257.

Singer, Jerome, and Kenneth S. Pope (eds.). *The Power of Human Imagination*. N. Y. and London: Plenum Press 1978.

Skinner, B. F. *Science and Human Behavior*. N. Y.: Macmillan, 1953.

Smirnov, A. A. *Problems of the Psychology of Memory*. N. Y.: Plenum Press, 1973.

Solso, Robert L. *Cognitive Psychology*. N. Y.: Harcourt Brace Jovanovich, Inc., 1979.

Spielberger, Charles. *Anxiety and Behavior*. N. Y.: Academic Press, 1966.

Spielberger, Charles (ed.). *Anxiety: Current Trends in Theory and Research.* Vols. I and II. N. Y.: Academic Press, 1972.

Spielberger, Charles, and Irwin Sarason (eds.). *Stress and Anxiety.* Vols. I and IV. N. Y.: John Wiley and Sons., 1975, 1977.

Spreen, Otfried, Frank J. Spellacy and J. R. Reid. "The Effect of Interstimulus Interval and Intensity on Ear Asymmetry for Nonverbal Stimuli in Dichotic Listening," *Neuropsychologia*, Vol. 8, 1970, 245-250.

Stanislavski, Constantin. *An Actor Prepares.* Trans. Elizabeth Reynolds Hapgood. N.Y.: Theatre Arts Books, 1948.

Straus, Roger A. *Strategic Self-Hypnosis: How to Overcome Stress, Improve Performance, and Live to Your Fullest Potential.* Englewood Cliffs, N. J.: Prentice-Hall, 1982.

Sudnow, David. *Talk's Body.* N. Y.: Alfred A. Knopf, 1979.

Sudnow, David. *Ways of the Hand.* N. Y.: Bantam Books, 1979.

Sullivan, Harry S. *Conceptions of Modern Psychiatry.* Washington, D. C.: William Alanson White Psychiatric Foundation, 1947 (Reprinted from *Psychiatry*, 3:1 and 8:2.).

Suzuki, D. T. *Zen Buddhism.* Selected Writings of D. T. Suzuki. Ed. William Barrett. Garden City, N. J.: Doubleday and Co., Inc., 1956.

Sweeney, Gladys Acevedo, and John J. Horan. "Separate and Combined Effects of Cue-Controlled Relaxation and Cognitive Restructuring in the Treatment of Musical Performance Anxiety," *Journal of Counselling Psychology*, Vol. 29 (5), 1982, 486-497.

Tart, Charles T. (ed.). *Altered States of Consciousness.* Garden City, N. Y.: Anchor Books, 1969.

Tart, Charles T. *States of Consciousness.* N. Y.: E.P.Dutton, 1975.

Tart, Charles T. *Transpersonal Psychologies.* N. Y.: Harper Colophon Books, 1977.

Ter-Pogossian, Michel M., Marcus E. Raichle and Burton E. Sobel. "Positron-Emission Tomography," *Scientific American*, October, 1980.

Treisman, A. M. "Selective Attention in Man," *British Medical Bulletin*, 1964b, 20, 12-16.

Vernon, Philip E. "Absolute pitch: A case study," *British Journal of Psychology*, 1977, Nov., Vol. 68 (4), 485-489.

Vernon, Philip E., Georgina Adamson, and Dorothy F. Vernon. *The Psychology and Education of Gifted Children.* London: Methuen and Co. Ltd., 1977.

Verny, Thomas, and John Kelly. *The Secret Life of the Unborn Child.* Toronto: Collins, 1981.

Wagner, Christoph. "Die Messung rheologisher Grössen an Gelenken der menschlichen Hand in vivo." In Hartmann, F. *Biopolymere und Biomechanik von Bindegewebssystemen.* Berlin/Heidelberg/New York: Springer, 1974.

Wagner, Christoph. "Physiologische Voraussetzungen für das Geigenspiel." In..... Schwarz, V. *Violinspiel und Violinmusik in Geschichte und Gegenwart.* Wien: Universal Edition, 1975.

Walsh, Roger N., and Frances Vaughan (eds.). *Beyond Ego*. Los Angeles: J. P. Tarcher, Inc., 1980.

Ward, W. Dixon. "Absolute Pitch," *Sound*, Part 1, May-June 1963, 14-21, Part 2, July-August 1963, 1-41.

Wardle, A. "Behavior Modification by Reciprocal Inhibition of Instrumental Music Performance Anxiety." In C. K. Madsen, R. D. Greer, and C. H. Madsen, Jr. (eds.). *Research in Music Behavior: Modifying Music Behavior in the Classroom*. N. Y.: Teachers College Press, 1975.

Whiteside, Abby. *Indispensables of Piano Technique*. Second edition. N. Y.: Coleman-Ross, 1961.

Wilber, Ken (ed.). *The Holographic Paradigm*. Boulder and London: Shambhala, 1982.

Wilson, G. Terence, and K. Daniel O'Leary. *Principles of Behavior Therapy*. Englewood Cliffs, N. J.: Prentice-Hall, Inc., 1980.

Wolpe, Joseph. *Psychotherapy by Reciprocal Inhibition*. Stanford: Stanford University Press, 1958.

Yerkes, R. M., and J. D. Dodson. "The Relation of Strengths of Stimulus to Rapidity of Habitformation," *Journal of Comparative Neurological Psychology*, 1908, 18, 459-482.

Zaidel, Dahlia, and R. W. Sperry. "Memory Impairment After Commissurotomy in Man," *Brain*, 97, 1974, 263-270.

NAME INDEX

SUBJECT INDEX